AUTHORITY AND PASSION

Demetrios Trakatellis

Metropolitan of Vresthena

AUTHORITY AND PASSION

Christological Aspects of
the Gospel according to Mark

Translated from the Greek by
George K. Duvall
and Harry Vulopas

HOLY CROSS ORTHODOX PRESS
Brookline, Massachusetts

Reprinted 1998
© Copyright 1987 by Holy Cross Orthodox Press
Published by Holy Cross Orthodox Press
50 Goddard Avenue
Brookline, MA 02146
USA

Cover design by Mary C. Vaporis

Icon: Codex A113, folio 210v., fourteenth century
Monastery of Megiste Lavra, Mount Athos

Library of Congress Cataloging in Publication Data
Trakatellis, Demetrios.
Authority and Passion. Translation of Exousia kai pathos.
Translated into English by George K. Duvall and Harry Vulopas.
Bibliography: p. Includes index.
1. Jesus Christ—History of doctrines—Early Church, ca. 30-600.
2. Bible. N. T. Mark—Theology. I. Title.
BT198.T6913   198   232
87-16812
ISBN 0-917651-45-6
ISBN 0-917651-46-4 (pbk.)

To my mother Georgia

εὐχαριστήριον

FOREWORD TO THE ENGLISH EDITION

The English translation and publication of my book Ἐξουσία καὶ Πάθος (Athens, 1983) is the result of the handsome work and the multifarious contributions of several people who deserve my deep gratitude. I should mention in particular the two translators: Mr. George Duvall who translated chapters 2, 3, 4, 5, and part of chapter 1, and Fr. Harry Vulopas who translated the introduction and the greatest part of chapter 1. Both worked with remarkable industry and sensitivity in order to offer a translation faithful to the original and, at the same time, standing on its own as a literary piece. My most special thanks belong to Fr. N. Michael Vaporis, the Director of the Holy Cross Press, for his unfailing support of the translation project throughout its course and for his decisive role in the transformation of the English manuscript into the printed volume now in hand.

The present translation follows exactly the original. There is one difference: in the final bibliography, a number of new items has been added, selected books or articles on Mark published after 1983.

As stated in the Preface of the Greek edition, the purpose of this christological commentary on the Gospel of Mark remains the same: to contribute to the search for and the discovery of the real, the true, and the genuine person of Christ.

Holy Cross Greek Orthodox
School of Theology
Brookline, Massachusetts
July, 1987

† Demetrios Trakatellis
Bishop of Vresthena

PREFACE

This book is part of a more general research project. A project which aims at exploring, analyzing, and interpreting the basic aspects and ideas about Jesus Christ encountered in the texts of the New Testament and early Christian literature. Such a task demands hard work and long multifaceted efforts. It rewards, however, the biblical scholar with deep spiritual satisfaction and joy.

The research and writing of the present monograph was facilitated by many people in Greece and elsewhere. I hereby express my whole-hearted appreciation to all of them. Special thanks go to my students at Hellenic College-Holy Cross Greek Orthodox School of Theology in Brookline, Massachusetts to whom I presented significant portions of this book during the academic year 1980-1981. Their animated participation in the exegetical course on Mark contributed to the delicate task of clarifying difficult or unclear points. I express also my particular thanks to Angeliki Goutzi who helped in the collection of the Greek bibliographical material, the typing, and the compilation of the indices, and to Penelope Konstantinidis who assisted me in the checking of the non-Greek bibliography and the selection and presentation of the research data. My particular thanks close, without having been exhausted, with the mention of the publishers Demetres Mavropoulos and Spyros Davris of the Domos Press. They were tireless in their creative cooperation throughout all the phases of the preparation and publication of the present work.

This book has been written with only one purpose: to offer to the reader, even though inadequately and dimly, the vision of the true person of the Lord as it is revealed by the Gospel according to Mark.

TABLE OF CONTENTS

CHAPTER FIVE

INTRODUCTION

The person of Jesus Christ as portrayed in the Gospel according to Mark is the subject of a great many works published in the last few decades. The majority of these studies have more or less utilized the exegetical approach in examining the Christology of the Gospel. Their purpose has been to shed light on the various aspects of this Christology, to identify its presuppositions and to determine its place in the overall theological scheme of the Gospel. In several of these recent books, inquiry into Mark's Christology has gone hand in hand with the examination of literary, historical, history of religions or theological questions within the Gospel text. Still others have combined the christological quest with an inquiry into the sources used by the Evangelist, and his work as an author, while many have sought to discover the underlying theological tendencies of Mark as he was writing his Gospel and the ecclesiological data from which these tendencies sprang.

The selection and application of exegetical methods found in the various works are analogous with the diversity of approaches and goals in the study of the Christology of Mark's Gospel. Methods such as those of historical, literary, form and redaction criticism, and that of structural analysis have been utilized by numerous interpreters in their attempts to understand and describe the Christology of this Gospel, a Christology which, inspite of extensive research, still remains open and, in large part, unfathomable. The pursuit of this inquiry into the Christology of Mark's Gospel continues to beckon the researcher into an unbelievably attractive and profoundly spiritual world.

The present monograph presupposes a tremendous amount of exegetical work as well as specific christological studies done with the Gospel of Mark. This study is not bound up with any particular exegetical method, even though several of these have been employed, hopefully with a degree of critical discernment. It should also be stated that the present work does not attempt a detailed exegetical analysis of the text. Our purpose is to view the main characteristics of the image of Christ as presented by the Gospel of Mark. This means that in the pages which follow, we will treat the Christology of the second Gospel only in its fundamental aspects.

At this point, three methodological clarifications should be made:

a) By the expression "the Christology of the Gospel according to Mark" or "Christology of Mark" we refer to a Christology expressed in this Gospel as a self-sufficient, and unified text, morphologically complete. It is, of course, known that contemporary scholars differentiate between the material which Mark is supposed to have found in extant sources of tradition and the material directly attributable to him, derived specifically from his own literary-theological activity and initiative. The discernment of various layers within the text is important; however, it is likely to introduce, to a certain degree, subjective elements, with their attendant personal judgments which might lead to conclusions that are not always generally accepted. On the other hand, the Gospel of Mark is a clearly defined and objectively existing text. In addition, the Gospel has, as already noted, a complete and finished literary form and expression, revealing a document which possesses independence and unity, apart from the probable sources which are organically integrated into the text. It is precisely the Christology of this concrete, established and integral text which constitutes the object of the present study.

b) The results of this work are presented in a descriptive and analytical manner, always based on the exegetical data. The Gospel according to Mark is analyzed from the first verse to the last from the standpoint of christological concepts. No pericopes have been omitted. Thus, the text is examined in its entirety and within the framework of its sequential development. The christological concepts are examined in their proper context and in the order they appear in the development of the Evangelist's account. In this manner, it is possible to determine the emphases, the shades of difference, and the alternation of christological aspects exactly as they appear in the text. At every step, a continous and determined attempt had been made to convey in a manner as precise and complete as possible the christological image found in any particular pericope or broader unit of the Gospel. On the basis of the clarifications set forth above, the present monograph may be described as a concise commentary on the Gospel according to Mark with an emphasis on interpreting the christological dimensions of the text.

c) The third methodological clarification has to do with the synthetic character of this work. A study in biblical theology could not be complete if its area of inquiry were confined to an analytical description of christological data. For this reason, considerable time has been spent in research and considerable space set aside for the presentation of the respective data in the form of a synthesis. The reader may therefore have an integral and complete concept of the basic christological features of Mark's Gospel. The synthetic and systematic manner of presenting the material also makes possible a deeper understanding of the christological aspects, their inter-relationship as well as their relationship to other significant areas of theological expression, such as anthropology and ecclesiology. One should also bear in mind that this synthetic presentation facilitates the perception of the essential correlation between Christology and the problems of human existence, between "faith in Christ Jesus" and the imprisonment of man in this world.

The research which preceded the writing of this volume leads to the fundamental conclusion that the Gospel of Mark refers continuously and chiefly to two significant christological aspects. They are conventionally referred to as the "Christology of Authority" and the "Christology of Passion." These two designations are to be understood in their broadest possible application. The former expresses the ideas associated with the works, words, and activity of Jesus which reveal his supernatural authority and power, his divine sovereignty and lordship. The latter embodies ideas which refer to his Passion, i.e. that broad spectrum which ranges from the lack of understanding on the part of his disciples to the betrayal, from the humbling of himself at the baptism to his agony at Gesthemane, from the opposition of the Pharisees to his crucifixion. Viewed from another standpoint, the Christology of Authority expresses the reality of Jesus' divine hypostasis, it describes the manifestation of his divinity. Conversely, the Christology of Passion reveals the humanity of the Lord, it sets forth his subjection to human situations of humiliation, suffering, and death.

The predominance of these two fundamental christological aspects, Authority and Passion, in the Gospel according to Mark has inspired the title of the present work and has determined its content. The christological study which follows has as its focal points the two christological concepts described above. The contents of each of these, their varied forms, their position in the Gospel of Mark as a whole and in its major sections, their coexistence and interpendence as well as their anthropological implications, constitute central themes which interact continuously in the pages which follow. From this interaction, we can clearly see the tremendous accomplishment of the Evangelist Mark: with the two fundamental christological aspects of Authority and Passion, he presents the image of Jesus Christ with a unique authenticity, vibrancy, veracity, dynamism, and wholeness. This is the image which is, and shall remain, the irreplaceable criterion of every Christology.

The present study has a clear framework. The five chapters which make up the body of the work are divided into two main sections. The first section, which comprises the first three chapters is, generally speaking, exegetical in character. The Gospel according to Mark is followed step by step, the pericopes are analyzed one after the other in their normal sequence and the christological facets of Authority and Passion are studied in detail exactly as they appear in the flow and development of the Gospel account. The first three chapters contain a great many footnotes. In these footnotes, the interested reader will find significant patristic observations in regard to the particular pericopes or individual verses being examined. Also to be found are numerous bibliographic references to current research in the Gospel of Mark. Attention is drawn to the selection and inclusion of a specific bibliography for each pericope. The reference works listed in this regard are volumes which have been published, for the most part, since 1970 and usually mention the most important studies circulating before 1970.

The second main section of the present work contains the fourth and fifth chapters which more or less have a synthetic character. Based on the exegetical data from the first part of this study, an effort was made to bring about a synthesis of the two fundamental christological concepts of the Gospel according to Mark. An attempt is made here to approach the Christologies of Authority and Passion from the perspective of the content and function of each, as well as from the standpoint of their interconnection and interdependence in Mark.

In researching the present work, extensive use has been made of the commentaries of church writers such as Victor presbyter of

Antioch, Theophylact, and Zigabenos. Many insights have been gained from patristic interpretations of various passages in the Gospel of Mark and relevant observations on parallel passages found in the commentaries on the Gospel of Matthew by Origen and by Chrysostom. Two of the most recent Greek commentaries on the Gospel of Mark, those of N. Damalas and P. Trembelas, have been used. From the vast bibliography in various languages, selection was made of those works deemed most representative of the commentary genre, theological trends, confessional origins, and current exegetical methods.

Bibliographic information about these commentaries and specific books and articles which refer either directly or indirectly to christological themes in the Gospel of Mark is found at the end of this volume and in numerous footnotes.

Chapter One

THE MANIFESTATION OF AUTHORITY
AND THE PRELUDE TO THE PASSION
(Mark 1.1-8.26)

In a captivating narrative flow, the first part of the Gospel according to Mark (Mark 1.1-8.26) gives us a series of events having a common theme: the revelation by various means of Jesus Christ's divine authority, supernatural power, and supreme prerogative. The emphasis and denotative variations differ as we go from dialogues to healings, from theophanic events to human confrontations, from teachings to exorcisms, and from resurrections of the dead to theological affirmations. The christological essence, however, remains the same. One after the other, the events in Mark 1.1-8.26 either indirectly suggest or directly project a Christology of Authority, an understanding, image or sense of Christ as a unique bearer of divine authority.

This dazzling manifestation of authority and power, however, is not alone on the Gospel scene. From the very first chapter, Mark has begun referring and alluding to Jesus' state of humiliation. As the narrative develops, the hints become more profuse and are imperceptibly transformed into clear indicators which point toward the Passion of Christ. Thus, the Christology of Passion also appears early and is already operative in Mark 1.1-8.26. Of course, in this section it has nowhere near the intensity, breadth or dominance had by the Christology of Authority. It moves on a secondary, parallel level, less noticeable than the latter; however, it is present and does not allow the Christology of Authority to become the sole and exclusive christological expression in the Gospel. As a result, the first part of Mark's Gospel is a masterpiece in which the manifestation of Jesus' divine authority is accompanied by the clearly discernible prelude to his Passion.

MANIFESTATIONS OF JESUS' AUTHORITY: PHASE ONE (1.1-3.6).

1. The Gospel of Mark begins with the solemn phrase-heading, "The beginning of the gospel of Jesus Christ, the Son of God" (1.1).[1] Mark is the only Evangelist who uses the expression "gospel of Jesus Christ." The term "gospel" is missing entirely in John and Luke, while Matthew uses the phrase "the gospel of the kingdom" (Mt 4.23). This comparison clearly emphasizes the christological significance this formulation has in Mark.[2] For him, the object and content of his gospel is Jesus, the Messiah and Son of God. The text also validates the interpretation that Jesus Christ is the one who proclaims and offers the gospel.[3] In this way, Jesus can simultaneously be the creator of the gospel and its content, the herald and subject of its message.

The inaugural declaration of Mark 1.1 places Christ at the absolute center of the action and development which is to follow. With solemnity, conceptual density, and verbal frugality, Mark unequivocally proclaims the divine prerogative and preeminence of the Messiah.[4]

2. The Mesiah's preeminence begins to be methodically presented in the pericope which follows (1.2-8),[5] referring to John the Baptist. This narrative describes John as being vested with the undisputed authority of the Old Testament. This authority, however, is exclusively connected with his role as Forerunner. In final analysis, the prophecy of Isaiah (1.2-3) focuses our attention on the Messiah.[6]

The Messiah's preeminence is expressed unequivocally in the concluding verses of the passage (1.7-8). There, John declares that he who is coming is "mightier than he,"[7] that he is the one "the thong of whose sandals he is not worthy to stoop down and untie," and that the one who is coming is also the one who will baptize in "the Holy Spirit," while John merely baptizes "in water."[8] This multifaceted proclamation couched in a series of comparisons, immediately reveals the vast difference between Jesus' authority and that of John.

The latter, his great stature notwithstanding, does not function autonomously, but rather in a christological mode. Evidence of this is the fact that throughout the entire passage (1.2-8), Mark does not mention the other aspects of John's preaching as do both Matthew (Mt 3.7-12) and Luke (Lk 3.7-14) in their parallel accounts. The John of Mark 1.2-8 speaks exclusively about the Messiah and prophetically propounds his incomparable prerogative.[9]

3. The pericope of the baptism (1.9-11)[10] is also expressive of Jesus' unique authority.[11] The heavens open, an occurrence which the apoclayptic literature of Israel relates to unusual events of a divine order.[12] At the same time, "the Spirit descended like a dove" upon Jesus, who is being baptized, to show divine recognition and confirmation of his messiahship.[13] The language here, reminiscent of the typical messianic passage of Isaiah, "the Spirit of the Lord is upon me" (Is 61.1), indirectly suggests the powerful idea of Old Testament promises being fulfilled. The most important single point in the narrative, however, is the information that "a voice came from heaven, 'You are my beloved son, with you I am well pleased' "(1.11).[14] The unique and supernatural Sonship of Christ is revealed here through an inbreaking of the transcendent into worldly reality. The baptism has a magnificent theophanic[15] character which is also underscored by the passage's impressive simplicity of language. Mark, in his brief introductory verses, firmly establishes Jesus' divine authority. The stage is already set for the Christology of Authority.

The baptism account, however, also contains the first elements of Jesus' humiliation and subjection to the circumstances of the human condition. Here we may have a faint suggestion of the Christology of Passion. It is found in the information that "In those days Jesus came from Nazareth to Galilee and was baptized by John in the Jordan" (1.9-10). The Messiah comes to his Forerunner and is baptized in the same manner as many of his Jewish contemporaries. The impression of humiliation is unavoidable and nothing in the text itself diminishes this effect.[16] Mark's christological concept in the present passage is more clearly perceived when compared to the parallel verses in Matthew and Luke. Luke does not use the phrase "by John," and in place of "he was baptized," he uses the participial form of the same verb. Thus, the verb grammatically becomes part of a subordinate clause, thereby diminishing the emphasis on Jesus' humiliation (Lk 3.21). The phenomenon is set forth with even greater clarity in Matthew, who retains the basic phraseology of Mark, but also includes a brief dialogue between Jesus and John: "John would have prevented him saying, 'I need to be baptized by you and do you come to me?'' (Mt 3.14). In Mark, we do not encounter any descriptions or explanations of this type; therefore, in the baptism account, Jesus is presented as humiliated, though he is at the same time proclaimed the unique bearer of divine authority.[17]

4. In the account of Christ's temptation in the wilderness, this same authority is clearly perceptible. Mark's text (1.12-13)[18] is exceptionally short in comparison to the parallel texts of the other Evangelists (Mt 4.1-11 and Lk 4.1-13). There are no dialogues, and the whole terrible ordeal of the forty days is expressed in the laconic participial expression "tempted by Satan." This condensation of language suggests the idea that Christ is superior to Satan.[19] The same idea is inherent in the statement: "And the angels ministered to him" (1.13).[20] The Messiah is being tempted but at the same time he is served by angels as one having authority over the spiritual world. His living among the "wild beasts" reveals the might of his authority on yet another level.[21]

In any event, no matter how much the image of messianic grandeur has restricted the element of temptation, this element is still quite present. Jesus encounters resistence in the initial stages of his work, and this resistence appears to come from non-human, demonic powers.

5. The passage following the temptation describes the beginning of Christ's preaching and his fundamental programmatic declaration (1.14-15).[22] Only in Mark is the first part of this proclamation recorded declaring that "the time is fulfilled." The idea is eschatological and refers to a radical break in the course of history effected by God; however this "time is fulfilled" has its consummation in the person and work of Christ, a fact which underlines his uniqueness.[23] A similar emphasis is detected in the statement "repent and believe in the gospel." Here, the exclusive meaning of the term "gospel" is made clear;[24] it is nothing else but the very words of Jesus. Mark 1.14-15, therefore, places Christ at the center of fundamental eschatological processes and attributes ultimate authority to his words.[25] At the same time, the same passage seems to hint faintly at the Passion with the statement, "Now after John was arrested." This piece of information is used to establish a specific time frame.

The verb παραδίδομαι, to be arrested, however, a key-verb in the Gospel of Mark, points toward the Passion of the Messiah,[26] and warns the reader that the tragedy will be repeated.

6. The programmatic pericope Mark 1.14-15 is followed by the narrative of the calling of the first disciples (1.16-20).[27] With the addition of a new plane of reference, Mark further advances the idea of Jesus' authority and power. The narrative elements have been restricted to those which are absolutely necessary: names, places, occupations. Thus, Christ's injunction "Follow me and I will make you become fishers of men" (1.17)[28] takes on special meaning and absolutely dominates the scene. The tremendous authority inherent in this injunction is underscored by the response: "And immediately they left their nets and followed him" (1.18). This immediate, radical response is even more striking in the calling of the brothers John and James: "And they left their father Zebedee in the boat with the hired servants, and followed him" (1.20). In this case, the Messiah's word seems to have incomparable power, a force which produces radical changes on the level of familial and vocational relationships.

7. The unique and incomparable authority of Jesus' words is portrayed graphically in the event which succeeds the call of the first disciples, and concerns the incident in the synagogue of Capernaum (1.21-28).[29] Here, Christ's words bear his supreme authority in two ways: teaching, and subjugation of evil spirits.

In regard to the first, Mark notes that those who heard Jesus in the synagogue "were astonished at his teaching, for he taught them as one who had authority and not as the scribes" (1.22) The verb ἐκπλήττομαι, to be astonished, is encounterd in Mark in similar contexts and is a "strong word" (6.2, 7.37, 10.26). It is obvious that Christ's teaching made an unusual impression on his audience. The reason for this phenomenon is the fact that Jesus spoke "as one who had authority." It is at this point that the term *authority* (ἐξουσία) first appears in Mark in connection with the Messiah. The qualification added by the Evangelist, "and not as the scribes," immediately reveals the special meaning of this term. The scribes, as teachers of the Law, did not lack authority and power among the people, but in Mark 1.22, the Evangelist changes the relative meaning of "authority," applying it in an absolute sense to Christ.[30] Thus at the outset, Mark establishes an essential, unbridgeable difference between the teaching Jesus and the teachers of Israel on the basis of the authority in their words.

The second dimension in which Jesus' authority is revealed is the world of evil spirits. Being confronted by Christ, the unclean spirit which possessed the man in the synagogue of Capernaum cries: "What have you to do with us, Jesus of Nazareth? Have you come to destroy us? I know who you are, the Holy One of God" (1.24). The evil spirit acknowledges the impossibility of any coexistence or interaction with Jesus. In addition, it discloses that the purpose of Jesus' coming is the annihilation of evil spirits. Since defeat of demonic powers belongs to the time and work of the Messiah, [31] the cry of the unclean spirit constitutes an unequivocal confession of Jesus' supreme authority. A corroboration of this view is found in the title "the Holy One of God." [32] This form of address is not found among the traditional messianic titles; however, its use in the Old Testament leads to the logical conclusion that in Mark 1.24, it serves as a declaration of messiahship, or, at the very least, an indication of a very special charisma. [33]

Provoked by the evil spirit, Jesus responds with a clear expression of authority: "But Jesus rebuked him, saying, 'Be silent and come out of him' " (1.25). The words used here are verbs indicative of superiority and power: "rebuked," "be silent," "come out." Here Jesus expresses himself with two imperative verbs, emphatically projecting his supernatural power, which results in the immediate expulsion of the unclean spirit. Christ speaks and his words are filled with an energy that destroys the power of demonic powers.

The impression made on the crowd is one more building block forming the concept of Christ's authority. Mark notes that "they were all amazed" (1.27). Here, the narrative, depicting an atmosphere of extraordinary wonder and general amazement, directs our attention to the protagonist of these events, Jesus, and his almighty word. [34] The crowd unreservedly proceeds to acknowledge the unique might of Christ's word: "What is this? A new teaching with authority; he commands even the unclean spirits and they obey him" (1.27). For the second time in the same pericope the term ἐξουσία (authority) appears in connection with Jesus. It is worth noting that the text here does not refer to a word spoken with authority, but rather to a "a new teaching with authority." It is evident that the crowd's observations are made in reference to the wider context of Jesus' teaching which, in fact, they describe as "new." [35] The meaning is therefore broader and is not restricted only to his ability to perform an exorcism. [36]

At any rate, its breadth notwithstanding, the main emphasis is on Jesus' authority over evil spirits: "With authority he commands even the unclean spirits and they obey him" (1.27). The verbs ἐπιτάσσω ("to command") and ὑπακούω ("to obey") belong to a vocabulary defining relationships of authority and obedience, of subjection and might. They are indicative of a christological understanding which conveys Christ's unquestionable sovereignty over the tenebrous world of demonic forces. This sovereignty is so unique that it is imposed without struggle or effort. In Mark 1.23-28, the unclean spirits do not fight against Jesus or violently oppose him. They simply acknowledge the Messiah as ruler and obey the word of his divine power.

8. After the events in the synagogue of Capernaum, Jesus comes to the house of Simon and Andrew. Here he is informed that Peter's mother-in-law "lay sick with a fever." He approaches her and lifts her up, having "taken her by the hand." "And the fever left her; and she served them" (1.29-31).[37] The narrative moves along the same christological lines as the preceding one, in that it expresses the idea of Jesus' authority. The domain of authority in this case is physical infirmity.[38] Perhaps Mark reports this event because of the importance of the persons involved in it. Then again, it is not unlikely that Mark may have included this episode in his Gospel account because this event had no causal dependence on pre-existing belief, on suffering due to long-term illness, or on the persistent plea of those present,[39] as is the case with other healing miracles. The impression made here is that Jesus acts on his own initiative, without setting terms or demanding specific prerequisites. The image derived from the text is that of a Messiah who reveals his beneficent authority freely, abundantly and voluntarily, without awaiting the entreaties of those who need his help.[40]

9. This beneficent authority of Jesus is graphically projected in the next pericope (1.32-34),[41] which also contains a general description of healings for a variety of illnesses and demonic possession, all of which took place "that evening at sundown." Here, Mark's narrative technique incorporates terms expressive of mass movements and large numbers. We are thus informed that they brought to Jesus "all who were sick or possessed with demons," that "the whole city" gathered there, that he healed "many" who were sick with "various

diseases," and cast out "many" demons.[42] We spontaneously evoke images of limitless therapeutic power. Christ brings healing to large numbers of people, to a broad spectrum of infirmities, and frees a great many demoniacs.

Once again, the Evangelist points out that demons acknowledge Jesus' messianic identity ("because they knew him," 1.34), as in Mark 1.24. In Mark 1.34, however, Christ imposes silence on the demons ("And he would not permit the demons to speak"). The Evangelist, perhaps, wishes to convey the idea that, either Jesus rejected and excluded any demonic testimony, or he wanted to avoid the danger of an untimely expression of excitement and enthusiasm on the part of the people. [43] The Messiah is opposed to any recognition of this type.

10. The following passage (1.35-39)[44] again gives us examples of a narrative technique using concepts of mass movements. Jesus withdraws to a "lonely place" to pray. Simon and the others, however, follow and find him there. The verbs used here are indicative of the anxiety, the intensity of the search ("pursued him," "and they found him," 1.36). As soon as they find him, they "said to him, 'Everyone is searching for you' " (1.37). This "everyone" evokes the image of a general rally or group action, tacitly underscoring the Messiah's importance. Further on, an even more universal example is given, this time geographically. Jesus "went throughout all Galilee." He covers the entire region, "preaching" and "casting out demons" (1.39). Mark has already given a lucid presentation of the unbeatable power and authority in the Messiah's word and his supernatural might over demons. When he then shows the Messiah accomplishing this two-fold work "throughout all Galilee," he instantly gives the reader a feeling of an achievement unusual in nature and scope.[45] This achievement in itself alludes to Jesus' divine authority.

11. The first chapter of Mark's Gospel closes with the narrative of the healing of the leper (1.40-45).[46] The narrative has a lively tone and contains some unforgetable details. Here too, because of the nature of the illness and the consequent magnitude of the miracle, the awesome power of Christ stands out.[47]

Clear testimony of this miraculous power is provided by the words which bring about the healing: "I will; be clean," and the immediate result: "and immediately the leprosy left him" (1.41-42). It has been correctly observed that the healing command in this instance is characteristic of Jesus as the all-powerful eschatological prophet who acts as the bearer of God's power.[48]

A similar impression is conveyed by the fact that the person healed does not appear to obey Jesus' command, "See that you say nothing to anyone" (1.44). The text informs us that "he went out and began to talk freely about it" (1.45). The inference drawn from this is that the leper's healing was so striking and unusual that he was unable to remain silent; in fact, he declared it with unbridled enthusiasm. Not even the Messiah's insistence on silence could prevent him from proclaiming the event.[49]

12. In the second chapter of the Gospel, the concept of the Messiah's authority is decidedly expanded. This augmentation begins with the episode relating the healing of the paralytic in Capernaum (2.1-12).[50] Here too, the scene reflects a characteristic seen in the first chapter: the gathering of large numbers of people. The press of the crowd is so great that in order to bring him to Jesus, the paralytic's friends lower him through the roof of the house (2.4). We have already noted the indirect, yet clear christological character underlying references to the gathering of large crowds to see the Messiah.[51]

Christ addresses the paralytic with the assurance-command, "My son, your sins are forgiven" (2.5). There can be no doubt that Jesus' action presupposes a relationship between sin and sickness and underscores it. Emphasis, however, is not laid on the connection between sin and disease, but on the divine authority of Jesus.[52] This becomes clear as the narrative develops. Indeed, the scribes present at the event react most vehemently: "Why does this man speak thus? It is blasphemy! Who can forgive sins but God alone?" (2.7). The provocation is unreservingly direct and the questions raised demand a response. Equally unequivocal and direct is Jesus' reply: "the Son of man has authority on earth to forgive sins" (2.10).[53] This is the third consecutive episode at the beginning of Mark's Gospel in which the word "authority" is used in reference to the Messiah. In this case, however, there is an essential expansion of the term emphasizing the forgiveness of sins. This is a gigantic step, because it reveals that Christ possesses power and authority which belong only to God. The scribes identify the issue without hesitation: "It is blasphemy! Who can forgive sins but God alone?" The forgiveness of sins is the exclusive prerogative of God and any departure from this constitutes an act of blasphemy;[54] yet, Jesus, with complete certainty, proclaims that he is the bearer of exactly this kind of authority which may be attributed only to God.

This assertion constitutes a christological aspect of divine lordship and power, one which finds complete corroboration in most of the elements in this passage (2.1-12). The entire discussion about the forgiveness of sins takes place in conjunction with the healing of a grave, incurable illness as was paralysis. At Jesus' command, the paralytic arises and immediately takes up his pallet and walks out before them all (2.12). Three important points can be made in regard to this passage. First, the healing of the paralytic constitutes a visible and tangible demonstration of Jesus' authority to forgive sins. Second, according to the narrative, the views of the scribes are not expressed openly, not even whispered among themselves. They are inner thoughts which have not yet been expressed in words; yet, the Messiah knows them: "perceiving in his spirit that they thus questioned within themselves, (he) said to them. 'Why do you question thus in your hearts?' "(2.8). The Messiah is presented as having the power to know the secret thoughts and motives in people's souls. This type of power is presented as supernatural.[55] Finally, at the end of the narrative, we have a third verification of Jesus' divine authority, this time an indirect one. It is based on the impression that the healing of the paralytic has on the crowd which witnessed the event. The sight of the former paralytic carrying his wooden pallet as he passed through their midst was so unbelieveable, "that they were all amazed and glorified God saying, 'We never saw anything like this.' " (2.12). The verb ἐξίσταμαι used here conveys a sense of overwhelming astonishment, admiration, rapture, and even mental shock, as a result of the intensity of the impression made by this event.[56] The declaration, "We never saw anything like this," graphically propounds the unheard-of character of the event. The observation that they "glorified God" indicates that this occurence is in fact a revelation of divine power,[57] and for this reason the people offered praise to God.

The entire pericope (2.1-12) is saturated with the concept of Jesus' superhuman prerogative, especially in regard to the matter of forgiving sins. In the same passage, however, there is an element associated with the Christology of Passion. It is the opposition of the scribes, which appears in Mark for the first time (2.6-7). This opposition is laden with an animosity which is difficult for them to control. It is worth noting that the first accusation the scribes and Pharisees hurl against Jesus is that he "blasphemes." The same accusation will be repeated at the end of this Gospel by the chief priest, and will ultimately be the reason for Jesus' death sentence (15.63-64). While describing manifestations of Christ's divine authority, Mark also foretells the Passion, and the Passion casts its shadow over the present even though its fulfillment is in the relatively distant future.

13. After the healing of the paralytic, Mark describes a series of events and discussions which have many features in common and belong essentially to the same thematic group. These may be found in the successive pericopes of Mark 2.15-17; 2.18-22; and 2.23-28. In these passages, the Messiah's authority is presented in a new frame of reference.

The series begins with the narrative account of the calling of Levi (2.13-14),[58] a laconic passage not unlike the one describing the calling of the first four disciples (1.16-20). In the present pericope, however, the condensation of the language is even more profound, thereby placing greater emphasis on Jesus' authority.[59] Thus, the word Jesus uses to call Levi to discipleship is a single verb in the imperative: ἀκολούθει μοι ("follow me"). The Messiah's authority appears here with singular force. Levi's response is equally terse: "And he rose and followed him." The immediacy of this reaction is quite striking and underscores the radical impact[60] Christ's word has on peoples' lives. In final analysis, it clearly reveals his unique authority.

The account of the call of Levi contains another very significant point which can also be catalogued in the Christology of Authority. It is the fact that Levi is a tax collector in the service of Herod Antipas. The meaning of the term "tax collector"[61] is graphically defined as the account unfolds ("with sinners and tax collectors," 2.16). It is this type of person, however, that the Messiah calls to become his apostle. It is this very act, unprecedented and unacceptable to everyday Judaic piety and to the established religious ethos, that demonstrates his tremendous authority. Here, an authority is at work which could only have been inconceivable, even to the most distinguished teacher of the Law in Israel.

As the narrative progresses, the tension mounts to a peak. The Messiah does not stop with the call of Levi. Mark informs us that in the banquet which ensued, "many tax collectors and sinners were sitting[62] with Jesus" (2.15). The Messiah acts in a manner totally at odds with the code of behavior followed by the religious teachers of the day. The contrast is pronounced and the text expresses it with the repetition in the same verse of the key-phrase, "Why does he eat with tax collectors and sinners?" which depicts Jesus as acting in a manner unacceptable to the Pharisees.[63] Here is an expression of incomparable superiority. This superiority, however, is not based on blind or instinctive rebelliousness. Jesus interprets his revolutionary ministry as a product of profound love and in fulfillment of his divine mission of salvation: "Those who are well have no need of a physician, but those who are sick; I came not to call the righteous, but sinners" (2.17).[64] In this instance, the authority of Christ appears to operate on a level far above the ethical and religious perception of Israel's teachers of the Law; it is divine and its goals are divine.

14. Mark 2.18-22[65] presents another facet of Jesus' authority. This incident involves a question of religious law, that of fasting. According to the Markan account, the disciples of the Pharisees and of John the Baptist fasted,[66] whereas Jesus' disciples did not (2.18). For this reason, Jesus was severely criticized because he was obviously responsible for his disciples' actions. The Messiah dares to ignore and disregard the daily practice of the fasting regulations and customs of the powerful religious circles of Palestine, and this fact reveals his unique authority.[67] The authority of the Messiah is not attributed merely to his refusal to follow the prescribed fasting practices; Jesus places the subject of fasting on new theoretical basis. His disciples will fast "when the bridegroom is taken from them,"[68] because, "as long as they have the bridegroom with them, they cannot fast" (2.19-20). This theoretical position introduces the novel view that from this time on, the meaning and purpose of fasting are defined, determined and dependant on the person of the Messiah-Bridegroom.[69] This view is instrumental in coming to recognize the Messiah as holding "the place of God," and it declares forth rightly that he may act and legislate as God.

This conslusion is corroborated by the two parabolic sayings attached to the narrative which refer to "unshrunk cloth" and "new wine" (2.21-22). New Testament commentators have observed that here, we encounter a characteristic example of what is revolutionary in Jesus' teaching.[70] The revolutionary newness of his teaching, however, presupposes the Messiah's supernatural authority.

15. The third pericope of this series (2.15-17, 2.18-22, and 2.23-28)

is closely tied with the two preceding ones in terms of form and content. Here again, we have (a) a basic event which differs from established religious practice; (b) the opposition of the Pharisees; (c) Jesus' response to this opposition—a response which reveals his divine authority.

The particular theme which constitutes the focus of Mark 2.23-28[71] is Sabbath observance. The Pharisees criticize Jesus' disciples because they gathered ears of grain to eat as they walked through a field on the Sabbath.[72] The Messiah's reply justifies his disciples' action with three cogent arguments. The first refers to the example of David and his companions "when Abiathar was high priest" (2.25-26). This example is not used only as a historical precedent; it is not by chance that, in this context, mention is made of David, who is directly associated with the Messiah. Subsequently, the analogy immediately leads back to the unique authority of Jesus, which derives from his messianic identity.

The second argument Jesus advances against the Pharisees' criticism constitutes a revolutionary reassessment of the whole question of the Sabbath. "And he said to them, 'The Sabbath was made for man, not man for the Sabbath' " (2.27). This logion introduces a new concept, based on the understanding that man takes precedence over even the holiest of days.[73] This type of radical reevaluation and changing of priorities, could not be achieved without the presence of a divine authority.

The third argument is set forth in the form of a conclusion which brings the entire narrative to a close: "so the Son of man is lord even of the Sabbath"(2.28). This passage does create difficulties in exegesis; however, the interpretation which commends itself most strongly is that of the Messiah's lordship over the Sabbath.[74] Consequently, his disciples' action of breaking the Sabbath regulations, over any other reason, is based on Jesus' authority. Thus, Christ's authority, which permits abolition of the Sabbath observance is parallelled to the authority of God, who declared the Sabbath to be holy. There is no doubt that the inferred comparison projects the idea of Jesus' authority as being equivalent to that of God.[75]

Analysis of the three pericopes forming the general unit of Mark 2.13-28 has shown the marked degree to which these texts are defined by the concept of the Messiah's divine authority. In the same passages, however, we can readily detect elements which belong to the Passion.

Thus, in all these episodes, we observe Jesus facing confrontations which have a spirit of hostility so pronounced that it cannot be hidden or curbed. His adversaries belong to the wider circle of Pharisees. The element of Passion is found not only in their opposition to the Messiah's salvific work, but also in the fact that this opposition comes from the religious leaders of the people and is, in fact, put forward in the name of God and the law of God. An especially painful tone seems to exist in the common reference to the Pharisees and John's disciples on fasting. If John's followers share[76] the sentiments of the Pharisees against the Messiah, this would certainly create an additional source of distress for Jesus.

Perhaps the clearest element referring to the Passsion is the prophetic utterance, "The days will come when the bridegroom will be taken away from them, and then they will fast in that day" (2.20). The expression "is taken away from them" is reminiscent of Isaiah's " . . . his life is taken away from the earth (Is 53.8 in the Septuagint version) where reference is made to the sacrificial death of the "servant" of the Lord. Apart from this parallel, the reference in Mark clearly has to do with something terrible that will befall the Messiah, something which will generate so much sorrow that fasting will be an integral part and expression of it. It is reasonable to interpret Mark 2.20 as a clear reference to the death of Jesus. Indeed, the change from "days" to "in that day" in the second part of the passage points to a specific day on which anguish will reach its culmination. Such is the day of the expiatory death of the Messiah.

16. The first pericope in the third chapter of Mark's Gospel (3.1-6)[77] completes a cycle of narratives relating verbal confrontations between Jesus and the Pharisees. In this passage, the confrontation again has the Sabbath observance as its theme. The immediate cause of this dispute is the healing of a man "who had a withered hand" (3.1).

Here again, the narrative projects the Messiah's unique authority. The first suggestion of this is reflected in the initiative which Jesus shows in posing a hard question-dilemma to the Pharisees. Jesus' initiative presupposes a knowledge of the Pharisees' thoughts similar to that in Mark 2.8, and consequently suggests a supernatural spiritual perspicacity. This is emphasized in the subsequent information that Jesus was deeply saddened "at their hardness of heart" (3.5). This last phrase shows the advanced state of the Pharisees' spiritual callousness. The only element of this narrative which might explain

Jesus' strong judgment is that the Pharisees did not respond to Jesus' question; however, this element is insufficient to justify the diagnosis of so profound and complex a condition as "hardness of heart." Again, the necessity-presupposition of a supernatural knowledge is intimated in explanation of this advanced diagnosis.

Certain exegetes have viewed Mark's comment, "and he looked around at them with anger" (3.5) as an expression of Jesus' divine majesty.[78] This view is certainly justified in light of the series of events described in this same verse: "He (Jesus) said to the man, 'Stretch out your hand!' He stretched it out, and his hand was restored." Here once again, Christ's divine authority is clearly manifested. At the same time, the miraculous results of his intervention clearly reveal his incomparable superiority to the Pharisees in the theoretical dispute over the Sabbath.

While suggesting and supporting Jesus' divine authority, Mark 3.1-6 simultaneously creates a parallel image of his unavoidable violent end; therefore, it is the first pericope in Mark's Gospel where the Christology of Passion has decisively shaped substantial aspects of the text.

There is a clear initial trace of this Passion Christology in the manner in which Jesus' adversaries are introduced: "and they watched to see whether he would heal him on the Sabbath, so that they might accuse him" (3.2). Their animosity is undisguised. The verb κατη-γορεῖν, to accuse, will be used again by Mark in a similar construction in one other case: Jesus' trial before Pilate (15.3-4), and there, it will lead to his death sentence. In Mark 3.2, the expression "that they might accuse him," derived from the cycle of Passion narratives, constitutes a distinguishable prelude to the baneful events to follow.

In the succeeding verses, the tension and distance between Jesus and his opponents increases and the breach becomes unbridgeable. The terminology acquires an unprecedented acerbity: "with anger," "grieved," "hardness of heart" (3.5).[79] This enormous tension foretells the now growing climax and the final, mortal confrontation which will end in the sacrificial death of Christ. It is pre-announced at the conclusion of the pericope: "The Pharisees went out and immediately held counsel with the Herodians against him, how to destroy him" (3.6).

This passage embodies certain Passion elements, four of which are the following:

a) The conspiracy against the Messiah has no features of doubt or hesitation. It enters its final stage "quickly."[80] The sentence is irrevocably decided immediately after the episode in the synagogue.

b) The decision to destroy Jesus is made by groups that are at variance with each other, as were the Pharisees and the Herodians.[81] We have already mentioned the unusual nature of such a collaboration; however, it is not the first time in history that bitter rivals had come together to do away with a common adversary. The alliance between the Pharisees and Herodians reveals the magnitude of their hatred for Jesus. Heterogeneous religious and political factions converge inexorably with the same goal.

c) The statement, "they held counsel against him"[82] seems to indicate that the conspiracy against Jesus is carefully worked out and organized. His execution is not the result of a sudden urge or instinctive, blind reaction, but a well-thought plan which was conceived very early in Jesus' ministry.

d) The coalition of the Pharisees and Herodians does not seek to defame Jesus or intimidate him into ceasing his activities. Their purpose is to have him put to death: "to destroy him." The verb ἀπολέσωσιν[83] means "to kill" or "to put to death" and is used in exactly this same sense in Mark 11.18.

The existence of the four elements enumerated above demonstrates that Mark 3.6 was clearly written with the Passion in mind, and this has strongly influenced its wording. A number of scholars have considered the appearance of this clear Christology of Passion so early in the Gospel of Mark to be somewhat paradoxical.[84] Be that as it may, its prematurity is justified by the conflicts previously recorded in Mark 2.[85] The emphasis on the Passion, however, may further justify, or rather reveal Mark's christological design. In the first two chapters of the Gospel and in Mark 3.1-6 as well, the dominant image of Christ is one of sovereignty, authority and divine power, working dynamically on numerous levels. In Mark 3.6, we are reminded that this same Christ has been proscribed by his adversaries from the very beginning of his ministry, and he now presses on accompanied by an irrevocable death sentence.[86] Here, the Christology of Passion does not allow a one-sided and exclusive development of the Christology of Authority. In Mark 3.6, we are alerted that, at some point along Jesus' course there lies a violent death, planned by specific groups of people. The Christology of Authority, therefore does not end up in triumphalism.

MANIFESTATIONS OF JESUS' AUTHORITY: PHASE TWO (3.7-6.6).

1. With Mark 3.7-12,[87] we enter a new unit of the Gospel. The narratives which follow futher develop and widen the concept of Authority. This text constitutes a kind of general synoptic narrative imbued with the concept of Jesus' supernatural power and authority.

This concept is suggested by the information that great crowds of people gather everywhere Christ appears.[88] The expression "a great multitude" is used twice. The disciples are told to have a boat ready "because of the crowd, lest they should crush him" (3.9),[89] which can only mean that the press of the crowd was unbearable. Mark notes that the people gathered in response to Jesus' miraculous works (3.8), in particular, the healings he effected. The vividness of the scene is admirably conveyed by Mark's comment, " . . . he had healed many, so that all who had diseases pressed upon him to touch him" (3.10). The Evangelist's observations here immediately convey the idea of a vital benevolent power, which Christ dispenses without limit.

The same impression is supported by the numerous geographic references in verses 7 and 8. These mention a considerable number of regions, from southernmost Idumea to Tyre and Sidon in the northwest, to regions "beyond the Jordan." For the first time in the Gospel, reference is made to Jerusalem. This geographic listing includes all of Palestine with its heterogeneous population and immediately conveys a vivid image of general mobilization caused by Jesus' miraculous works.[90] It is highly likely that at this point, there is suggestion that Jesus' authority is also being recognized by non-Jews.

The clearest recognition of Jesus' authority, however, is on the part of evil spirits (3.11-12). The text is especially emphatic. "When the unclean spirits beheld him, they fell down before him," to express their total submission to his divine authority. At the same time, they proceed to make a complete confession which they declare quite loudly ("they cried out"), "You are the Son of God." Their confession is tantamount to an acceptance of Jesus' divine sonship, of his divine authority, as may be deduced by a comparison of this passage with corresponding phrasal parallels in Mark.[91] This confession has extra significance in that it is not an abstract one, but is accompanied by complete submission.

Yet, Jesus does not permit the evil spirits to make his divine identity known; "And he strictly ordered them not to make him known"

(3.12). Ostensibly, he forbids them because he rejects even their involuntary participation in his ministry, as recorded also in Mark 1.34. Jesus insists on their silence, in all likelihood because, as noted elsewhere, an untimely revelation of his divine sonship would cause an equally untimely acceleration of his end. If this latter hypothesis is correct, then an indirect reference to the Passion can be discerned.[92]

2. The account in Mark 3.13-19[93] concerns the calling of the twelve Apostles[94] and shows us a new dimension of Christ's authority. Jesus "went up on the mountain, and called to him those whom he desired; and they came to him" (3.13). The scene is alive with grandeur and power, and reference to the mountain suggests an Old Testament atmosphere of divine revelation. The process of choosing and the persons chosen are exclusively at the will of the Messiah. No other factors, criteria or presuppositions are mentioned; the will of the Messiah alone determines the call. This indicates an authority of absolute degree. Their direct response, with no trace of hesitation, underscores this: "and they came to him."

As the narrative unfolds, a new function of Jesus' divine authority is revealed in the naming and appointing of the Twelve: " . . . he appointed twelve, whom he also called apostles" (3.14 and 16). The verb ποιεῖν, to appoint, in this case is being used in a manner similar to particular instances in the Old Testament[95] and refers to the act of commissioning someone by divine authorization. It is typical of the Messiah's authority that, even in the first stages of his activity, he establishes a divinely ordained institution, a body charged with an extraordinary mission.

The work and mission of the Twelve is a variation of the corresponding messianic mission: "to be sent out to preach, and have authority to cast out demons" (3.14-15). It is here that Christ imparts to the apostles not only his preaching authority, but something even more significant: his matchless power to cast out demons. The expression used is impressive, because it refers to authority even over evil spirits. The bestowal of this kind of authority on the apostles emphasizes its immeasurable magnitude and irresistible power. Not only does the Messiah himself possess an abundance of immense power, but he is also capable of granting this power undiminished to his apostles.[96]

The account about the creation of the apostolic institution is an eloquent example of a text having the Christology of Authority as its theme. It is not by chance, however, that the account ends with a reference to Judas, "who betrayed him" (3.19). The Passion concept is never out of sight.

3. The narrative relating the selection and appointment of the Twelve is followed by a text (3.20-30)[97] which is composite both morphologically and christologically. The text begins with the report of an especially large gathering of people and Jesus' rather intense activity. Mark offers the characteristic comment "that they could not even eat" (3.20). At this point the first major theme of the narrative is introduced: "And when those who were with him heard it, they went out to seize him, for they said, 'He is beside himself'" (3.21). "Those who were with him" are in all likelihood Jesus' relatives,[98]who came to prevent him from continuing his ministry at such a relentless pace. Here, the text hints that the Messiah's activity and mode of life are unusual and incomprehensible from a human point of view; therefore, the people, in an attempt to classify or describe his condition, resort to categorizing him as irrational or behaving in a uniquely ecstatic manner ("he is beside himself").[99] Such a conclusion, however, will point out the singular character and rhythm of Jesus' ministry and way of life. His relatives' intervention clearly shows that the Messiah transcends human measures, and finally, it sheds light on the superhuman way he exercises his ministry.

This same episode, however, essentially belongs to that category of material which expresses a negative view of Jesus. It contains a very serious accusation ("he is beside himself") which stems either from a lack of understanding in its most favorable light, or out of hostility, as is more likely the case.[100] It also includes a decision to take decisive action, if "seize him" may be understood to mean "restrain him," "interfere with his activities," "engage him so that he cannot continue at the same pace," or "seize and incarcerate him," as would be done in the case of one dangerously unbalanced. Although the episode brings out elements of Jesus' supernatural character, it is more nearly aligned with texts of the Christology of Passion, and is written in a stark manner.

The episode of Mark 3.22-30 which follows also belongs to these texts and makes up the largest part of the pericope under analysis. It is at this point that the scribes "who came down from Jerusalem" appear on the scene and proceed to hurl a horrible accusation against

Christ: "He is possessed by Beelzebul, and by the prince of demons he casts out the demons" (3.22). This accusation is worse than that of blasphemy (2.7). It suggests a condition that is much more than deceit, sin or impiety. With an unhesitating reversal of the basic understanding of things, the religious leaders of Jerusalem declare that Jesus is possessed by the infamous evil spirit Beelzebul,[101] and that his ministry is satanic and not messianic, since everything he does is brought about by the prince of evil spirits. This fiery, extreme attack (in terms of accusations), issued by the established religious leadership, demonstrates that there is no room to retreat, that the decision to destroy Jesus is now rushing inexorably on course toward fulfillment. The Christology of Passion emerges from the events recorded with absolute clarity, mainly in the scribes' incredible accusation.

This accusation, however, also contains a fundamental element of Authority Christology. We can detect a tacit but nonetheless unquestionable acknowledgment of Jesus' amazing work in the scribes' declaration. This acknowledgement presupposes the fact that it is impossible to explain Jesus' deeds as the result of human factors or powers. On the human level, Christ's power is inexplicable. The scribes maintain that it can be explained only by demonic manifestation. Jesus retorts that it can be nothing other than divine, refuting the argument of his adversaries and supporting yet another facet of the Christology of Authority with unassailable logic (3.23-28).

In this instance, Jesus uses two arguments. The first is the elementary fact that it is impossible for Satan to do battle against himself or destroy himself. How can Jesus' ministry be motivated by Satan if the purpose of his ministry is precisely to neutralize and ultimately destroy demonic power? The second argument doubtlessly alludes to lines from a parable scene: "But no man can enter a strong man's house and plunder his goods unless he first binds the strong man; then indeed he may plunder his house" (3.27). In this pericope, it is clear that Jesus' exorcism of demons is not merely an incidental expression of a special power, but a much broader expression of Jesus' authority over the devil and his forces.[102] The Messiah has neutralized, subjugated and bound Satan, the "strong man," and has plundered his "household." By declaring this, Jesus not only repels the attack of the scribes, but reveals his divine identity and authority. Sovereignty over evil spirits and the destruction of their sinister rule is exclusively and absolutely the work of God.

The last three verses of Mark 3.20-30 further support the concept of Jesus' divine authority. They bring in the announcement-affirmation[103] that accusing Jesus of having an unclean spirit is equivalent to blasphemy against the Holy Spirit. Blasphemy of this sort will not be forgiven, because the sinner "is guilty of eternal judgment" (3.28-30). The sentence is final and absolute.[104] Jesus' work against evil spirits is the work of the Holy Spirit; consequently, the scribes' ascription of Jesus' work to demonic power is interpreted as conscious opposton to God and incurable depravity.[105] The Christology of Authority in light of the pneumatological opening made in Mark 3.28-30 belongs to the sphere of the absolute.

4. The third chapter of Mark's Gospel ends with the passage about Jesus' mother and brothers (3.31-35).[106] This account deals with family relationships[107] in connection with the Messiah's work, and brings up another, heretofore unknown aspect of Jesus' unique authority. The episode unfolds in two phases.

In the first phase, according to the Evangelist's account "his mother and his brothers came; and standing outside they sent to him and called him" (3.31). The request is relayed by the crowd surrounding Jesus, listening to his teaching. The repetition of the request reveals its intensity as well as the certainty that it reached the Messiah. "And he replied, 'Who are my mother and my brothers?'" (3.33). This reply may allude to the preceding episode (3.21), but the foremost meaning here is that Christ refuses to allow family ties to take precedence over the gospel.[108] When we consider the great importance the Jews placed on close family relationships, Jesus' attitude is extremely bold,[109] upsetting the complicated fabric of ideas concerning familial ties. Such radical action presupposes a superior authority.

In the second phase of the story, a further step is taken. Jesus, "looking around on those who sat about him. . . said, 'Here are my mother and my brothers. Whoever does the will of God is my brother and sister and mother.'" (3.34-35). Here, in place of blood relationships, Jesus introduces another form of human relationship and interpersonal association. The criterion and fundamental factor of a relationship is now the word of Christ and the will of God. This new and greater relationship is based on hearing and doing God's will as expressed by Jesus.[110] This new consideration of human relationships, this innovative change through the establishment of new criteria, underline the divine authority of the Messiah. His is an authority which, while definitively changing the basic forms of human relationships and interdependency, does not disorganize, but rather creates balance and restoration.

5. The fourth chapter of Mark's Gospel differs from the preceding ones. The greater part of it (4.1-34) is not a narrative, but presents extensive teachings of Jesus in the form of parables. This section contains the parables of the sower (4.3-20), the grain of wheat (4.26-29) and the mustard seed (4.30-33). In verses 21-25, Mark has inserted the sayings about the light hidden under a bushel and the giving of fair measure. The content of the three parables, the textual structure of Mark 4.1-34, and especially the position and function of this section in Mark's entire narrative scheme have been the objects of extensive exegetical debate.[111] These discussions properly belong to another area of research and therefore will not concern us here. Of considerable interest in this section is the fact that the pericopes forming the didactic unit of Mark 4.1-34 conceal some noteworthy elements of Authority Christology on one level and Passion Christology on another.

In the parable of the sower (4.2-20),[112] a serious means of exalting Jesus' authority is the use of parabolic teaching itself. The great gulf between Jesus' knowledge and that of his listeners is thereby emphasized. He possesses all knowledge, the entire "mystery of the kingdom of God" (4.11), and he communicates and interprets this to those whom he deems capable of actually hearing.[113] Seen from a negative standpoint, his authority is spotlighted because of his listeners' hopeless inability to understand these parables (4.11-12),[114] in that they have only limited ability to hear ("as they were able to hear it," 4.33), and because of the obvious difficulty experienced by the disciples: "Do you not understand this parable? How then will you understand all the parables?" (4.13).[115]

This same material, however, could be viewed as indirect reference to a Christology of Passion. The "inability" of the Messiah's word to tear down the obstacles to understanding and lead the multitude into the wonderful mystery of God's kingdom is a tribulation for him, a cross to bear before the Cross.[116] This concept dominates the greater part of the parable of the sower in alternating dramatic variations. It deals with the seed-word of Christ which falls on the beaten path, among the rocks or thorns, and therefore bears no fruit. This time, we do not encounter the inflexible and hostile attitude of the Pharisees.[117] We do, however, encounter human situations which prevent Jesus' words from entering the inner person, which hinder its growth and fruition. This phenomenon must surely be considered a source of deep pain for the Messiah and should be placed within the general area of the Passion.

Aside from that, one of the two main themes of the parable of the sower has to do with extraordinary fruition:[118] "But those that were sown upon the good soil are the ones who hear the word and accept it and bear fruit, thirtyfold and sixtyfold and a hundredfold" (4.20). The growth is wondrous, and with a ratio of one hundred to one, it borders on the unbelievable. Here, we can observe an aspect of the supernatural power of Christ's word which brings results of unusual size and scope. It is likely that his word will encounter resistance, that it will be choked by thorns, but it never stops effecting miraculous changes and generating incredible fruition.[119] Finally, the parable of the sower should be understood as a metaphorical reflection of Jesus' limitless authority.

In the parables of the grain of wheat and the mustard seed (4.26-32) the focus is on the kingdom of God, which constitutes one of the basic themes in Mark's Gospel. In his programmatic introductory proclamation, Jesus announced that "the kingdom of heaven is at hand" (1.15) and in his explanation of the parables, he speaks about the "secret (mysterion) of the kingdom of God" (4.11). We shall return to this topic in a later section. Here, we will restrict ourselves to a study of the specific elements which give the two parables in Mark 4.26-32 their distinctive color. In the first parable (4.26-29),[120] the growth and character of the kingdom of God are compared to the growth and fruition of a grain of wheat. Emphasis is placed on the silent process through which the sown seed develops into a ripened ear. The change takes place imperceptibly, almost automatically (4.28) from sowing to reaping, because of the concentrated power hidden in the grain of wheat.[121] The parable centers our attention on the tremendous esoteric power of God's kingdom and its quiet growth into eschatological perfection. It also underscores the idea that a considerable period of this growth process takes place in a completely quiet, unseen manner, while human society goes about its activities at a "regular" pace (4.27).

In the second parable (4.30-32)[122] as well, the main concept is the tremendous and concentrated inner dynamism of the kingdom of God.

The mustard seed, "the smallest of all the seeds upon the earth," is transformed by rapid growth to become "the greatest of all shrubs" (4.31-32). The antithesis "smallest of all . . . greatest of all,"[123] reveals the magnitude and character of the power which brings about this change.

The limitless power of growth, change and fruition of God's kingdom[124] stands out graphically in the two parables of Mark 4.26-32. The kingdom, however, is directly associated with the preaching, person and work of the Messiah. Such a correlation automatically ascribes to Jesus the incomparable dynamism of the kingdom of God.

6. This lengthy parabolic teaching is followed by the narrative pericope of Mark 4.35-41.[125] With this material we return to accounts which describe miracles that Jesus performed. The particular event in Mark 4.35-41 is that of the calming of the storm on Lake Tiberias. This incident, which is also reported by the Evangelists Matthew (8.23-27) and Luke (8.22-25), contains eloquent evidence of Jesus' supernatural authority.[126] The divine power of Jesus is revealed to the disciples in a situation filled with mortal danger from which there is not apparent escape. The cause of their peril is a violent storm: "And a great storm of wind arose, and the waves beat into the boat, so that the boat was already filling" (4.37). And even though the boat is in danger of sinking from moment to moment and the disciples are panic-stricken, Jesus is "in the stern, asleep on the cushion" (4.38). Jesus' demeanor is so incompatible with the circumstances that the disciples awaken him in a boldly petulant tone: "Teacher, do you not care if we perish?" (4.38). Jesus' bearing in this account, highlighted by the diametrically opposite behavior of his disciples, clearly reveals a divine authority which emanates total tranquility and the assurance that the crisis will pass.

Jesus' divine authority is painted in vivid colors in the magnificent scene which follows: "And he awoke and rebuked the wind and said to the sea, 'Peace! Be still!' " (4.39). Christ acts by his word alone; without becoming agitated, without being carried away,[127] he remains calm in a situation of general upheaval and terror caused by the high winds and surging waves. The Evangelist uses the verb ἐπετίμησεν ("rebuked"), characteristic of relationships of authority and subjection, superiority and dependence. Jesus' rebuke, i.e. his command, is restricted to two imperatives, "Peace! Be still!" As was observed in other incidents,[128] Jesus' word is as brief as possible, yet most powerful. It is both definitive and final, uttered without introduction, periphrase or elaboration. It clearly reveals divine authority.

The consequences are astonishing: "And the wind ceased, and there was a great calm (4.39). The immediate transformation of the "great storm" into a "great calm" proclaims the incomparable power of Jesus.

Two more details from the final scene of the sea-storm episode reinforce the idea of Christ's limitless power. The first is the disciples' reaction in witnessing the sudden, dramatic change in the weather. Mark observes that "they were filled with awe" (4.41). Here is to be understood an impression of fear, awe, astonishment and amazement experienced by the disciples as they observed an unprecedented supernatural phenomenon.[129] The second detail concerns the words spoken by the disciples: "Who then is this that even wind and sea obey him?" (4.41). The question posed by the disciples unequivocally acknowledges Jesus' sovereignty over the forces of nature.[130] Their recognition does not refer to areas in which Jesus' power is already known (illness, evil spirits, the Law, family ties), but to something entirely new. For the first time, the Messiah manifests his lordship over the forces of nature.

Special attention should be paid to the fact that the particular elements refered to are the wind and the sea. Jewish theological thought considered these elements to be bearers of gigantic power. The sea especially, according to the Old Testament and apocalyptic writings constituted a menacing entity from which came terror and monstrous beings.[131] Therefore, when the sea is described as "obeying" the Messiah, it is of great christological significance.

Some exegetes have observed a certain similarity between the narrative of the quieting of the storm in Mark 4.35-41 and the story of Jonah.[132] It is not inconceivable that the account of the sea tragedy of Jonah was in the thoughts of the Evangelist as he related the episode on Lake Tiberias. The parallels in the two narratives are quite striking. The sovereignty of God over the sea in Jonah's situation has been transferred to Jesus in Mark 4.35-41. Christ has dominion over the sea exactly as did the all-powerful Lord of the Old Testament.[133]

The incident of the stilling of the storm also appears to contain an indicator of Passion Christology. After the calming of the sea, Jesus reproaches his disciples with the words: "Why are you afraid? Have you no faith?" (4.40). His rebuke is sharp,[134] especially when compared to the milder expressions in the parallel accounts of Matthew 8.26 and Luke 8.25. The intensity and relative harshness of Mark 4.40 betrays Jesus' grief, caused by his disicples' lack of understanding, their terrible difficulty in comprehending whom they really encounter in the person of this Jesus who is with them. Building by degrees of intensity, this theme runs through the entire Gospel of Mark. Its conclusion, which is reached in Judas' betrayal (14.43-46), the disciples' flight (14.50) and Peter's denial (14.66-72), numbers it among the primary themes of Passion Christology. Consequently, Jesus' reprimand in Mark 4.40 belongs within this same christological framework.

7. The healing of the demoniac in the country of the Gerasenes (5.1-20)[135] is yet another occurence which proclaims Jesus' divine authority. The narrative is rather lengthy and presents a dramatic plot in miniature. Here again, Jesus' divine authority and power over evil spirits is demonstrated emphatically. This concept was encountered in earlier chapters of Mark (1.23-28, 34, 39; 3.14-16, 22-30); however, in Mark 5.1-20, it is presented analytically with a number of significant elements.[136] The three main elements are the following:

The first deals with the condition of the Gerasene demoniac, who lived "night and day among the tombs and on the mountains always crying out and bruising himself with stones," and "no one could bind him any more, even with a chain," and "the chains he wrenched apart and the fetters he broke in pieces and no one had the strength to subdue him" (5.2-5). One can readily determine from the foregoing description[137] that here, Jesus is confronting a tremendous demonic force. Indeed, as the narrative unfolds, it is revealed that the Gerasene is possessed by a great number of evil spirits ("My name is legion, for we are many," 5.9), and they are so powerful that they cause the immediate drowning of two thousand swine (5.13). Jesus finds himself the opponent of a veritable army of violent demons.

Yet, this satanic legion is decidely powerless before and submissive to the Messiah's authority. The demoniac, "when he saw Jesus from afar, ran and worshiped him, and crying out with a loud voice said, 'What have you to do with me, Jesus, Son of the Most High?' "(5.6-7). There is complete recognition, followed by a loud affirmation of Jesus' identity and accompanied by an attitude of worship. The demoniac's affirmation is at the same time a declaration of Jesus' divine authority and of the unbridgeable gulf between him and the demonic powers.

To their declaration of submission the horde of evil spirits adds the entreaty, "I adjure you by God, do not torment me" (5.7). This urgent plea is made by terror-stricken supplicants confronted by an all-powerful adversary whose authority to punish cannot be ignored.[138] The intensity of the scene is magnified by the addition of two more petitions which the demons direct to Jesus through the Gerasene demoniac (5.10, 12). The entire pericope dramatically depicts the demons' state of humiliation and submission when they encounter the Ruler-Messiah. In this framework Mark will say characteristically of Jesus that "he gave them leave" (5.13), i.e. he permitted the evil spirits to enter the swine. The verb ἐπέτρεψεν indicative of supremacy and lordship, once again underscores the Messiah's limitless power and authority over demonic forces.[139]

The second point which emphasizes Jesus' divine authority is found in the description of the consequences following the Gerasene's liberation-healing. He who just a short time before was demon-possessed is now seen "sitting there, clothed and in his right mind" (5.15), near Jesus. The sight is not simply astonishing—it is a tangible affirmation of a unique, divine intervention.[140] The people of the city are therefore paralyzed with fear when they come upon the scene (5.15). Their fear assumes the dimension of panic when they are informed in detail about the events which have just transpired. "And they began to beg Jesus to depart from their neighborhood" (5.17). In essence, this entreaty is a striking declaration of Christ's supernatural power. The Gerasenes immediately acknowledge this power which brings about incalculable changes in individuals and causes extraordinary occurances. They fearfully beg him to remove this power from their midst.[141] They seek to increase the distance between themselves and Jesus in order that they might avoid the consequences of being confronted by an individual who has such authority over demonic powers.

The third point is encountered in the final verses of the narrative. When Jesus is preparing to embark, he says to the Gerasene who was healed, "Go home to your friends and tell them how much the Lord has done for you, and how he has had mercy on you" (5.19). "The Lord," in this passage is used instead of "God." Jesus' ministry is viewed as God's work. Mark observes characteristically that the former demoniac "began to proclaim in the Decapolis how much Jesus had done for him" (5.20). In the pericope of the healing of the Gerasene, a shift is made from "what the Lord (God) has done" to "how much Jesus had done." At this juncture, it is acknowledged that the power and authority which Jesus has over demons is in reality the power and authority of God.[142]

8. In the pericope of Mark 5.21-43,[143] the account of the two miracles shows Jesus' supernatural power in ways heretofore unknown. There can be no doubt that the healing of the woman with an issue of blood and the raising of the daughter of Jairus demonstrate unique aspects of the Messiah's divine authority. This too may have prompted the Evangelist to weave these two narratives together.[144]

The uniqueness of the incident involving the woman with the chronic hemorrage lies in the fact that her healing is effected neither by Jesus' word nor by the laying on of his hands. According to Mark's description, the ailing woman "having heard the reports about Jesus came up behind him in the crowd and touched his garment. For she said, 'If I touch even his garments, I shall be made well.'" (5.27-28). Healing takes place without the woman's begging and with no initiative shown in the matter on the part of the Messiah. This is emphasized as the events of the pericope unfold, when Jesus, "perceiving in himself that power had gone forth from him" asked, "Who touched my garments?" (5.30). This miraculous restoration of health is accomplished by power "going out" from Jesus, and it is at this point precisely that the uniqueness of the event becomes evident. Despite a diversity of opinions, New Testament scholars appear to agree that, in Mark 5.30, the term "power" refers to a divine healing power which abides in Jesus.[145] For the first time in Mark's Gospel, mention is made of the Messiah's healing energy as a palpable force transmitted by touch. Jesus' immediately perceptible, tangible and abundant miraculous healing power radiates throughout the narrative of the woman with the issue of blood.

The dramatic episode dealing with the daughter of Jairus reveals yet another aspect of Christ's unique authority. Mark 5.35-43 methodically sets the stage for the great revelation by assuring us that the child is dead. The dreadful opening announcement ("Your daughter is dead; Why trouble the teacher any further?" 5.35) is followed by a description of the mourners at Jairus' house ("people weeping and wailing loudly" 5.38). The climax is reached on a note of tragic irony. When Jesus, using his own language, says to the bystanders, "the child is not dead but sleeping" (5.39), they ridicule him ("And they laughed at him" 5.40).[146] The death of the child is so incontrovertible that any other assertion merely evokes bitter, deriding laughter.

When the crisis has reached the irrevocable finality of death, Jesus' supernatural authority is revealed. Holding the dead girl's hand, the Messiah utters the divine command, "Little girl, I say to you, arise" (5.41).[147] That which ensues is astounding: "And immediately the girl got up and walked" (5.42). The impression made by this turn of events cannot be adequately described. The Evangelist informs us that those present "were immediately overcome with amazement" (5.42). It has already been noted (2.12) that the verb ἐξίσταμαι expresses a combination of emotions such as intense astonishment, amazement, ecstacy, and even a type of insanity (cf. 3.21) resulting from the impact of powerful existential situations on an individual. The usage here of the cognate object accompanied by an emphatic quantitative adjective (ἔκστασις μεγάλη) imparts an even greater intensity to the verb.

The magnitude and character of impression Jesus created can be explained only by the magnitude and character of miracle he performed. The resurrection of a dead girl certainly constitutes a mighty expression of divine power. The Messiah appears as the lord of life and death. This supreme authority is also evident in his statement: "The child is not dead but sleeping" (5.39),[148] and it is precisely because he has lordship over death that he can give it a new name, thus completely transforming its nature.

We should not fail to observe that Jesus takes only three disciples with him to the house of Jairus: Peter, James and John (5.37). These three alone will be with Christ at his Transfiguration (9.2) and again during his agony at Gesthemane on the night his enemies arrest him (14.33). The two latter episodes have a fundamental christological character, and this point at once underscores the significance of referring to these three leading disciples in the framework of the raising of Jairus' daughter. It thereby establishes the christological importance of this miracle. It becomes clear that his authority over death not only manifests a supreme expression of Jesus' divine authority, but could be considered a kind of theophany as well.[149]

9. Jesus' visit "to his own country" (6.1-6),[150] with which Mark begins the sixth chapter of his Gospel, is defined by aspects of the Christology of Passion. From the emphasis on Jesus' authority observed in the fifth chapter, we now move to a keen reminder of the trials and tribulations which await him.[151]

This reminder is introduced by a series of questions which the Nazarenes ask themselves. The initial queries in this section display an inherent acknowledgement of authority in Jesus' words and an awareness of his power: "and many who heard him were astonished, saying, 'Where did this man get all this? What is the wisdom given to him? What mighty works are wrought by his hands!' " (6.2). When we take note of the comments accompanying these questions, we perceive that the latter reflect a decidedly hostile tone; however, this does not inhibit their becoming a reference to particular data showing an unusual potency of word and deed.[152]

In the verses which follow, however, the questions of the Nazarenes become increasingly hostile, expressing an attitude of disbelief and disdain: "Is not this the carpenter, the son of Mary and brother of James and Joses and Judas and Simon, and are not his sisters here with us?" (6.3). This is the only place in the entire New Testament where Jesus is referred to as "the carpenter."[153] The use of this occupational term for Jesus in the present context is certainly derogatory. This disdainful attitude continues unabated in the use of the phrase, "the son of Mary." The Jews did not ordinarily identify an individual through his mother, but almost always through the father. In parallel passages, Luke writes, "He is the son of Joseph" (Lk 4.22) and Matthew, "the son of the carpenter" (Mt 13.55). The only plausible explanation for Mark's retention of the phrase "the son of Mary" is that it is an expression of contempt and, consequently, indicative of the hostile attitude of the Nazarenes.[154]

Similar observations can be advanced for the remaining question (6.3) of Jesus' fellow citizens. The relatives of Jesus[155] who were mentioned in this passage were obviously ordinary inhabitants of Nazareth, whose origins, in the opinion of the Nazarenes, were so humble that no prophet or important teacher could come from them. It was inconceivable to the Nazarenes that the Messiah could be related to so undistinguished a family, and this propels the questions of the Nazarenes, and it is this very inconceivability that manifests their great contempt.

The queries result in a mental condition the Evangelist describes with the phrase, "And they took offense at him" (6.3). The verb here ἐσκανδαλίζοντο is a blend of insult,[156] wrath and, especially, disbelief, as one can readily ascertain from the text which follows: "And he marveled because of their unbelief" (6.6). Jesus himself describes the situation precisely when he applies to himself a well-known Hebrew maxim: "A prophet is not without honor, except in his own country" (6.4). In this maxim, the term "without honor" (ἄτιμος) has particular significance. It represents a judgment as well as the Nazarenes' emotional attitude regarding Jesus. It constitutes a keyword in the magnificent prophecy of Isaiah concerning the suffering of "the servant of the Lord."[157] The presence of the term "without honor" in Mark 6.4 may well be an echo of the passage in Isaiah 53.2-3.

The image of Christ as drawn in Mark 6.1-6 is of a Messiah who is disdained, repelled, cruelly insulted and finally rejected. It can therefore be readily classifed within the framework of Passion Christology because it also reveals a mode of human behavior which, as it develops and intensifies, will ultimately lead to the death of Christ. This particular element has been retained fully in the parallel passage in the Gospel of Luke, in which an attempt on Jesus' life is reported.[158]

In his account of the Nazareth episode, Mark includes another revealing comment when he states: "And he could do no mighty work there, except that he laid his hands upon a few sick people and healed them" (6.5). This statement has been characterized as exceptionally daring, because it calls attention to a situation in which Jesus could not perform miracles.[159] Mark's boldness shows a broader understanding of the Messiah's Passion. The Passion does not consist only of an affliction which springs from enmity, persecution or martyrdom, but also of an "inability" to act because of human resistance. According to Mark 6.1-6, the Nazarenes' resistance which actually arises from a number of factors, is so persistent that it impedes the manifestation of Jesus' unique power.[160] This is undoubtedly a source of distress for the Messiah and belongs to the wider circle of Passion elements which permeate the narrative in Mark 6.1-6.

MANIFESTATIONS OF JESUS' AUTHORITY: PHASE THREE (6.7-8.26)

1. Following the events at Nazareth, which turn our attention to the Passion Christology, comes the pericope of the mission of the Twelve (6.7-13), a text indicative of the Christology of Authority.[161] This pericope has points in common with Mark 3.13-16, but also contains special added features.

The main theme in Mark 6.7-13 is the granting to the twelve Apostles a special authority to exorcise: "and gave them authority over the unclean spirits" (Mk 6.7). The fundamental word used is "authority" as in Mark 3.15, and the emphasis is obvious. The added element in Mark 6.7-13 is the information that the Twelve "cast out many demons." This authority is confirmed by the results of its application. Futhermore, Mark 6.12 informs us that the Twelve did not only receive authority to expel demons, but that "they went out and preached that men should repent." This suggests that the Messiah also entrusted them with a preaching mission on a par with his own, which would indicate an added gift of authority.[162] In the same passage, we are also told that the twelve Apostles "anointed with oil many that were sick and healed them." The nature of this information confirms the fact that the Twelve worked miraculous healings similar to those of Jesus.[163] Consequently, Mark 6.7-13 describes not only the giving of further powers to the Apostles, but also the embodiment of these powers in astonishing works sealed by the Messiah's authority. Mark's interweaving of the above bits of information paints a picture of the many-faceted and boundless authority of Jesus.[164]

We should not forget that, at this point in the Gospel story, the Twelve are not what they became after the Resurrection. Further on, Mark will offer examples of the Apostles' imperfection, weakness, pusillanimity, little faith, and spiritual blindness (7.18; 8.17-21; 8.33; 9.33-34; 10.41-45; 14.32-41; 14.66-72). To these same men, however, the Messiah gives enormous powers. This is an extra indication of his divine power which is not threatened by the Twelve's contingent inadequacies or poor use of those messianic powers. Jesus' divine authority is able to control and safeguard the correct functioning of the messianic gifts given to the Twelve against their apparent weaknesses.[165]

The tone of the guidelines Jesus gives in Mark 6.8-11 is likewise one of lofty authority. Their content presupposes absolute poverty and a voluntary divorce from all resources. The Twelve, with their known personality traits, could not have been thrown into this new adventure of missionary work if the authority and divine lordship of the Messiah had not offset their doubts and fears.[166] Jesus' guidelines also contain an especially serious side: "And if any place will not receive you and they refuse to hear you, when you leave, shake off the dust that is on your feet for a testimony against them" (6.11). The authority which dictates the above guidelines is truly divine because it gives the Apostles the power of irrevocable judgment on a soteriological and eschatological level.[167]

2. Between the passages of the mission of the Twelve (6.7-13) and

their accounts of it (6.30-33), Mark inserts the narrative of John the Baptist's execution (6.14-29).[168] This narrative has been the cause of many discussions between exegetes on theological, historical and philological grounds.[169] Apart from specific answers to these questions, we believe that the form, content, and position of the pericope in the general context of this section of the Gospel are better understood on the basis of Mark's christological views which we have already pointed out. It seems that here is a passage intensely allusory of Passion Christology from which traces of the Christology of Authority are not entirely absent.

Mark 6.14-29 is obviously martyrological.[170] Already at the beginning (6.16), the beheading of John is reported as a historical fact, so that what follows is a retrospective description of the dramatic events leading up to it. The successive steps of the passage lead to the inevitable execution of the protagonist. The arrest and imprisonment follow the original conflict which is laid out in a climate of unforeseen developments (6.17-20). Just when the situation in the passage seems to be relaxing (6.21-23) the beheading of John is brought in with all its blood-curdling cruelty (6.24-28).

Obviously, Mark 6.14-29 has the noble figure of the Baptist at its center and in most vivid colors projects the martyr's death he undergoes in the course of the events described. The last part of the narrative (6.24-28) is typical in that the head of John is mentioned continuously (four times in five verses). The final scene in Herod's palace, with the horrible procession of the Forerunner's head "on a platter," displaces every other image and impression, confirming the passage's martyrological character.

It seems strange at first sight that the Evangelist interrupts the narrative of the Messiah's activities to insert a long[171] passage about the execution of John. The emphasis on the latter with an inordinately long passage at this point in the Gospel story is not explicable by Mark's narrative technique. More convincing here is the view that John's violent death is a clear indicator and preamble to the tortuous end of the Messiah, and it is with this perspective and this thought that the Evangelist refers to it.[172]

The parallelism lies precisely in the violent and martyrly death. There are, however, other correlations on particular points. John is executed by the political power which governs under the direction and tolerence of the Romans. Similarly, the Messiah will be executed by a Roman political authority. In John's case, the leader seems not to desire his execution, but rather has respect for him ("knowing that he was a righteous and holy man," 6.20). In Jesus' case too, Pilate apparently tries to prove him innocent (15.2-15, especially 15.10, "he perceived that it was out of envy that the chief priests had delivered him up"). There are also parallels in the entombment. After John's execution, "when his disciples heard of it, they came and took his body, and laid it in a tomb" (6.29). Here, there are phrasal similarities to the description of Jesus' entombment: "And he (Joseph)... taking him down, wrapped him in the linen shroud, and laid him in a tomb." (15.46)

This analysis presumes that Mark 6.14-29 is in its excellent vividness, composition and parallelism a prelude to the painful death of the Messiah; and it therefore is placed within the area of Passion Christology. This moreover explains its position at this point in the Gospel. All that came before built on the idea of Jesus' divine authority and supernatural power with accentuated rhythm. The insertion of John's martyrdom abruptly changes our point of view and gives us another christological aspect. We suddenly become conscious of the concept and image of the Messiah's Passion, and this helps us see the divine power and glory of the Messiah in its right perspective.

At any rate, the pericope Mark 6.14-29 lacks no distinguishable traces of Authority Christology. The introductory verses (6.14-16) have the wondrous works of Jesus as an informative substratum. The people's lack of a reasonable explanation and the fact that they resort to theories about John's being resurrected or the Prophet Elijah having returned[173] underscores the supernatural character of these works and implicitly stresses the uniqueness of Christ's power.

3. In the following pericope (6.30-44),[174] the main theme is once again Christ's unique power and authority. In the opening section (6.30-33), the Apostles come to give account to Jesus of all "that they had done and taught" (6.30). The material confirms that the authority the Messiah gave to the Twelve (6.7) has already been translated into authoritative words and unusual works not unlike his own. The gamut of messianic powers are now manifested in the Apostles, and the impression of Christ's divine power becomes deeper. This picture is completed with supplementary material about great numbers of people flocking around them to an unbearable degree. Even when Jesus and his disciples go off in a boat to the opposite shore, "they ran there on foot from all the towns and got there ahead of them"

(6.33). We have already explained that the motif of the mobilization of the enormous crowd, and the mass gathering of people wherever Jesus happens to be, is a constant expression of Authority Christology in Mark.

The greater part of Mark 6.30-44[175] describes the miracle of the feeding of the five thousand. This miracle is described in all four Gospels (Mt 14.13-21, Lk 9.10-17, Jn 6.1-14), which shows its significance and important position in ancient tradition. In Mark 6.30-44 we find one of the most notable manifestations of Jesus' divine power.[176] With captivating realism, the passage alludes to the negative factors which show off this power. The place where these events occur is "lonely" (ἔρημος) (6.35).[177] It is not a city, nor is it a center where food supplies would be readily available. The time for dinner had already passed. The food the Apostles had with them was little, while the crowd was enormous, in that men alone numbered five thousand. At the request of his disciples in regard to feeding the crowd, the Messiah orders, "You give them someting to eat." He gets an answer which shows the magnitude of the problem: "Shall we go and buy two hundred denarii worth of bread and give it to them to eat?" (6.37).[178] These drawbacks describe a situation which would appear not to have a "natural" solution.

At this critical juncture, Jesus intervenes, miraculously multiplying the "five loaves and two fish" which the disciples had with them (6.38-41), and supplies the whole crowd. The narrative excellently propounds the abundance of food and the overcompensation of need: "And they all ate and were satisfied. And they took up twelve baskets full of broken pieces and of the fish.[179] And those who ate the loaves were five thousand men" (6.42-43). This case reveals Jesus' divine authority over physical elements and their yields. It is manifested in an unusual way which creates amazing processes within the physical world and its produce. The miracle is of such an order and magnitude that as the Evangelist John remarks in his parallel pericope: "When the people saw the sign which he had done, they said, 'This is indeed the prophet who is come into the world!'" (Jn 6.14). Mark makes no such comment, because he considers it rather obvious, as we can surmise from Mark 6.52.

The feeding of the five thousand has two special characteristics. The first is the warm manifestation of Jesus' affection. This was shown in the first sentence, "he had compassion on them, because they were like sheep without a shepherd" (6.34),[180] and because the miracle is exclusively the result of the Messiah's initiative. The disciples sought another way, but in a matchless gesture of compassion, Jesus prepares the miraculous dinner. Jesus' divine power works in a way that shows his infinite affection for people even when it is not sought, while at the same time, it emphasizes the significance of filling, not only spiritual needs, but material ones as well.

The second characteristic is the special wording with which the main phase of Christ's miraculous intervention is described: "And taking the five loaves and the two fish he looked up to heaven, and blessed, and broke the loaves, and gave them to the disciples" (6.41). In this passage, the verbs "taking," "looked up," "blessed," "broke," "gave" are mentioned successively. Four of these five verbs also exist in the Markan description of the institution and tradition of the Eucharist during the Last Supper: "he took bread, and blessed, and broke it, and gave it to them" (14.22). The coincidence cannot be accidental, as exegetes have already pointed out. It is obvious that the phrasing of the miracle of the Feeding of the Five Thousand has been affected by that of the Last Supper.[181] This means that the atmosphere of the Passion which dominates the Last Supper and the sense of the Lord's death as embodied in Holy Eucharist are suggested, even though indirectly, in Mark 6.41.[182] The description of a miraculous and magnificent manifestation of Jesus' divine power and authority is recoreded using words associated with his Passion.

4. The narrative following the feeding of the five thousand (6.45-52)[183] is another clear indicator of the Christology of Authority. The topic of this passage is Jesus' saving his disciples from a tempest which developed from a strong wind. The incident is reminiscent of the calming of the storm and the terrible disturbance of the sea in Mark 4.35-41 and therefore needs no detailed anaylsis.[184] We shall point out only two noteworthy differences. In Mark 6.45-52, the disciples are alone[185] in the boat, tossed by the opposing wind. Jesus is on dry land, absorbed in prayer (6.46). His disciples' plight on the water had gone on for some time when Jesus, around three in the morning, takes the initiative to help them, and for this reason "he came to them, walking on the sea" (6.48). The incident is unprecedented,[186] it oversteps natural law, and fills the disciples with astonishment and fear: "but when they saw him walking on the sea they thought it was a ghost, and cried out; for they all saw him and were terrified" (6.49-50). Here, Christ appears with manifest supernatural authority over nature, in that he can walk on the sea. In this

respect, the Christology of Authority in the present episode is more
advanced than that in Mark 4.35-41. There, Jesus was "in the stern,
asleep on the cushion," while here "he comes, walking on the sea."
His appearance and manner of coming are an amazing manifestation of divine power.[187]

There is yet a second difference between the two like incidents,
and this has to do with Jesus' manner of calming the tempest. In
Mark 4.35-41, the Messiah gives the command, "Peace! Be still!"
while in Mark 6.45-52, he simply "got into the boat with them and
the wind ceased." In the latter incident, Jesus has no need of speaking. His mere boarding the boat, battered by the storm on Lake
Tiberias, is enough to immediately change the harsh weather into mild.

The description of the calming of the storm in Mark 6.45-52 does
not fail to mention the disciples' astonishment at witnessing these
supernatural events. Mark's wording is declaratory of the impression
made: "And they were utterly astounded" (6.51). The words charge
one another with intensity. The use of such wording again graphically
alludes to a recognition of Jesus' divine authority and prerogative.
In Matthew's description of the same incident, this element has been
expressed openly and directly: as soon as "the wind ceased," "those
in the boat worshiped him, saying, 'Truly, you are the Son of God.'"
(Mt 14.33).

Mark accompanies the information about the disciples' astonishment and fear with the explanation that "they did not understand
about the loaves, but their hearts were hardened" (6.52). This seem-
ingly strange explanation is appending a grave rebuke against the
disciples. They are characterized as having "hardened hearts," and
advanced spiritual blindness. This rebuke, however, indirectly shows
the uniqueness of the Messiah's power, because it certifies that his
divine authority was manifested with such magnificence and intensity
at the still recent event of the Feeding of the Five Thousand, that
his disciples must not have been amazed at seeing him walk on the
sea or calm a storm.

At the same time, however, there is an allusion to the Christology
of Passion in the expression "they did not understand about the loaves,
but their hearts were hardened." This elementary difficulty in understanding, this advanced hardness of heart in the disciples doubtlessly
constitutes a source of distress for the Messiah, and for this reason
it is a Passion element in the general sense. The reactions of the
disciples, without being reactions like those with the scribes and

Pharisees, they still belong to the same general circle of human weakness and spiritual blindness which lead up to Jesus' execution.[188]

5. The sixth chapter of Mark's Gospel closes with a general description of the Messiah's healing activity in the region of Gennesaret (6.53-56).[189] The description epigrammatically emphasizes Jesus' multifaceted and inexhaustible power to heal infirmity with two basic points of information.

The first refers to the masses of people that rush to meet Jesus requesting and expecting healing, and the people's tumult upon learning of his arrival. Very indicative are phrases like "immediately the people recognized him, and ran about the whole neighborhood;" "(they) began to bring sick people on their pallets to any place where they heard he was," and "wherever he came, in villages, cities, or country, they laid the sick in the marketplaces" (6.54-56). The impression is one of general excitement and mass refuge to Christ's miraculous healing power. As we have repeatedly pointed out, this stresses the Messiah's divine authority and power.[190]

The second point relates to the manner of healing. Mark describes it briefly: "And (they) besought him that they might touch even the fringe of his garment; and as many as touched it were made well" (6.56). This manner of healing is reminiscent of the healing of the woman with the issue of blood (5.25-34); but here, Christ permits them to touch his garment, and his healing affects many people and not just one. These special bits of information build an impression more intense than that of the episode with the woman with the issue of blood. In Mark 6.53-56, Jesus works in a manner which shows the use of an enormous, boundless power which only God could have.

6. The greater part of the seventh chapter (7.1-23)[191] contains Jesus' teachings about ritual and ethical purity, prompted by questions.[192] Here, the Evangelist returns to the subject of Christ's prerogative as divine lawmaker and bearer of absolute truth.

Already in the opening verses (7.2-4), Jesus' superior authority appears when it is written that some of his disciples "ate with hands defiled, that is, unwashed." The disciples' action, as is evident from the context, constitutes a clear deviation from the rule which "the Pharisees, and all the Jews" followed. It is evident that not keeping this rule was causally bound with Jesus and presupposes his divine lordship. Behind the disciples' act in the question of washing hands, one can see the prerogative of the Messiah as lawmaker. This is also corroborated by the subsequent accusation which the Pharisees direct at Jesus in the form of a question (7.5). The reproachful tone of the question signifies that blame is placed on him, but such blame for overstepping strong general rules of religious conduct betrays a superhuman lordship.

The idea of Christ's divine authority as teacher and lawmaker is expressed in his answer to the Pharisees (7.6-13).[193] The answer places the discussion about washing hands on a new level, and using a concrete example (7.10-13), it shows the sharp opposition between the tradition of the Pharisees and the law of God. The Messiah's language in this incident is biting: "You leave the commandment of God, and hold fast the tradition of men" (7.8); "You have a fine way of rejecting the commandment of God in order to keep your tradition!" (7.9); "thus making void the word of God through your tradition which you hand on" (7.13). The basic verbs here are very strong: ἀφέντες, ἀθετεῖτε, ἀκυροῦντες. Such an intense, inexorable indictment, which essentially overturns the almighty tradition of the Pharisees and scribes, shows Christ's incomparable prerogative and that he is on a distinctly higher level than Israel's teachers of the law.[194]

The same is true of the continuation of Christ's teaching about "what defiles a man" (7.14-23). Here Jesus accomplishes a revolutionary change of criteria and perspective in discussing ethical purity.[195] For the Jews who heard his words, the Messiah's teaching was something very advanced theologically,[196] inexplicable if the Messiah had no divine authority.

The pericope Mk 7.1-23 is not deprived of data suggestive of the Christology of Passion. There are two. The first is the hostility present in the questions of the Pharisees and scribes. There is obvious conflict which shows that the conspiracy against Jesus (3.6) is undergoing full development, racing implacably toward his martyrly end. The second fact is the renewed weakness and spiritual blindness of the disciples: "And he said to them, 'Then are you also without understanding? Do you not see that . . .'" (7.18). These questions preserve all the Messiah's pain, which his own disciples do not even comprehend. We do not have to repeat here how this lack of understanding significantly shapes Jesus' Passion.

7. In the remaining part of the seventh chapter of his Gospel,

Mark relates two healing miracles (7.24-37), adding two fresh examples of power which reveal new sides of Jesus' divine authority.

The new element in the first miracle (7.24-30)[197] is that the healing is performed in the family of a Gentile woman, not Jewish,[198] and in pagan territory. Despite the apparent opposition present in the dialogue between Jesus and the Syrophoenician woman (7.27), the entire incident expounds the idea of Christ's benevolent power being extended also to Gentiles. Indicative is the information that Jesus "entered a house, and would not have anyone know it; yet he could not be hid" (7.24), which suggests that he was already well known in Gentile circles in the region of Tyre.[199] The siginificance of the passage is that it reveals the truth that the miraculous power of Christ is not confined or limited to the people of Israel or her own geographic territory.[200] The world of the Gentiles, in the person of the Syrophoenician woman, becomes a recipient of Jesus' healing energy.[201]

Another new element is present in the same incident: the healing is done at a distance (7.29-30). That this manner of healing especially stresses the Messiah's divine authority needs no further explanation.[202]

The specialness of the second miracle in the pericope (7.31-37)[203] is in the manner of healing. Jesus takes the "man who was deaf and had an impediment in his speech" and "he put his fingers into his ears, and he spat and touched his tongue" (7.33). This therapeutic technique is reminiscent of similar occurrences very familiar to people in New Testament times.[204] As different commentators hold, however, Mark's description has special points, such as Jesus' prayer and sigh (7.34). Thus, the scene is solemn while Jesus' sigh, expressive of his love for a suffering human being, fills the air with the reality of God's mercy and affection. We should include that the specific therapeutic technique based on touch is applied to a deaf man, i.e. to a person who could understand the language of touch but not the sound of words. Thus, it turns out that this is a further expression of understanding and affection. Here, the miraculous healing authority of Jesus is expressed in direct relation to special human needs.[205]

The end of the pericope describes the people's amazement and admiration at the healing of the deaf man (7.36-37). The sentence used is typical: "And they were astonished beyond measure, saying, 'He has done all things well; he even makes the deaf hear and the dumb speak.'" It has been correctly observed that the wording is reminiscent of Isaiah 35.5-6, and belongs to that famous thirty-fifth chapter which describes the eschatological coming of God.[206] On the other hand, the expression, "he has done all things well," verifies the perfectness and completeness of the works he has done and seems to parallel the work of God on the six days of creation.[207] Here, it is clear that, in the Messiah who works miracles, we encounter God the Creator (Gen 1.31), coming to save (Is 35.4).

8. The healing of the deaf man is followed by yet another great miracle,[208] the Feeding of the Four Thousand (8.1-10).[209] The narrative presents significant similarities with the Feeding of the Five Thousand (6.35-44)[210] and therefore needs no analysis. We will comment only on two points.

First: the miracle is the result of Jesus' initiative, more specifically his love: "I have compassion on the crowd, because they have been with me now three days, and have nothing to eat; and if I send them away hungry to their homes, they will faint on the way" (8.2-3). The miracle of multiplying the bread and feeding the people is an act of the Messiah's divine power,[211] motivated by his immense compassion.

Second: as in Mark 6.30-44, the four verbs which Mark 8.1-10 uses to describe the teaching about the multiplication are noteworthy: "he took," "having given thanks," "he broke," "and gave." These are very similar to those used in the description of the institution and tradition of the Eucharist, not only in Mark (14.22 "he took," "he blessed," "broke," "gave,") but in Paul as well (1 Cor 11.23-24 "he . . . took bread, and when he had given thanks, he broke it").[212] This means that the signs of the Passion are present and shape the vocabulary of a passage describing a series of Jesus' supernatural works.

9. Signs of the Passion are felt much more in the brief pericope which follows (8.11-13).[213] In this passage, we read of another attack by the Pharisees against Christ. As we have already pointed out, episodes of this type are ever-present signposts on the fated road to Jesus' painful end. In this particular case, the Pharisees' ill-willed attack is expressed as a request for a "sign from heaven" (8.11). Their motives are hostile, as can be deduced from the phrase, "to test him."[214] Jesus, in no uncertain terms, responds to this provocation with an unreserved and absolute denial: "Truly, I say to you, no sign

shall be given to this generation" (8.12).[215] His response widens the unbridgeable gap and increases the certainty of his inevitable, tragic end. The particular seriousness of this situation is also apparent in the statement that Jesus "sighed deeply in his spirit" (8.12). Here, all Christ's anguish and spiritual distress unfolds as he confronts a tragic human attitude, as was that of the Pharisees.[216] After so many miraculous works at every level, they ask him for "a sign," showing their incurable blindness, a spiritual callousness which will be a fundamental factor in Jesus' execution.

As with other answers Jesus gives, however, his absolute denial to satisfy the malevolent request of the Pharisees places him on a level of divine superiority. His authority is divine and is manifested in miracle-working always within the spectrum of greatest discernment and freedom.

10. The theme of spiritual blindness also dominates the very next pericope (8.14-21),[217] and therefore, christologically, it is placed within the general cycle of the Passion. In this instance, interest is centered on the disciples.[218] By reason of their concern over bread, Jesus hurls a strong rebuke at them: "Do you not yet perceive or understand? Are your hearts hardened? Having eyes do you not see, and having ears do you not hear? And do you not remember? . . . Do you not yet understand?" (8.17-21).[219] The language here appears very sharp.[220] The words echo like continuous hammering. The intensity is explained by the fact that not only the Pharisees, but even his own disciples, who have attended everything, have not come to understand the meaning of the Messiah's miraculous works. They are therefore rebuked for their spiritual blindness,[221] hardness of heart, and inability to understand the special acts of God. Aside from the significance this diagnosis has, it stresses the uniqueness of the Messiah, his distance[222] as yet from those people closest to him. Here is described a phenomenon of sharply differentiated levels of existence, a phenomenon which begets indescribable pain.[223] Such pain constitutes an essential part of Jesus' Passion.

11. The first major section of Mark's Gospel (1.1-8.26) closes with a pericope which again places the Messiah's incomparable authority in the forefront. It deals with restoring sight to a blind man (8.22-26).[224]

A special characteristic of this passage is that the healing comes in two phases. This, perhaps, is done for pedagogical reasons.[225] At any rate, the central thought here again is the dynamic expression of Jesus' absolute authority over every type of infirmity, weakness, or chronic illness.

It is not by accident, however, that in this particular case, Jesus gives sight to a blind man. Rather, it helps explain the placement of the miracle at this point in Mark's Gospel.[226] In the episodes which preceded, there was word of the Pharisees' spiritual hardness and the disciples' inner blindness. The language used was pointed, sufficient to drive the disciples into despair. Now, with the miracle of the blind man, Jesus is seen as the Messiah who opens the eyes of the blind, who restores sight. The symbolism is quite obvious.[227] The Messiah can also turn one from spiritual blindness, can grant a new inner sight, a new power to see and understand God's miracles, as worked by Jesus.[228] The miracle of the blind man, a fresh sign manifesting Jesus' tenderness, also becomes a new sign, renewing the hope of his disciples.

Chapter Two

BALANCE WITHIN ALTERNATING CONCEPTS OF AUTHORITY AND PASSION (8.27-10.52)

As previously pointed out, the first part of the Gospel of Mark (1.1-8.26) is characterized by successive manifestations of Jesus' divine authority. There are at the same time more or less explicit references to the Passion; however, priority indisputably belongs to the Christology of Authority, while the Christology of Passion unfolds on another level, and is often expressed in allusory language.

Moving on to the second major section of the Gospel (8.27-10.52), the two basic christological concepts of Authority and Passion are found to manifest themselves in continuous alternation, offsetting each other. In this major section of his gospel, Mark retains the fundamental image and depiction of a Messiah who dispenses supernatural power and works with the prerogative of a divine authority. At the same time, the Evangelist introduces the reality of the Passion with unmistakably clear design. The violent death of Jesus is portrayed as a factual certainty and is described in continuous stages and a variety of indicative connotations. In this part of the Gospel, these two great lines of christological thought move parallel to each other, each keeping the other in balance. The transition from Authority to Passion and back again occurs in repeated cycles throughout the narratives, dialogues, and teachings.

1. The initial pericope (8.27-30)[1] belongs among the more indicative examples of the Christology of Authority. It deals with the account of that very significant confession of Peter which occurred in the region of the city Caesarea Phillipi, north of Lake Tiberias.

The entire pericope is built on two questions which Jesus asks his disciples: "Who do men say that I am?" (8.27) and "who do you say that I am?" (8.29).

The disciples answer the first question by expressing three different opinions. Accordingly, some people identify Jesus with John the Baptist, others with Elijah, and still others with one of the prophets (8.28). Mark brought in these same three opinions in his narrative about the beheading of John (6.14-15). In Caesarea Phillipi the same scheme is repeated unaltered, a scheme that comprises outstanding figures connected with the coming of the Messiah, but not the Messiah himself.[2]

To the second question, "But who do you say that I am?", Peter answers in a way which in all likelihood[3] represents the thinking of the other disciples: "You are the Christ" (8.29).

Peter's confession-response is most clear as of its underlying content. Jesus is the Christ, i.e. the Messiah, the one uniquely "anointed" by God to carry out his steadfast promises and his eternal plan for the salvation of Israel and every nation on earth. "You are the Christ," considered against the rest of the text, denotes something essentially different from the great prophets who came before. It underscores Jesus' unique and incomparable nature, and intimates his immeasureable authority inasmuch as he is the Messiah.[4] These views are reinforced by two additional elements offered in the text and should be noted.

The first is the text's dialectic process. Peter's opinion comes directly after a lay opinion mentioning prophet and forerunner. If Peter had wanted to give a similar opinion, he would have been able to use a like answer. Counter to this, however, he immediately jumps to a higher theological plane and responds with an absolute confession in tone and spirit. The placement of "You are the Christ" directly after a series of variations on the theme of prophet and forerunner emphasizes the uniqueness of Jesus' identity with the Messiah and the gulf which separates him from any other prophetic figure, no matter how great.[5]

The second element is the term "Christ." Attention to the use of this term in Mark's Gospel has much to offer. Three particular examples are brought to mind: a) the introductory statement "the beginning of the gospel of Jesus Christ" (1.1) in which the soteriological dimension of the term is presented; b) the eschatological speech of Jesus in Mark 13, where the term "Christ" is connected with the eschatological coming of the Son of man with incomparable power and glory (13.21-26); and c) the dialogue between Jesus and the high priest during his trial before the Sanhedrin (14.61-62), where the best witness is to be found for the meaning of this term in Mark ("again the high priest asked him, 'Are you the Christ, the Son of the Blessed?' And Jesus said, 'I am; and you will see the Son of man seated at the right hand of Power, and coming with the clouds of heaven'"). A very poignant implication develops during this dialogue: the absolute connection of Christ and God; the connection is such, that the acceptance of the title "Christ" by Jesus is interpreted by the Sanhedrin as his crowning blasphemy and not as a mere messianic pretension (14.64).

The passages above shed light on the essential meaning of the term "Christ" in Mark and it is with this definition that the term should be interpreted in the confession of Peter at Caesarea Phillipi.[6] Here we have a fundamental proclamation of Jesus' messiahship placing him over and above the greatest prophets, considering him an unmatched bearer of divine power and authority. It may be for this reason that Jesus, immediately after Peter's confession, "charged them to tell no one about him" (8.30). At this stage, spreading the idea that Jesus was the Messiah could have resulted in particular danger due to its ethno-political connections.[7] Perhaps this grave prohibition is also due in large part to the disciples' marked ignorance relative to Jesus at this stage of the gospel story.

2. Directly after the very representative example of the Christology of Authority just analyzed comes an equally representative example of Passion Christology (8.31-33).[8] A many-jointed prediction or prophecy of the Messiah's Passion comprises the backbone of this pericope. The main points of this warning announcement are the following:

a) The revelation of painful death comes from Jesus himself, at his own discretion and initiative; moreover, it does not have the quality of fleeting observation or incidental allusion. The Evangelist is clear: "and he (Jesus) began to teach them (the disciples)" (8.31). The disclosure of the Passion's complex reality composes a teaching, i.e. a complete and methodical presentation that begins at this point in the gospel story. This perforce brings the Christology of Passion to the forefront of the evolving situation.

b) Christ's prediction begins with the statement, "the Son of man must suffer many things" (8.31). This expresses the necessity (δεῖ)

of the Messiah's terrible affliction.[9] Judging from the meaning of
the verb δεῖ ("must") in Mark,[10] this necessity touches upon God's
great plan for the salvation of the world.

Noteworthy in the same passage is the term "Son of man." It
appears again and again in fundamental passages predicting or
describing the Messiah's Passion (9.12, 9.31, 10.33, 10.45, 14.21, 14.42)
as well as in others expressing his singular authority and divine
prerogative (2.10, 2.28, 8.38, 9.9, 13.26, 14.62). Especially notable is
Mark 14.61-62 where the title "Son of man" indicates the highest
power and authority both in the present and in the eschatological
future. Mark 8.31 is the first passage in which the Evangelist uses
the term "Son of man" in conjuction with the Passion. The capacity
of this term to also conceptually embody conditions of suffering, affliction, and martyrdom renders it especially useful in Jesus' teaching
about the path to Golgotha.[11]

c) Following the statement "the Son of man must suffer many
things" comes the phrase "and be rejected by the elders and the
chief priests and the scribes" (8.31). The verb ἀποδοκιμάζω used
here means "to reject or consider unsuitable or useless."[12] The action of the Jewish religious leaders is especially grievous to the
Messiah, because it betrays these leaders' appalling spiritual condition and their poor criteria for evaluating Jesus. It is also noteworthy that the three groups, elders, chief priests, and scribes, are mentioned as one body by Mark exclusively in texts referring to the Passion (11.27, 14.43, 15.1). This spotlights the agreement of all the
religious factions in their rejection of Jesus as well as the wide gulf
that separates him from these religious teachers and leaders. Thus,
the groundwork is laid for the following phase, which is also the final
one.

d) This phase consists of a single act described in Greek by one
verb: καὶ ἀποκτανθῆναι, "and be killed" (8.31). This verb, ἀποκτείνω
is found in the passage describing the beheading of the Forerunner
(6.19); in passages predicting the suffering of the Messiah (8.31, 9.31,
10.34); in the violent deaths related in the parable of the vineyard
(12.5-8); and in the last stage of the conspiracy against Jesus (14.1).
The eloquent martyrological character of these texts leaves no doubt
as to the meaning of this word in Mark 8.31: a violent martyr's death.

As appears from the other Evangelists' use of ἀποκτείνω, the verb
was applied as well to prophets of the Old Testament[13] and disciples
of Christ.[14] This evidence leads to the conclusion that ἀποκτείνω

was a martyrological word of ancient tradition,[15] having Jesus at its roots.

e) The many-faceted disclosure of the Passion ends with an unexpected formulation: "and after three days rise again" (8.31). Having established the certainty of his sacrificial death, Jesus now gives assurance of his resurrection.[16] Here again, a profile of Christ's singular authority and divine might is presented. This profile, however, is left undeveloped because the main theme is the Passion. But the Passion does not imperiously shroud the future in impenetrable darkness: the light of the resurrection gives the true form and magnitude of these events. The Christology of Authority is yet present in instances such as Mark 8.31, although the Passion Christology is playing the lead role.[17]

The prediction of Christ's suffering is followed by an episode that consolidates this prediction. Jesus' message is frank and cannot be misinterpreted ("And he said this plainly," 8.31), and it is to this message Peter reacts with extraordinary perturbation: "and Peter took him, and began to rebuke him" (8.32).[18] Here, the Evangelist shows how strange and unacceptable the concept of Christ's martyrdom was for the disciples.

Christ's sacrifice, however, is a part of the plan of divine economy and disavowal of it is tantamount to opposing God. This is indicated in the course of events as described in Mark 8.31-33. To Peter's criticism Jesus responds with a most severe reprimand: "Get behind me, Satan! For you are not on the side of God, but of men" (8.33).[19] There is no other case in the New Testament where the name "Satan" is given to a man. This observation highlights the extraordinary seriousness of the situation in Mark 8.33.[20] The avoidance or rejection of the Passion is essentially related to the devil, while its acceptance is bound to a spiritual state described as being "mindful of the things of God."[21] Jesus' response to Peter's provocation establishes the Christology of Passion on an unshakable foundation. Christ's accepting the cup of final affliction and death is the supreme act in God's plan, an act that by all means must occur. Perhaps here is hidden the greatest example of Jesus' authority: the authority to freely accept the Passion.[22]

3. The same line of thought that runs through the preceding pericope is continued in Mark 8.34-9.1[23] with the difference that here, we have a change in perspective—the Christology of Passion is

presented in connection with its underlying anthropological consequences. This teaching develops with four successive declarations.

The first introduces the conditions for a faithful following of Jesus:
"if any man would come after me, let him deny himself and take
up his cross and follow me" (8.34). The main theme is taking the
cross, which means going to one's execution and being prepared to
undergo it.[24] Other phases in this section express related ideas.
Mark 8.34 connotes the priority of the suffering and martyrdom of
Jesus' disciples as an element of genuine faithfulness to the Messiah.
In this pericope, the Christology of Passion with its radical anthropological consequences has been brought into the everyday situation of the disciples.[25]

The second declaration complements the first by arguing that giving up one's life for Jesus' sake and the gospel is in essence saving
one's life (8.35). This explanation confirms the opinion that the first
declaration indeed speaks of death.[26] Noteworthy is the phrase
"whoever loses his life for my sake and the gospel's," for in it Jesus
reveals that he is the reason and purpose for sacrificing one's life.
There seems to be a blending of the Christology of Passion with that
of Authority here.[27] The disciple needs to accept the idea of suffering and sacrifice as Jesus does, but at the same time he needs to carry
this act for Jesus to its endpoint, a thing that accentuates the authority
and divinity of the suffering Messiah. The suffering Jesus is at the
same time the Messiah of divine authority, who is worth even the
sacrifice of one's life.[28]

The third declaration gives another reason. Essentially, it presents
the immeasurable consequences of sacrifice for Jesus, contrasting a
denial of this sacrifice on a par with gaining the entire world (8.36-37).
The text extols the incomparable value of the soul while applauding
the uniquely important act of offering one's life for Jesus' sake.

The fourth declaration is a corroboration of the first three: it
underscores the soteriological consequences of refusing to confess
Jesus and his words in public (8.38).[29] Not confessing seems to be
attributed to not accepting a suffering Messiah, refusing to offer one's
life for his sake, or both. The consequences are tragic and are connected with the eschatological coming of the Christ.[30] This stresses
the significance of the Messiah's Passion as much as it does the
disciples' suffering for him. At the same time, however, reference
to the eschatological glory of the Son of man brings the Christology
of Authority to the forefront.[31]

It is this Christology which seems to dictate the last words of the pericope: "Truly I say to you, there are some standing here who will not taste death before they see that the kingdom of God has come with power" (9.1). There has been much debate over the exact meaning of this passage. It is indisputable, however, that it stresses the powerful coming of the kingdom of God and its imminence.[32] Thus, the immediate future is not shaped merely by the suffering of Christ and his disciples, but by the unique power of God's kingdom, a power which is organically and etiologically bound with Jesus.[33]

4. The two preceding pericopes are determined, as was mentioned, by the Christology of Passion. The pericope of Mark 9.2-8,[34] which follows, however, belongs to the classic texts of Authority Christology. This text describes Jesus' theophanic transfiguration before three of his disciples, Peter, James, and John.

The information contained in the initial verses is significant, laying an offhand emphasis on the event. An accurate time designation, "after six days" (9.2), connects the christological confession of Peter (8.29) chronologically with Christ's transfiguration. This "after six days" also warns of the impending presentation of significant events.[35] This impression of importance is reinforced by the selection of only three disciples to be present for what was about to happen. As previously pointed out, the presence of three disciples in two other very important events[36] accentuates the special significance of the present one as well.

Proceeding along the same lines, the report adds that he "led them (i.e. the three disciples) up a high mountain apart by themselves" (9.2). The phrase "apart by themselves," which adds to the already distinctive action of their selection, intensifies the air of exclusiveness and anticipation of the events to be unfolded. The ascent "up a high mountain" is one more point in the same category of data. As has been observed, this ascent can be compared to Moses' climbing Mt. Sinai to receive the Law from God (Ex 24 and 34). The parallelism, which is supported by certain similarities in wording,[37] places the transfiguration of Jesus on a special level, putting it on a par with the foremost theophanic event of the Old Testament.

The transfiguration event (9.3-7) consists of four basic aspects or reference points which reveal the divine authority, prerogative, and person of Jesus.[38] We will analyze them briefly without retaining the chronological order of the events.

The first consists of the transfiguration itself: "and he was transfigured before them, and his garments became glistening, intensely white as no fuller on earth could bleach them" (9.3). Here, the transfiguration of Jesus' face is described along with the transformation of his garments into clothing of brilliant whiteness.[39] The image he presents is one of astonishing brilliance and indescribable whiteness, which cannot be compared to anything on earth.[40] The intensity of the glory and light is such that it even affects his clothes and is not confined to his person. The Messiah is revealed in all his wondrous glory and divine splendor in a pure theophanic scene exuding divine magnificence.

The second aspect is the scene of Jesus conversing with two great figures of the Old Testament: "and there appeared to them Elijah with Moses; and they were talking to Jesus" (9.4). This graphically expresses the concept of Jesus' recognition by two leading men of the Old Testament, who are connected with basic messianic predictions and eschatological anticipations, and who, at the same time, personify the Law and the Prophets.[41] At this point, the Law and the Prophets converge in the person of Jesus, who is revealed to be superior in divine glory, power and authority to any predecessor.

The third aspect of the transfiguration deals with the reaction of the disciples: "and Peter said to Jesus, 'Master, it is well that we are here: let us make three booths, one for you and one for Moses and one for Elijah.' For he did not know what to say, for they were exceedingly afraid" (9.5-6). Peter's words betray the tremendous impression made by this event. It is an impression blending boundless joy with indescribable fear and awe. We often run across the verb φοβοῦμαι as expressing the state of the disciples at manifestations of Jesus' unique power.[42] It is with this meaning that the expression ἔκφοβοι ἐγένοντο ("they were exceedingly afraid") is used in Mark 9.6,[43] to describe the disciples' intense reaction and shock at the sudden, magnificent manifestation of Jesus' divine person and power at the transfiguration.

The fourth aspect adds a new theophanic dimension to the transfiguration: "and a cloud overshadowed them, and a voice came out of the cloud, 'This is my beloved Son; listen to him'" (9.7). The cloud here is affiliated with the presence of God, as it was in the theophany on Mt. Sinai (Ex 24.15-18).[44] The voice of God, issuing from the cloud, sanctions the new eternal law in the word of the Messiah: "listen to him." On Sinai, God gave the Law to Moses, while on the mount of Transfiguration, he declares Jesus his beloved Son, whose word is now a new Law. The solemn phrase recognizing the divine Sonship of Christ in Mark 9.7 is similar to that uttered at his Baptism (1.11) with the difference that there, it was addressed to Jesus, while here, it is addressed to the others present at the transfiguration;[45] moreover here, the "listen to him," is added. This suggests that the Christ is endowed with the absolute authority of the Son of God: he is the divine Commander and Lawgiver. [46]

In its entirety, the description of the transfiguration reveals the divine person of Jesus in successive scenes and at differing levels of reference.[47] Christ, who shines in supernatural glory, converses with leading figures of the Old Covenant, evokes joy and trembling fear in his disciples, and is pronounced by divine voice to be the beloved Son and eminent Lawgiver holding the place of God, is undoubtedly the divine Son, having singular and absolute divine authority and Sonship.[48] The transfiguration passage constitutes a masterly text for the Christology of Authority.

It should be noted that this text functions to confirm the truth of the two great concepts developed in the two preceding pericopes. The first is the concept of the Messiah's Passion ("the Son of man must suffer many things," 8.31). The transfiguration, which comes directly after the prediction of suffering and death, seals what is said with a magnificent theophanic revelation. In particular, the phrase "listen to him" aside from the general application, implies a divine sanction of the Passion teaching.[49] The second concept is Jesus' absolute messianic identity ("You are the Christ," 8.29), as it was formulated by Peter. At the transfiguration, Peter's confession is confirmed[50] in an excellent manner, because the multifarious theophanic scene graphically projects the unique and indisputable divine hypostasis of Jesus-Messiah.

5. The grandiose scene of the transfiguration terminates abruptly ("and suddenly looking around they no longer saw any one with them but Jesus only," Mark 9.8), and there follows a short dialogue (9.9-13).[51] The first part of the dialogue moves in the christological sphere of authority, for it connects the transfiguration with the resurrection. The connection once more manifests the supernatural character of the transfiguration[52] and places it within the events that disclose the divine hypostasis of Jesus. Even the difficulty of the disciples in understanding the exact significance of Christ's words concerning the resurrection (9.9-10) is expressed in a manner which

betrays an eschatological aspect, and consequently, an aspect of the highest expression of God's power.

The second part of the discussion, which is built on this eschatological aspect-question (9.11-13) turns the train of thought in the direction of the Passion. Jesus, by reason of his disciples' mention of the Prophet Elijah, lets it be known that the Elijah about whom they were speaking is the Forerunner, and that a basic element in the parallelism was martyrdom ("and they did to him whatever they pleased, as it is written of him" Mark 9.13).[53] He then poses a question, one that hints at the absolute certainty of the Messiah's sacrificial death: "and how is it written of the Son of man, that he should suffer many things and be treated with contempt?" (9.12). With this, the truth of the Passion is established with implacable clarity in the middle of the conversation, the very moment when the impression of the glorious transfiguration is still very much alive in the souls of the three disciples.[54]

6. The pericope that follows, Mark 9.14-29,[55] describes the miraculous healing of a demoniac, and again, the christological perspective changes. Parallels are again drawn between the events described in Mark 9.14-29 and events that marked the descent of Moses from Sinai.[56] What is of greatest importance in this pericope, however, is not likely Old Testament influences, but the event itself as an expression of the unique might of Christ.[57]

Mark 9.14-29 has all the characteristics of narratives about miraculous healings encountered elsewhere in Mark. Certain facts should be pointed out, however, that make this pericope special:

The first is the fact that the crowd shows its admiration before, and not after[58] the astonishing healing. It is an admiration mixed with adorational cordiality: "and immediately all the crowd, when they saw him, were greatly amazed, and ran up to him and greeted him" (9.15). The people were "greatly amazed" (ἐκθαμβοῦνται), i.e. they were moved by a condition of ineffable astonishment and awe, hardly having come face-to-face with Christ, even before becoming witnesses of a miracle. There are two explanations for this phenomenon: the first presupposes that Jesus' face still retained vestiges of the wondrous radiation from the transfiguration; the second, that, unrelated to the transfiguration, Jesus' appearance begat a feeling of awe and astonishment.[59] Both views, however, make the same christological point: the person of Jesus radiates the presence of the ultramundane, the divine.

Secondly, in Mark 9.14-29, the inability of the disciples to free the demoniac child from the "unclean," "dumb and deaf spirit" is prominently presented. The child's father ("and I asked your disciples to cast it out, and they were not able" Mark 9.18) and the disciples themselves confess this to be true ("why could we not cast it out?" Mark 9.28). This truth, however, suggests a contrast to the supreme authority of Jesus. The excellence of the Messiah's might is built upon the inability of the disciples.

The third special element in the pericope of Mark 9.14-29 is the preservation of an unusual number of details indicating the tragic condition of the child. The Evangelist returns four times to this theme (9.17-18; 9.20; 9.22; and 9.26),[60] thus stressing the painfulness and horror of demons' oppressive power over humanity. The passage, however, extols the unique might of Christ,[61] who has authority and power to liberate mankind from the rage and oppression of the demonic. Noteworthy at this point is the final scene of the healing: "and the boy was like a corpse; so that most of them said, 'He is dead.' But Jesus took him by the hand and lifted him up, and he arose" (9.26-28). The wording here immediately summons up images of the resurrection (corpse, dead, lifted . . . up, arose). Parallels between liberation from demons and resurrection from the dead become inevitable,[62] and with them the emphasis on the authority of the Messiah.

Finally, it should be noted that the subject of the conversation between Jesus and the demoniac's father, i.e. faith, outlines the almighty strength of Christ. The declaration "all things are possible to him who believes" (9.23) does not acclaim the unlimited power of faith by itself as much as it does the unlimited power of Jesus, which is given and revealed in its full dynamism through faith.[63]

7. The weighty passage of Mark 9.30-32[64] returns us to the Christology of Passion.[65] Here we find the second prediction of the Messiah's martyrly end. In form and content, this message is in many ways similar to the first (8.31), and for this reason a detailed analysis will not be given. It does, however, contain certain noteworthy characteristics.

In Mark 9.30-32 the initial declaration of the Passion is stated in the phrase "The Son of man will be delivered into the hands of men, and they will kill him." The verb παραδίδοται, to be delivered,

is very denotative. It is a verb which Mark uses repeatedly in referring to the betrayal of Judas (3.19, 14.10, 14.18, 14.21). Consequently,
its use in Mark 9.31 alludes to Judas' act.[66] The same verb is encountered in passages about the Baptist (1.14), Christ's disciples (13.9,
13.11-12) as well as about Jesus himself (10.33, 15.1, 15.10, 15.15).
In all these examples, the meanings and associations are of a pre-
dominantly martyrological type.

The passive verb παραδίδοται, to be delivered, in Mark 9.31 has
no agent. According to one hypothesis, Judas or the world hostile
to God would be considered the agents of this verb. Another opinion
holds that the agent is not in question, but that παραδίδοται in Mark
9.31 corresponds to the verb δεῖ (must) in Mark 8.31, which is indicative of more general factors and complex mechanisms within the
divine plan of salvation.[67] Accepting this, παραδίδοται in Mark 9.31
is exegetically parallel to παρεδόθη of Romans 4.25 ("who was put
to death for our transgressions"). The observations above lead to the
conclusion that παραδίδοται covers a wide spectrum of concepts
presenting the truth about the Messiah's suffering on a broader theological perspective.

The phrase "the Son of man will be delivered into the hands of
men" (9.31) is remarkable from yet another standpoint. The tension
between the terms "Son of man" and "men" is very perceptible and
painful. The formulation shows the depth of the Messiah's pain as
well as the tragedy of the men who will execute the Son of man, who
in turn is sacrificed for the salvation of men.[68] Here the Christology
of Passion, as preserved in Mark, presents the tragic paradox of Jesus'
execution by mankind with admirable, yet simple phrasal dexterity.

The end of the pericope adds to the gloominess of the Passion
image, because the disciples, as the Evangelist writes, "did not
understrand the saying, and they were afraid to ask" (9.32). Whatever
the exact meaning of the passage is, what prevails is the disciples'
difficulty in comprehending Jesus. Although they have heard repeated
teachings and explanations, they still do not understand; a thing that
leaves the Messiah alone in the dramatic march toward his dreary end.

Mark 9.31-32, as well as the corresponding text of Mark 8.31, is
not exclusively spent on Passion Christology. The prediction is not
only one of death, but also of resurrection: "and when he is killed,
after three days he will rise." The Christology of Authority is used
here as a counterbalance to restrain the sorrow of the Passion, thus
allowing a glimpse of the gentle face of him who will conquer death.

8. Following the second prediction of the Passion and up to the end of the ninth chapter come a series of Jesus' sayings (9.33-37, 9.38-41, 9.42-50).[69] Inspite of the loose connections between them, these sayings appear to be directly or indirectly related to the Passion message in Mark 9.31-32.[70]

a) The first group of sayings belongs to the pericope Mark 9.33-37. A basic passage in this set is Jesus' declaration: "if any one would be first, he must be last of all and servant of all" (9.35),[71] in answer to the disciples' agonizing question, "who is greatest" (9.34).[72] Here Christ sets the inalterable standard for judging a disciple as "first" or "greatest," and that is, that the disciple should be the "last of all and servant of all." The position is clear and will be repeated in variation in Mark 10.43-44, where it is shown that the Messiah also applies the rule to himself without restriction: ("For the Son of man also came not to be served but to serve, and to give his life as a ransom for many" 10.45).[73] The primary reference of the application above is to the Passion, which combines ultimate humility with perfect service.

In the declaration of Mark 9.35, the consequences of Passion Christology are transferred to the human level. At the same time it shows that the Passion is not an isolated christological event, but the perfect and absolute archetype of the zenith of human development.

Jesus accompanies his teaching with the example of the child (9.36-37). This example affirms the idea of being last in rank, but at the same time, it teaches that a person's value depends on his relationship with the Christ: "Whoever receives one such child in my name receives me" (9.37).[74] It is evident that a gradual and imperceptible movement toward the Christology of Authority is taking place. The last step in this direction occurs in the remainder of verse 37: "and whoever receives me, receives not me but him who sent me."

b) The sayings of the second group (9.38-41) strictly deal with the meaning of the expression "in the name" or "on the name" of Christ.[75] This pericope displays a christological perspective of divine power, and apparently functions to counterbalance what was said before concerning the Passion (9.31), being last, and being servant (9.35).

The concept of Jesus' divine power emerges in the initial sentence of the pericope: "Teacher, we saw a man casting out demons in your name" (9.38). Here the singular authority of Christ over demons is manifested in that demonic powers are banished merely by calling on his name. The incident, of course, acquires special significance in this particular passage, because the exorsist is not even a disciple of the Messiah ("he was not following us," 9.38). Jesus sanctions this act with a statement that shows he does not consider this a rare exception: "for no one who does a mighty work in my name will be able soon after to speak evil of me" (9.39). Doing "mighty" works by calling on the name of Christ, even by those who are not his disciples or followers, exhibits his supernatural authority.[76]

The last words of the pericope also show the scope of the Messiah's divine prerogative: "For, truly I say to you, whoever gives you a cup of water to drink because you bear the name of Christ, will by no means lose his reward" (9.41).[77]

c) The third group of Jesus's sayings (9.42-50) has scandal as its central theme. This theme is connected with the anthropological consequences of Passion Christology, consisting of service (διακονία) and readiness for sacrifice (cf. Mark 9.35).[78] Using especially descriptive language, Jesus teaches the need for his disciples to remain in the kingdom of God even in the face of painful sacrifice. The road he points out is a road of affliction, mortification, and severance, i.e. a path of suffering.[79] The text of Mark 9.42-50 is expressive, in its own style, language, and level, of a christological concept that focuses on the Passion and its consequences.

As occurs in many other instances, here too, the text presents the christological concepts of Authority graphically. Jesus warns of the grave implications for the one who "causes one of these little ones who believe in me to sin" (9.42). This grave responsibility stems not only from the fact that the scandal involves "little ones" as much as it does little ones who "believe" in Jesus. The Messiah is the highest point of reference and the greatest of relationships, and when this relationship is disturbed or broken, it places the salvation of the one responsible in jeopardy.[80]

9. The tenth chapter of Mark's Gospel begins with the pericope concerning divorce (10.1-12),[81] and in this text, consequent with the development of the main theme,[82] profiles of the two familiar christological types show through.

The discussion is introduced with geographic information: "And he left there and went to the region of Judea and beyond the Jordan" (10.1). This information conveys the idea of a steady advance toward Jerusalem, which is organically linked with the Passion (10.33). Consequently, Mark 10.1 is an indicator of the Christology of Passion. Along these same lines, the Pharisees' motives for their discussion with Jesus are to be noted: "And Pharisees came up and in order to test him asked: Is it lawful for a man to divorce his wife?" (10.2). With the expression "in order to test him" (cf. Mark 8.11 and 12.15), the Evangelist again brings to the forefront the irreconcilable enmity of the Pharisees[83] and their blatant, evolving conspiracy against Jesus, i.e. the actualization of the Passion.

On the other hand, the answer Christ gives to the "test" question yet again validates his divine authority and legitimacy, and it does so by essentially refuting the provision in Mosaic law for divorce. Answering Jesus' counterquestion, the Pharisees unhesitatingly state their opinion that "Moses allowed a man to write a certificate of divorce, and to put her (i.e. the wife) away" (10.4). They expressly quote Deuteronomy[84] to support their opinion that divorce is permitted under certain circumstances. Jesus, however, does not accept this idea and acclaims the indissolubility of marriage using the imperative, i.e. the command form: "What therefore God has joined together, let not man put asunder." (10.9). This fact is most significant, because the Messiah is legislating here—surpassing the given provision of Mosaic law with his own new commandment; which is to say, he is legislating as God.

Jesus' supreme authority is exhibited as well in the way he puts the entire discussion about divorce on a new level. He explains to the Pharisees that the provision for divorce in Deuteronomy (24.1) is simply God's concession due to man's hardness of heart, while it is God's will to have a permanent and indissoluble union of man and woman so that "the two shall become one flesh" (10.6-8).[85] Jesus raises the discussion about divorce up to the level of marriage, focusing attention on the essence and nature of marriage;[86] moreover, he passes from a concession ("allowed") of God to that which is the will of God. He lays down as a steadfast rule that "they are no longer two but one flesh" and that "God has joined (them) together." An immediate consequence of these positions is the *a priori* impossibility of divorce. On this basis the Messiah characterizes marriage after divorce as adultery (10.11-12).

Here Christ's absolute prerogative is evinced as he makes radical declarations and substantial re-evaluations. His definitive statements and commands suggest his authority to be that of God.

10. Mark 10.13-16[87] preserves a most beautiful and tender expression of the Messiah's affection for children while at the same time offering basic points in the teaching about the kingdom of God. The passage also exhibits the divine authority and power of Jesus.[88]

Christ's special authority and singular benevolent might is evinced by the fact that "they were bringing children to him, that he might touch them" (10.13). The verb ἅπτομαι, to touch, in Mark as well as in Matthew and Luke is connected with miraculous healings Jesus performed (1.4, 3.10, 5.27-31, 6.56 et al., Mt 8.3, 9.20, 14.3-6 et al., Lk 5.13, 6.19, 8.44-47 et al.), and is an eloquent allusion to his supernatural saving power.[89] The end of the passage, where it is stated, that the Messiah "took them (the children) and blessed them, laying his hands upon them" (10.16), expresses the same idea. This passage is descriptive of his boundless affection and benevolent energy.[90]

Christ's authority is also demonstrated when he opposes his disciples in the matter of the children. They turned away the ones who brought children to Jesus, "but when Jesus saw it he was indignant, and said to them, 'let the children come to me, do not hinder them'" (10.14). This opposing stance, most certainly delivered with strong emotion,[91] reveals his eminent superiority.

Also indicative of the Christology of Authority are Christ's declarations about the kingdom of God in connection with children: "Truly, I say to you, whoever does not receive the kingdom of God like a child shall not enter it" (10.15), and "for to such belongs the kingdom of God" (10.14). These statements betray divine authority, because they lay down the lofty subject of God's kingdom[92] in an absolute manner. Jesus speaks once more with the authority of God.

11. Our last observation applies also to the pericope of Mark 10.17-27,[93] which deals with the question of the rich man, "What must I do to inherit eternal life?" (10.17). This pericope presents interesting exegetical problems,[94] and again evokes a strong sense of Christ's divine authority. This impression is related etiologically to certain data,[95] mainly three basic points which Jesus puts into words:

The first is identified with his telling the rich man: "You lack one thing; go, sell what you have, and give to the poor, and you will have treasure in heaven; and come, follow me'' (10.21). According to what we know of the general practices of the Jews at that time,[96] this precept required a revolutionary decision on the part of the rich man. Renouncing and giving away all one's possessions as a prerequisite to ''inherit eternal life'' was something the Jews had never heard of. The incident is given special emphasis by way of its phrasal brevity, absence of explanation, and accumulation of imperative verbs: ''go,'' ''sell,'' ''give,'' ''come follow me.'' Such language betrays divine prerogative and supreme authority, in that it sets the standards for entry into God's inheritance. Worthy of special attention is the phrase ''and come, follow me.'' Here, the act of following Jesus is seen as the final criterion for inheriting eternal life, the last link in a chain of radical actions. The special relationship with the Messiah within such a plan is of absolute value[97] and automatically projects his divine person.

The second point refers to the conclusion of Christ, certainly filled with sadness when the rich man ''went away sorrowful'': ''How hard it will be for those who have riches to enter the kingdom of God'' (10.23). This comment is not merely a general truth declared by the Gospel, but a definite judgement having decisive soteriological significance for the rich man. The Messiah is seen as an eschatological judge with all the authority of the judging God.

The third point is hidden in Jesus' answer to his disciples' agonizing question, ''Then who can be saved?'' (10.2), asked directly after the episode with the rich man: ''With men it is impossible, but not with God; for all things are possible with God'' (10.27). Here again divine prerogative shines through. The Messiah speaks with finality about human possibilities for the salvation of humankind: the impasse is insurmountable. He likewise speaks in an absolute manner about God's ability to save mankind: the possibilities are unlimited and infinite. This type of soteriological definitions[98] veils a complete and perfect knowledge of eschatological truth, i.e. a knowledge which only God could have. The christological implications of these observations are so evident as not to require further examination.

12. In Mark 10.28-31[99] alternative examples to the rich man in the preceding story are given in the persons of Peter and the disciples: ''Lo, we have left everything and followed you'' (10.28). Jesus uses Peter's words as an opening to present great truths related to this decisive act of the Apostles. Two points about these truths should

be given attention:

In Mark 10.29 the Messiah teaches solemnly that "there is no one who has left house or brothers or sisters or mother or father or children or lands for my sake and for the gospel, who will not receive a hundredfold . . . " Listing all these forsaken persons and things strikes an emotional chord. This sacrifice is enormous and covers all those persons and things to which people are by necessity bound. The important thing is that this sacrifice is made for Jesus. Here Christ becomes the reason for changing relationships and abandoning elementary human goods. This puts emphasis on the divine authority in the person of Jesus. The Messiah's divine authority is also emphasized by the promises-effects of sacrifice for the Christ's sake. The eschatological promises ("and in the age to come, eternal life," 10.30) are promises dictated by an authority like that of God.[100]

The second point that should be noted is the expression "with persecutions" (10.30), which accompanies the promises. Such an expression belongs to the Christology of Passion. A genuine disciple of Jesus cannot avoid suffering, a form of which is persecution. Partaking of the eschatological glory of the Messiah also means partaking in his suffering in one form or another.

13. Mark 10.32-34[101] begins one of the most excellent and complete presentations of Passion Christology. This text contains the third prediction of Christ's sacrificial death.

The prediction is prefaced by a sequence of informative data which builds an atmosphere of solenmity and awe.[102] The first is geographic: "And they were on the road, going up to Jerusalem," (10.32). Approaching Jerusalem is identified exclusively with the Passion in Mark's Gospel,[103] and consequently, reference to the city warns that the end is coming much closer. A second piece of information develops the idea of proximity on another dramatic level: "and Jesus was walking ahead of them, and they were amazed, and those who followed were afraid" (10.32). The verbs here depict mental states which anticipate unusual events to come.[104] Finally, Mark 10.32 shows that the announcement of the Passion was made only to the Twelve, a fact that adds solemnity and gravity to the situation.

The prediction itself (10.33-34) is the third encountered in this general section (8.27-10.52). The two preceding ones (8.31 and 9.31) are shorter, while Mark 10.33-34 is more elaborate, exploring every phase of the Messiah's Passion in miniature.

a) The first phase is described with the words "Behold, we are going up to Jerusalem; and the Son of man will be delivered[105] to the chief priests and the scribes" (10.33). Already, the text indicates the exact place and the particular people to whom Jesus will be betrayed. For the first time the verb παραδίδομαι, to be delivered, is connected with the chief priests and scribes.[106]

b) The words "and they will condemn him to death" (10.33) briefly depict the second phase. Again, for the first time, the exact role of the Jewish religious leaders is defined, and the act of the condemnation of the Messiah is separated from his execution. Jesus' condemnation to death is the exclusive work of the chief priests and scribes.[107]

c) Likewise, it is also their deed which is described in the third phase: "and deliver him to the Gentiles" (10.33). The chief priests are to be responsible for condemning Christ to death, and delivering him to the "Gentiles" for execution. Here, the disciples are told that Jesus will be handed over a second time, which augments the magnitude of his humiliation and degradation. The Messiah will be delivered mercilessly into the hands of the Gentiles and this will add insult to the pain of his sacrifice.

d) The fourth phase concerns the suffering of Christ at the hands of the Gentiles: "and they will mock him, and spit upon him, and scourge him" (10.34). This passage lists Jesus' specific tortures, a point which is absent from the two earlier predictions.[108] The Passion is not limited to a harsh death. It is accompanied by a series of painful, degrading, and ominous tortures. The three verbs of this passage cover successive forms of contempt, from irony and sarcasm to bodily torment.

e) A single verb describes the fifth phase: "and they will kill him" (10.34). In this, the third prediction is similar to the other two ("and be killed," 8.31 and "and they will kill him," 9.31). With but one word,[109] with the maximum conceivable brevity, the circle of terrible sacrifice is closed. The inexorable bounds of death impose this phrasal bareness especially after the preceding painful phases about the Passion.

It is evident that Mark 10.33-34 is a masterful epitome of the Christology of Passion. With impressively clear and decisive language,[110] Jesus unfolds the reality of his death to his amazed and frightened disciples.

As it happens constantly in Mark's gospel, however, the Christology

of Passion does not retain a sole and unchecked dominance. After
the "kill him" follows the declaration "and after three days he will
rise" (10.34)[111] on a firm note of certitude. The resurrection is
foretold with a certainty on a par with the announcement of the Passion. The Christology of the Messiah's supreme authority limits the
intensity and power of the Passion Christology, even though the latter remains the dominant Christology of Mark 10.33-34. Here, Jesus'
word is primarily and deliberately one that shows the realness of the
Passion.[112]

14. The same factuality also permeates the complicated pericope
of Mark 10.35-45.[113] The Christology of Passion is immediately
sensed in the attitude of the disciples. They show a serious lack of
understanding. Even before the echos of Jesus' words about his violent
and imminent death are extinguished, they begin looking for seats
of honor (10.37) and dispute over them (10.41). Their spiritual blindness is serious and their inability to comprehend their Teacher, even
in elementary matters, seems incurable.[114] The disciples' blindness
and incompetence is a primary source of sorrow for Jesus and is therefore a phenomenon which belongs, as previously pointed out, in the
larger circle of Passion Christology.

The foremost expression of this Christology, however, is found
in Jesus' words which form the content of Mark 10.35-45, and which
can be divided into four interrelated units.

The first is dominated by the question, "Are you able to drink
the cup that I drink, or to be baptized with the baptism with which
I am baptized?" (10.38). Exegetes have pointed out that Old Testament texts make a connection of "cup" and "baptism" with suffering and death.[115] Mark himself, in describing the agony at Gethsemane, preserves Jesus' statement: "remove this cup from me" (14.36,
cf. Mt 26.39, Lk 22.42), where "cup" signifies a martyr's death. In
texts of the New Testament as well, we find expressions which indicate, that, very early a connection was made between baptism and
death.[116] Therefore, the Messiah's words in Mark 10.38 clearly refer
to his execution. The use of the present tense in the verbs of the above
passage create a distinct impression. This implies that the entry into
the area of the Passion has already occurred.[117] The limits of this
stage are found beyond the boundary line depicting the main events
of the Passion which develop after the entry into Jerusalem.

The second unit is centered around Jesus' answer to James and

John: "The cup that I drink you will drink; and with the baptism with which I am baptized, you will be baptized" (10.39). In this instance the Messiah is perfectly clear as to the sacrificial death awaiting him. He is also clear, however, that a similar lot is reserved for his disciples.[118] The verbs are alike: "I drink, you will drink," "I am baptized, you will be baptized." The chronological difference does not reduce the certainty, but rather emphasizes it, because here, the link between present and future is immediate. In Mark 10.39 the area of Passion Christology, which has Jesus at its center, is enlarged to comprise both Jesus and his people.

The third unit concerns Christ's words in the passage Mark 10.42-44. In this text is found his teaching about the leaders and great men who "rule over the nations [RSV 'Gentiles'],'' and his most emphatic order to his disciples: "it shall not be so among you; but whoever would be great among you must be your servant, and whoever would be first among you must be slave of all" (10.43-44). A part of this teaching was encountered in Mark 9.34-35. Here, however, the language and ideas are more developed, offering a sharp critique of "rulers" and "great men" among the Gentiles as well.[119] The terms "lord it over them" and "exercise authority over them" reveal the heavy, intolerable burden of their oppression and the full disapproval of such by the Messiah. The disciples are called to a completely different path, a path defined by the terms "servant" and "slave."[120] These terms, however, relate to the ideas of turning from all dominance, of humility, pain, and toil, i.e. ideas that conceptually border on suffering. Here the Christology of Passion has introduced into the human realm modes of behavior which are fundamentally different from the ones then prevailing.

The explanation for the above stance is to be found in the fourth unit of Jesus' sayings: "For the Son of man also came not to be served but to serve, and to give his life as a ransom for many" (10.45).[121] The reason the Messiah wants his disciples to be "servants" and "slaves" is that he himself came to serve and offer his life for human salvation. The principal meaning of this passage is that Christ offers his life for the sake of humankind. The fact that the Messiah suffers and dies for human salvation is indicated with marvelous clarity. The Christology of Passion is revealed as a Christology infused with and molded by love and service,[122] which in turn becomes the only way of life and code of behavior for Jesus' disciples.[123]

The four units of the Messiah's sayings in Mark 10.35-45 constitute an imposing network in expressing a Passion Christology. The special characteristics here are the particular aspects, or rather effects of this Christology in anthropological and soteriological matters.

In the same pericope, Mark 10.35-45, there are certain tangible elements of the Christology of Authority. The request of the sons of Zebedee (10.35) presupposes that they were cognizant of its potential fulfillment, that is, they recognized Jesus' supreme authority; moreover, the two disciples speak about the Messiah's "glory" (10.37).[124] In addition, Jesus' words in Mark 10.35-45 in every way exude the lofty prerogative and authority of God. Deep within the repeated images in Mark 10.35-45, images of the Passion, the Messiah is discerned, sometimes hazily, sometimes lucidly, "in his glory."

15. The major section of Mark 8.27-10.52 closes with the account of a miracle. While leaving Jericho, Christ gives sight to the blind Bartimaeus, thereby doing a supernatural work which signifies his divine power.

The narrative in Mark 10.46-52,[125] as do all miracle stories in Mark, conveys the idea of Christ's incomparable lordship and might. In the miracle of Bartimaeus, however, there is something of special note. The blind beggar addresses Christ as "Son of David," at least twice, loudly (10.47 and 10.48). This address is a messianic title.[126] Until this point in the Gospel, every spoken confession referring to Jesus as the Messiah, aside from the theophanic ones (1.11, 9.7) came either from the disciples or from demons.[127] This is the first instance of a simple layman, unassociated with the circle of disciples, making public recognition of Jesus as the Messiah. Here is a great new opening. The truth about the full identity of Jesus cannot be kept secret.[128]

This observation is confirmed by the fact that Jesus does not "forbid" Bartimaeus from using this form of address, nor does he command him to be silent. This happened for the last time at Peter's confession. Here, Jesus accepts the title "Son of David" and at the same time, by his silence, waives the prohibition against declaring his messianic identity.[129] From this point on, preaching Jesus' messiahship can go on without inhibitions or reservations. On the other hand, the time remaining is indeed short. With the impending entrance into Jerusalem, the final reckoning will begin.

In view of the beginning of the Passion[130] and of the final suffering view, the incident of the blind man works as a strong reminder of the divine authority and person of Christ.[131] At the same time, however, Mark 10.46-52 functions on yet another level of reference. Immediately before this major section, Mark 8.27-10.52, another miracle involving the healing of a blind man was related. Now at the conclusion of the same major section, Mark brings in the miraculous overcoming of blindness and Jesus' giving sight to Bartimaeus. These two miracles were preceded by several episodes which revealed the spiritual blindness of his disciples. The two miracles show Jesus removing physical blindness. The symbolism is all too clear and transference to the disciples' level is easy.[132] Christ has the authority and power to free his disciples from the spiritual blindness that torments them, to give them the vision and ability to clearly see and understand who he truly is.[133]

Chapter Three

THE FULFILLMENT OF THE PASSION IN THE LIGHT OF AUTHORITY (Mark 11.1-16.20)

With the eleventh chapter we enter the third major section of the Gospel according to Mark (11.1-16.20). The events described in this final section take place in Jerusalem; therefore, chapters eleven through thirteen present Christ's activities and teaching in the Holy City. Here, the conflict between Jesus and the Jewish religious leaders and teachers becomes noticeable, a conflict that climaxes with lightening speed, running headlong into the Passion. In chapters fourteen and fifteen the Passion is depicted in its successive stages, from the betrayal and arrest to Christ's crucifixion, death, and burial.

This section is governed by the Christology of Passion, especially in its final chapters, although the Christology of Authority is never absent. The careful reader of Mark 11.1-16.20 encounters repeated indications of the latter which do not allow a one-sided development of the other. In this section we have the opposite of what occurred in the first. There, the primary emphasis was on the Christology of Authority with constant reminders of Passion Christology. In Mark 11.1-16.20, the roles are reversed.

THE FIRST PHASE: THE CONFLICT REACHES A CLIMAX (11.1-13.36)

1. The eleventh chapter begins with the description of Jesus' entrance into Jerusalem (11.1-11),[1] which the other Evangelists also recount (Mt 21.1-11, Lk 19.28-40, Jn 12.12-19). There is no doubt that Mark considers the event as messianic;[2] therefore, we would expect fo find presentation of elements declaratory of Jesus' divine authority

in Mark 11.1-11. This, however, does not seem to occur. The episode about the colt (11.2-3) certainly shows Jesus speaking with indisputable authority and possessing unusual knowledge, but it is reported without comment or emphasis. The same observation applies to the term "Lord" ("the Lord has need of it," 11.3), which may have unique christological significance, but could have also been used here in the same sense it was used by the Syrophoenician woman (7.28).[3] Consequently, the preliminaries of the Son of God's entrance into Jerusalem present his matchless authority, but in a restrained, matter-of-fact way, using the most rudimentary language necessary to convey the information.

Similarly reported is the description of the entrance itself, in contrast to the corresponding passages of the other Evangelists. Three particular points can be distinguished with relative ease:

The first is the number of people present as spectators or accompanying Christ as he comes into Jerusalem. Mark uses the words "many," "others," "those who went before," and "those who followed." Out of all these, "many" alone seems to imply a great number, but it does not appear to be the term the Evangelist prefers when he wants to emphasize numbers.[4] In such instances, he uses expressions like "a great multitude" (3.7-8), "a very large crowd" (4.1), "all the crowd" (2.13), "a great crowd" (5.21). In contrast to the other Evangelists,[5] Mark 11.1-11, is sparing in his references to numbers, as though not wanting to stress the great number of those who received Jesus.

The second characteristic concerns the impression made by Christ's arrival in Jerusalem. Mark makes no comment that would indicate the city was in any way excited in welcoming Jesus. The end of the vignette most certainly creates an air of quiet, hushed solemnity, or rather, sacredness: "And he entered Jerusalem, and went into the temple; and when he had looked round at everything, as it was already late, he went out to Bethany with the twelve" (11.11). The passage here is impressive when compared with the corresponding passage in Matthew: "And when he entered Jerusalem, all the city was stirred, saying, 'Who is this?'" (Mt 21.10).[6] It is obvious that Mark does not place emphasis on the general excitement and intense agitation created by Jesus' arrival in the Holy City.

The laudations of those present constitute the third noteworthy point. All the Evangelists mention the phrase "blessed is he that comes in the name of the Lord" (Mt 21.9, Mk 11.9, Lk 19.38, Jn 12.13);

moreover, in three of them, we encounter either the word "king" or its concept.[7] In Mark we find the expression, "Blessed is the kingdom of our father David that is coming" (11.10). Why did the second Evangelist prefer to use this rather unusual expression?[8] It may be that he prefers to avoid words which directly proclaim Jesus a king. His reference is indirect; consequently, the tone becomes less triumphant, at least on a personal level.[9]

The above three characteristics underline the distinctiveness of Mark 11.1-11, which presents the Messiah's entrance into Jerusalem on a note of restrained festivity, moderate in excitement and intensity. This phenomenon can perhaps be explained by the influence of the impending Passion.[10] Here, the Christology of Passion seems to have influenced the report of a triumphant event, which itself expresses a Christology of Authority.

2. The pericope Mark 11.12-25, which follows the passage relating the entrance into Jerusalem, is a composite one. It consists of the episode about the "withered figtree" in two phases (11.12-14 and 20-25).[11] Between these is inserted the cleansing of the Temple (11.15-18).[12] These two incidents give us a number of examples of Authority Christology.

The episode of the withered figtree belongs to the category of miracles involving nature. Jesus censures a figtree and the following day the tree is seen to be "withered away to its roots" (11.20). The Messiah's word acts with supernatural power, having miraculous results. Here Christ's divine authority over nature and natural phenomena is clear.[13]

This supernatural power of his is also suggested in the discourse appended to the miracle. In response to Peter's comment, Jesus proclaims: "Have faith in God. Truly, I say to you, whoever says to this mountain, 'Be taken up and cast into the sea,' and does not doubt in his heart, but believes that what he says will come to pass, it will be done for him" (11.22-23). This message and the material it contains presuppose divine authority. At the same time, the accompanying sentences point out that the disciples are in a position to use the word to produce miracles on a par with those of Jesus.[14] It is obvious, however, that this power is directly connected with the Messiah, who has the fullness of the miracle-producing power.[15]

The account of the withered figtree, according to many interpreters, also has a symbolic side, most likely referring to the Jewish people:[16] many leaves that give a false sense of vitality and productiveness, but are desperately void of fruit, which will bring about their final withering. This symbolic interpretation, which is exegetically legitimate, again manifests lofty authority on Jesus' part, because it portends an ultimate divine judgment on the chosen people.[17]

Along the same lines, the Christology of Authority also shapes the account of the cleansing of the Temple (11.15-17). Here we have the depiction of a series of Jesus' acts which have a messianic character, in that the cleansing and renewal of the Temple is connected with the time of the Messiah.[18] Mark's account reveals the divine prerogative of God's Son in all its magnificence and might. His actions manifest divine wrath over the plight of the Temple and his words bring a condemning judgement against those responsible of changing the holy place into a "den of thieves" (11.17). Every word in the vignette goes to build an image of lofty supremacy, an image of one who acts as God.[19]

It may be Mark's intention here to accurately convey the christological concept of Christ's divine authority, and so he uses language indicative of judgment and divine wrath. His object is not to give an informative account of the incident in the Temple, but to show Jesus' attitude and behavior as to their nature and intent. Christ's behavior and actions in Mark 11.15-17 exceed human measures. They belong to the sphere of divine authority and prerogative.[20]

The passage of Mark 11.12-25 also contains an eloquent example of Passion Christology. It treats the opposition of the Jewish religious leaders to the cleansing of the Temple: "And the chief priests and the scribes heard it and sought a way to destroy him" (11.18). The Messiah's behavior in the Temple causes an eruption of enmity among his adversaries. These look for a way to rid themselves of Jesus. Strangely, the uniqueness and sacredness in the Messiah's words and actions cause his opponents' hatred to foment and this accelerates his sacrificial end. Each new revelation of Jesus' messianic identity brings stronger opposition, and the Passion closes in with breakneck speed.

3. Mark 11.27-33[21] begins a series of pericopes which describe discussions between Jesus and the Jewish religious leaders. These dialogues show an undisguised belligerency on the part of the religious leaders and a clear desire to reveal the truth on the Messiah's part.

Thus, conflict is suggested every step of the way, which intensifies the situation more and more. These passages have an air permeated with the Passion which is now very much closer.

In Mark 11.27-33, the conflict has as its starting point the question which the high priests, scribes, and elders ask Christ: "By what authority are you doing these things, or who gave you this authority to do them?" (11.28). Essentially, the question is a grave accusation, as the context reveals. It is grave because it comes from members of the Sanhedrin, the highest authoritative spiritual body of the Jews of that time,[22] and particularly because it mentions an authority that seems unusual. Whatever meaning is given to "doing these things,"[23] the fundamental meaning is revelatory of acts and words which are done in the name of a divine authority.[24] For reasons which are obvious, the high priests and scribes do not accept that Jesus has such divine legitimation for what he does and teaches. To them, he is essentially being sacrilegious. The penalties for this are known, and the impression made by the question in the form we saw it in Mark 11.28 is a preliminary to a final sentence.

The question of the Jewish religious leaders and teachers at the same time makes an indirect but eloquent recognition of Jesus' activities and teaching. Their accusation, as we have seen, is an accusation that what he does is in the name of a divine authority, as one sent by God. This is a tacit admission of his extraordinary authority, and because this admission comes from inexorable adversaries, it attains special importance.

The incomparable authority in Jesus' answer to the chief priests and scribes is described with unmatched style.[25] The crux of Jesus' answer is in his reference to John the Baptist, who acted as an agent of God, never pursuing nor receiving official recognition from religious leaders. The significance of this is that, in Jesus' case too, there is a special authority flowing directly from God which does not depend on official recognition. Here the immediacy of the Messiah's divine source of authority is strongly suggested.[26] At the same time, Jesus' supernatural capabilities are manifested throughout the entire scene, for he knows people's thoughts, especially the thoughts of his opponents, thereby confounding them (11.31-32).

At the end of the discussion yet another fact indicative of Christ's authority is related. When Jesus says to his opponents, "Neither will I tell you by what authority I do these things" (11.33), he expresses a unique power. Here Christ lets it be known that his prerogative cannot be put under censure even by the all-powerful Sanhedrin, that he does not require recognition by the high priests, scribes and elders, that he has a divine authority which comes directly from God, having God's recognition and approval.[27]

The outcome of this discussion is humiliating for the religious leaders of the Jews and of course causes their enmity to grow. Together with its intimation of divine supremacy, the phrase "Neither will I tell you by what authority I do these things," also contains an inevitable challenge of the type that creates a deadly danger. The next pericope deals with the immediacy of this danger and its final realization.

4. This pericope, Mark 12.1-12,[28] is the familiar parable of the vineyard[29] (parallel passages are found in Mt 21.33-46 and Lk 20.9-19), which with strong lines expresses the Christology of Passion. An interesting element is presented by this Christology. It relates, in parabolic form, the Passion of the Messiah to Old Testament precedents.

The parable stresses the repeated sending of God's servants[30] to his people: "When the time came, he sent a servant to the tenants" (12.2); "Again he sent to them another servant" (12.4); "And so with many others" (12.5). The description, though sketchy, excellently conveys the image of God's continual sending of persons and his immovable decision to keep contact with his people.

At the same time the parable suggests in relief the malevolence of Israel's religious leadership, symbolized by the tenants,[31] and the terrible martyrdom inflicted on the servants sent by God: "beat," "wounded . . . in the head," "treated him shamefully," "killed," "some they beat," "some they killed." These verbs, accumulated into two verses (12.3-5), expose all the harshness, fury and irreconcilability of the persecutions. The persecutions gain greater significance because they continue inexorably against God's attempts to send new representatives, attempts that reveal his long-suffering.

The next step in this long list of violent acts against those sent by God is the martyrly death of the son: "And they took him and killed him, and cast him out of the vineyard" (12.8). Here Jesus predicts his own death at the hands of those who have placed themselves in opposition to God. The verb is the same used in the three predictions of the Passion (8.31, 9.31, 10.34).[32] In this pericope, however, the Messiah's violent end comes as the last of a series of abuses and murders which began in the Old Testament period. The Passion of the Son of God covers a wider area and, on the part of the Jews, is shown not as an isolated event, but a repetition and continuation of what came before.[33] At the same time, there is a conspicuous difference: in the past they dealt with servants, while in the present they are dealing with the "only," "beloved son," "the heir"; therefore, the Messiah's Passion is manifested in simultaneous continuity and discontinuity with the past of the people of God, with all the consequences this christological concept could have.

Mark's comment after the parable confirms the idea of the imminence of Jesus' Passion (12.12). The Evangelist's remarks give the impression that, at this stage, Christ's violent arrest by the Jewish religious leaders was avoided at the last moment.

In the pericope Mark 12.1-12 there are also noteworthy references to the Christology of Authority. The Messiah is radically set apart from his precursors, the people sent by God throughout Israel's history. They were servants, he is the Son. The Sonship of Christ is denoted with unusual emphasis. He is the "only," the only-begotten and "beloved son."[34] This last term is the term par excellance acknowledging the Son's divine identity in the theophanic scenes of the baptism (1.11) and transfiguration (9.7).[35] Expression of the Christology of Authority is also seen at the end of the parable (12.9-11) where the final victory of God is proclaimed with recognition of the Messiah as the wonderful, ineffable foundation of life. The last word does not go to Christ's murderers, but to God's authority and that of his beloved Son.[36]

5. Mark 12.13-17[37] is also found in that series of dialogues which are prompted by hostility toward Jesus and are attempts to incriminate him. It therefore belongs to the texts of Passion Christology.

In this particular case we can distinguish three points which intimate the magnitude of the enmity and hidden threat:

The first is the identity of those who first question Jesus. They belong to the Pharisees and the Herodians (12.13). The fact that these two opposing factions are working together punctuates their common opposition to Christ;[38] but the likelihood that both were sent by the Sanhedrin unveils the seriousness of the threat against Jesus as well as the continuing conspiracy for his downfall.

The second point is the Pharisees' motives for the discussion: "to entrap him in his talk" (12.13). The verb ἀγρεύσωσιν is used here metaphorically and means they wish to ensnare Jesus in an argument, causing him to say something they could use to openly denounce him[39] and call for his arrest.

The third is the question itself which the Pharisees put to Jesus: "Is it lawful to pay taxes to Caesar, or not? Should we pay, or should we not?" (12.14).[40] The question was conceived with ingenious cunning. An affirmative answer would provoke the ethnic sentiment of those listening, a negative answer would be tantamount to revolution against the Romans.

This material serves to manifest not only the magnitude of the opposition against Christ, but the resoluteness, cunning and relentlessness which accompany it, mercilessly paving the way for the Passion.

Mark 12.13-17 does not lack references to the Christology of Authority. Christ's answer, which dumbfounds the Pharisees, his recognition of their hypocrisy and dark motives ("But knowing their hypocrisy, he said to them, 'Why put me to the test?' " 12.15), his changing the level of the discussion, suggest a unique prerogative. The final remarks of the Evangelist function along the same lines: "And they were amazed at him" (12.17).[41]

6. The pericope which follows (12.18-27)[42] is of the same conflict type as the one preceding. This is another aggressive act against Jesus intended to entrap, humiliate, and cause his destruction.

Christ's opponents in Mark 12.18-27 are the Sadducees, representing one of the stronger religious factions among the Jews of New Testament times.[43] The Sadducees in Mark appear for the first time in this passage. With their entrance, a new and powerful enemy is added to the deadly battle against Jesus; thus, the front against the Son of God is comprised of all the big religious factions of Judaism.

It is typical that the Sadducees who are introduced into the passage with the explanatory note, "who say that there is no resurrection" (12.18), ask a question as to the manner of the resurrection and human relationships within it.[44] The question is a blend of irony and contempt. The entire pericope of Mark 12.18-27 with its content and position within the developing events is a building block of the conspiracy against Jesus and his Passion.

In the same text, the attitude and answer of Christ express his prerogative and supremacy. "Unobstrusive, but clearly discernible

are the moral elevation of Jesus, the spirituality of his outlook, and
the force of his personality."[45] His divine authority is especially visible in the double rebuke he directs at the Sadducees: "Is not this
why you are wrong . . . " (12.24) and "you are quite wrong" (12.27).
Such a judgment against the strong Sadducees presupposes enormous
superiority.

7. With the text of Mark 12.28-34,[46] one more discussion is
added to the series of conflict pericopes which began in Mark 11.27-33.
This discussion, however, does not have a polemic or "entrapping"
orientation. The representative of the class of scribes, who is speaking with Jesus in Mark 12.28-34, asks him the initial question with
good intent: " . . . and heard them disputing with one another, and
seeing that he (Jesus) answered them well, asked him . . . " (12.28).
The scribe recognizes Jesus' correctness in answering the Sadducees
(12.18-27) and this is the basis of his own question.[47]

The scribe's good intent is also evident in the comment he makes
after Jesus' answer: "You are right, Teacher, you have truly said . . . "
(12.32).[48] Much more indicative of the friendly spirit of the talk is
the final verse of the passage: "And when Jesus saw that he answered
wisely, he said to him, 'You are not far from the kingdom of God'"
(12.34). Expressions of this sort are unthinkable in discussions of the
polemic, entrapment type like those in Mark 12.28-34.

The discussion in this pericope is not formed by elements of Passion Christology; on the contrary, it seems to be dictated mainly by
perspectives of Christology of Authority, because it presents Christ's
superiority as an authentic Teacher of the Law, being officially
recognized by one of the opposition. Here Jesus, after a series of in-
quisitions, has been shown to be an incomparably superb Teacher,
whom his enemies are incapable of confronting.[49] At the end of the
dialogue between Christ and the scribe, Mark will specifically note
that "no one dared to ask him any question" (12.34).

8. Thus, in the next two brief pericopes (12.35-37 and 12.38-40),
Christ himself takes the initiative to make a direct critique of his
adversaries. In his critique, he exposes their theological insufficiency
and ethical inferiority. Such action, having the spiritual leadership
of the Jews as its target and the Temple as the place of its delivery
("taught in the Temple," 12.35) presupposes an eminent authority.
In this view, the two pericopes of Mark 12.35-37 and 12.38-40 have

the Christology of Authority at their foundation; however, outside this general base, the two texts also contain particular christological aspects that are of special interest.

a) The main theme of the first text (12.35-37)[50] is the connection between David and the Messiah. Jesus develops an irrefutable dialectic for the scribes: the scribes say that "the Christ is the son of David." But David himself, speaking prophetically,[51] calls him his Lord. Inasmuch as he is his Lord, "how is he his son?" (12.35-37). The impasse is obvious and denudes the scribes of their superiority as interpreters of the scriptures and teachers of Israel.

The impasse is also revelatory of Jesus' ideas about the relationship between David and the Christ. What are these ideas? Exegetical opinions are of two categories. According to the first, Jesus here wants to deny the Davidic ancestry of the Messiah[52] and stress that the Messiah, inasmuch as he is David's Lord, cannot be his direct descendant. This position aims at eliminating the ethno-political elements from the image of the Messiah stemming from relationship with King David, the symbol of ethnic power and splendor. Such a position, however, cannot hold because the davidic ancestry of the Messiah was the foremost messianic belief.[53] If the above position is correct apart from this, then it shows the existence of a powerful Christology of Authority, because it suggests that Jesus' messiahship does not depend on descent from David. David, very simply put, is his servant, for which reason he calls him "his Lord."

According to the second exegetical opinion, Jesus in Mark 12.35-37 does not want to minimize or destroy the idea that the Messiah is the "son of David," but wants to impress the fact that he is someone incomparably greater, that he is David's Lord.[54] The main thought here is one of lordship, which emphatically points out the radical difference-supremacy of Christ over his great Prophet-King ancestor. Thus, new perspectives are opened up as to the uniqueness of the Messiah and his work, and his super-davidic and super-ethnic authority is revealed.[55] If this second exegetical hypothesis comes closer to the meaning of Mark 12.35-37, then we again have before us an expression of the Christology of Authority. The great and glorious David becomes a point of reference and comparison to emphasize the essential "otherness," superiority, and uniqueness of the Messiah and his authority.

Mark 12.35-37 with its quotation of Psalm 109 (LXX):1 makes a discernible allusion to the idea of Christ's pre-existence. In this instance we encounter yet another indicator of the Christology of Authority, in that the christological expressions of pre-existence are closely related to the divine person of Christ.[56]

b) The second pericope, Mark 12.38-40,[57] also contains christological material suggesting Christ's authority and excellence. His critique against the scribes, exercised with implacable and sweeping language, is a thing which presupposes enormous authority. Only a person endowed with divine prerogative could advance such a public censure of a mighty religious class like the scribes. Yet, the content of Jesus' censure of the scribes refers for the most part to honorary distinctions, recognition of their superiority and place of leadership. All this is bound in some way with the phenomenon of authority. When Jesus makes his sharp criticism, described in Mark 12.38-40, he shows the vanity and depravity in the scribes' authority while simultaneously revealing the superior and unattainable quality of his own.

Finally, the inferential statement of Jesus against the scribes should be noted: "They will receive the greater condemnation" (12.40). Here we have the matter of a final, condemning judgment.[58] The speaker is not only a unique teacher, but also the highest judge. He is one with authority who has the right to judge and condemn the bad religious leaders of the people.

9. The twelfth chapter of Mark's Gospel ends with the incident of the widow, who put all her money into the Temple treasury, "everything she had . . . her whole living" (12.41-44).[59] The Messiah recommends the example of this poor widow to his disciples, for she shows the essence of a true faith in God in a tangible way. After showing his disapproval and condemnation of the attitude of the religious leaders and teachers, Jesus dynamically ("Truly, I say to you," 12.43) points out the fundamental characteristic of the true people of God: generosity and the fully confident relegation of everything at their disposal to God ("everything she had," "her whole living," 12.44). Hidden in this teaching is not a mere statement of fact as it is the sanctioning of a new criterion, a new canon for evaluating a close relationship with God. Here the Messiah is seen as a supreme, divine[60] Lawmaker, having authority to define and sanction the form of a new piety.

This form of piety, however, has at its core the offering of "whole living" (ὅλου τοῦ βίου), something that can also mean sacrificing one's own life for God's sake. This interpretation, exegetically legitimate, is conceptually bound with the Passion, when considered from the point of view of voluntary offering.[61] The episode with the "poor widow" therefore turns out to be an implicit reference to the coming Passion, which will become the focal point of the new piety, proclaimed and installed by the Messiah.

10. The thirteenth chapter of the Gospel of Mark contains Jesus' message about the last coming and judgment in connection with the impending catastrophe in Jerusalem and Judea. This is the longest single discourse of Jesus in Mark's Gospel. This particular text has been well studied and continues to occupy interpreters because of its tremendous richness and exegetical problems.[62] Here, however, we will deal only with the christological material of Authority and Passion as it appears in the various pericopes of Mark 13.[63]

Mark 13.1-2 should be considered our first pericope.[64] It concerns Jesus' prophecy of the complete destruction of the Temple at Jerusalem: "Do you see these great buildings? There will not be left here one stone upon another, that will not be thrown down" (13.2). In this instance, Christ speaks as a prophet, predicting the horrible calamity which will strike that famous edifice, the Temple.

Prophecies similar to this can be found in the Old Testament;[65] however, this does not minimize the importance of Jesus' prophecy, which is absolute in its statement, terrible in its immediacy, yet excellently preserves vividness and expressive detail even in its terseness. One could rightly ask whether Mark 13.1-2 is not so much a prophecy as it is a condemning sentence[66] for a system that no longer functions with God at its center, and is essentially dead when it comes to worship. Here we have an image of a Messiah who prophecies with enormous authority. The introductory verses of Mark 13 bear the obvious stamp of Christology of Authority.

11. Mark 13.3-13[67] constitutes the first part of Jesus' eschatological discourse to a small group of four disciples ("Peter and James and John and Andrew" 13.3). In this text, describing the beginning of the "birth-pangs," i.e. the first phase of the dramatic events to come, there is notable evidence of the Christology of Passion. Surely, this passion refers directly to the Messiah's disciples, but further reference must be sought with the Messiah himself.[68]

The final, painful trial of the disciples is placed within a gigantic framework of universal apocalyptic affliction: wars, uprisings, earthquakes, famines (13.8).[69] Within this universal chaos, Christ's disciples will also have their own special lot of afflictions, mainly in the form of persecutions. "They will deliver you up to councils; and you will be beaten in synagogues; and you will stand before governors and kings for my sake, to bear testimony before them" (13.9). This description reminds one of the predictions of the Messiah's Passion in chapters 8, 9, and 10, especially Mark 10.33-34. Here as there, the verb "deliver" (παραδίδω) introduces a series of bitter sufferings.[70] Here as there, there is mention of Jewish religious rulers ("chief priests and scribes," 10.33, "councils" and "synagogues," 13.9), of pagan rulers ("Gentiles," 10.33, "governors and kings," 13.9), and bodily torments ("scourge," 10.34, "be beaten," 13.9). This comparison may very well show that Mark 10.33-34 is connected conceptually with Mark 13.9, inasmuch as the persecutions of the disciples are described with the same terminology describing the cycle of the Messiah's Passion. Here the Christology of Passion seems to function on an anthtropological and ecclesiological level.[71]

The same is true for the extreme expression of passion, i.e. martyrly death. As in the messianic predictions (8.31, 9.31, 10.34), this pericope fortells: "brother will deliver up brother to death, and the father his child, and children will rise against parents and have them put to death" (13.12). The verb παραδίδω reappears in connection with killings (as in the messianic examples in Mark 9.31 and 10.33), while the introduction of close relatives into the raging persecution introduced here make the situation gloomier. Also indicative of the increasing general fury is Christ's statement, "and you will be hated by all for my name's sake" (13.13). The martyrdom of Christ's people will occur in a heavy atmosphere of general animosity. This martyrdom is directly related to Christ and his Passion, so that what the disciples suffer, they suffer for his sake ("for my sake," 13.9 and "for my name's sake," 13.13). Their passion becomes an extension or continuation of the Messiah's Passion.

The monstrous dimensions of the tribulation in Mark 13.3-13 does not entail an omission of the Christology of Authority. The very fact that the text is a prognostic statement points to Jesus' supernatural knowledge and prerogative. The manifestation and description of shocking phenomena in the eschatological future depicts Jesus as having knowledge of divine plans and mysteries.

Aside from this, Christ's divine prerogative can also be detected in Mark 13.11, "And when they bring you to trial and deliver you up, do not be anxious beforehand what you are to say; but say whatever is given you in that hour, for it is not you who speak, but the Holy Spirit." Christ's words here express a lofty authority to give clear commands in the face of deadly confrontations. Moreover, the Messiah's absolute confidence that the Holy Spirit will speak through his disciples to the rulers and leaders of the people, punctuates the divine uniqueness of this Messiah.[72]

Finally, since the disciples' martyrdom is done for Jesus' sake and is grounded in him ("for my sake," "for my name's sake," 13.9-13), we should likewise consider this an expression of Authority Christology. The magnitude and character of this sacrifice lays stress on the great worthiness and excellence of the one for whom it is offered.[73]

12. The next part of Jesus' eschatological message, Mark 13.14-23,[74] refers to the unprecedented affliction which is to befall the inhabitants of Judea, accompanied by apocalyptic phenomena and signs of the last times. The starting point of this terrible series of events will be the appearance of the "desolating sacrilege . . . " . . . "where it ought not to be" (13.14).[75] The trials will come to a climax with violent rhythm and will reach unparalleled intensity: "For in those days there will be such tribulation as has not been from the beginning of the creation which God created until now and never will be" (13.19). At the apex of this affliction "false Christs and false prophets will arise and show signs and wonders, to lead astray, if possible, the elect" (13.22). This last phenomenon may belong on the wider circle of Passion Christology, because in essence it depicts a very intense opposition to Christ: an attempt to destroy his work on the human level, in the domain of salvation ("lead astray").[76] This attempt is made at a time of intolerable universal affliction, revealing the enormous evil behind it.[77]

The end of the pericope of Mark 13.14-23 seems to retrace christological concepts which are somewhat different from those mentioned above: "But take heed; I have told you all things beforehand" (13.23). The command for vigilance and care is a clear and succinct expression of unique supremacy. At the same time the information that Jesus predicted "all things," that he gave a detailed picture of all these things that are to happen long before their historical actualization, clearly indicates his supernatural knowledge.[78] If Mark 13.22 is related to the Christology of Passion, then Mark 13.23 is related to the Christology of Authority.

13. The pericope Mark 13.24-27[79]describes the glorious coming of the "Son of man." At every turn, the text reminds us of the Old Testament and the apocalyptic literature[80] in terms of images and language. The description in its entirety constitutes one of the more representative examples of the Christology of Authority.

The first strong evidence suggesting this authority is the radical change on a universal scale. The terrible affliction that Jesus predicted immediately before (13.14-23), was related to historical events having people as its protagonists. In Mark 13.24-27 we pass to an extra-terrestrial level, to the astral realm and to supernatural manifestations: "the sun will be darkened, and the moon will not give its light, and the stars will be falling from heaven, and the powers in the heavens will be shaken" (13.24-25). These phenomena describe a fundamental change in the order and function of heavenly bodies and forces, owing to the coming of the Son of man.[81] Thus, the Messiah is shown to be a divine being of supernatural dimensions, inasmuch as his final coming provokes extreme changes throughout the whole universe and the spiritual, extra-human world.[82]

The second strong point is what is to occur during the final coming of Christ: "And then he will send out the angels, and gather his elect from the four winds, from the ends of the earth to the ends of heaven" (13.27). Here the dominion of the Son of Man shines in all its splendor as Lord and Ruler of angels. He sends them as his servants and subjects[83] to carry out his plan, which is to gather his "elect." It is distinctive, that in this text, the verb "gather" refers to Christ (3rd. pers. sing.) and not to the angels.[84] This informs us that the gathering is a matter completely of his own. The expression "and gather his elect" intimates "selection" and with it, judgment[85] on a supernatural and eschatological level. In Mark 13.27, therefore, the Son of man appears simultaneously as Ruler of angels and eschatological Judge of humankind, i.e. one endowed with God's authority.

With the information above we can grasp the central message of Mark 13.24-27: "And then they will see the Son of man coming in clouds with great power and glory." The words and concepts of the message most likely come from the prophecy of Daniel (Dan 7.13). There, however, the symbolic figure, who is characterized "like a son of man," arrives and is presented before God, the "Ancient of Days." Here in Mark 13.26 the Son of man himself appears in a universal scene as absolute Lord and, by implication, as God.[86] The terms "with great power and glory" are declarative of divine authority and magnificence.[87] The visional figure of Daniel 7.13 becomes the concrete historic Son of man of Mark 13.24-27, who comes as Judge and God. It should be noted that the message of Mark 13.26 will be repeated by Jesus almost word-for-word at his trial before the high priest ("you will see the Son of man seated at the right hand of Power, and coming with the clouds of heaven," 14.62). There it will be considered the crowning blasphemy, enough to condemn him to death. The theological foundation is obvious. The message is tantamount to a claim to divinity.

It is impressive that in Mark 13.24-27 (and Mark 14.62) Christ appears as the "Son of man,"[88] exactly as in the Passion predictions (8.31, 9.31, 10.33). The name-title of eschatological glory is exactly the same as that of the Passion. The correlation and bond between the two is continuous and unbroken.

All in all, the Christology of Authority indubitably dominates the pericope of Mark 13.24-27, and is manifested in all its power and splendor. This does not happen by chance. In the two chapters which follow (14 and 15), the Passion of Christ will be related in a sequence of painful episodes. Experiencing the terrible scenes of that section, the reader will not be able to forget that the suffering Jesus is still the Son of man, who will come "in clouds with great power and glory."[89]

14. The last part of Christ's eschatological message, Mark 13.28-37,[90] comprises warnings as to the nearness in time of his predictions and his intense command for watchfulness. Also encountered in this part are elements of the Christologies of Authority and Passion.

Within the gamut of expressions of Authority Christology is the proliferation of information of a purely prognostic nature (13.28-30). Behind the predictions that refer to apocalyptic and eschatological happenings in the unknown future is the Messiah, presented as a person possessing supernatural knowledge.

The numerous imperatives found in the second part of the pericope (13.33-37) should be placed in the same christological cycle: "take heed" (v. 33), "watch" (v. 35), "watch" (v. 37). Here, Christ is speaking with divine authority,[91] an authority not only over his immediate listeners, but over the wider circle of people intimated by the phrase "And what I say to you I say to all: Watch" (13.37).[92]

The most significant expression of the Christology of Authority however, is found in the Jesus' statement in the middle of the pericope: "Heaven and earth will pass away, but my words will not pass away" (13.31). This statement of Christ is encountered almost to the letter in parallel passages of the other two synoptic Gospels (Mt 24.35 and Lk 21.33), a fact that certifies its exceptional position in the tradition of the ancient Church. This is an especially significant text which attaches an absolute meaning to Jesus' words, in that they surpass worldly order as much as they delimit eschatological events ("heaven and earth will pass away").[93] As such, Mark 13.31 shows a theological bond with passages in John, where Jesus' words are mentioned in an apparently absolute sense.[94] As there, so in Mark 13.31, it is obvious that Christ is speaking with the prerogative and lofty authority of God.

The Christology of Passion may very well exist as a premise behind Mark 13.32. In this passage, Jesus gives the eschatological information that "of that day or that hour no one knows, not even the angels in heaven, nor the Son, but only the Father." The phrase "nor the Son" has posed a difficult problem for interpreters from the beginning.[95] It is impossible to make an extensive exegetical analysis here. We believe that the passage can and should be understood in the light of the Christology of Passion and in context with where it appears in the text. "Nor the Son" could at best belong to the same category as the expressions "and he could do no mighty work there" (6.5), or "the Son of man must suffer many things . . . and be killed" (8.31). In these cases the phraseology becomes expressive of the Son's powerlessness as a human Messiah, the culminating point of which is the actual Passion and death. "Nor the Son" is not descriptive of the relationship between the Father and the Son on a divine level, but declarative of the limits which arise from Christ's human condition,[96] which in final analysis is superbly expressed in the Passion.

The above opinion is also supported by the context of the passage. Immediately before the "nor the Son" there is a declaration of absolute divine prerogative in the Messiah's words (13.31). The presence of this expression of divine authority hermeneutically checks the level of reference and meaning of "nor the Son." Moreover, the last phrase protects the passage of Mark 13.31 from any attempt to interpret it with a one-sided Christology. The successive statements in Mark 13.31 and 13.32 exist together to perform a mutual hermeneutic function: to suggest an integral christological image simultaneously manifesting aspects of Jesus' Authority with those of his Passion.

THE SECOND PHASE: THE PASSION (14.1-15.47)

1. Mark's fourteenth chapter begins a narrative dealing with the Passion of Jesus Christ.[97] From this point on, the language of Passion Christology develops quickly, finally dominating the text, while expressions of the Christology of Authority become more confined.

The first two verses open the narrative by pointing out the human factors taking the lead roles in Christ's annihilation: "the chief priests and the scribes were seeking how to arrest him by stealth, and kill him" (14.1). The pivotal role of the chief priests and scribes was made known in the predictions of Christ's martyrly death in Mark 8.31 and Mark 10.33. The appearance of these persons at the forefront of Mark 14.1 warns of the Passion's imminence. The verb ἀποκτείνω appears once more as a basic technical term connected with Christ's execution. Moreover, in Mark 14.1 the word δόλος ("stealth") is used for the first and only time,[98] which adds further gloom to the already dark atmosphere.

The sense of the Passion's imminency is intensified by the chronological information given in Mark 14.1: "It was now two days before the Passover and the feast of Unleavened Bread." The chronological point of reference, which seems to be very near, stresses the immediacy of the developing situation.[99] Yet, the presence of such a reference can be explained only if it involves narrating a uniquely significant series of events in the very near future, where a reference point is used to place it in time.[100] The supplementary information, "for they said, 'Not during the feast, lest there be a tumult of the people'" (14.2), functions rather to accelerate things chronologically.

2. After the introductory verses, there follows the scene of Jesus' anointing with myrrh at the house of Simon the Leper (14.3-9).[101] A woman pours pure, expensive fragrance on Jesus' head. The narrative of this event owes to its obvious connection with the Passion.[102] Two points indicate this connection: the first is Jesus' comment at the objection of "some," or the disciples:[103] "For you always have the poor with you . . . but you will not always have me" (14.7).[104] The allusion to the impending separation is eloquent. Even more eloquent is the reason Jesus gives to justify the woman's act: "She has done

a beautiful thing to me . . . she has anointed my body beforehand
for burying'' (14.6-8). With these words we pass to the burial. Christ's
Death is presupposed as an accomplished fact, and this psychologically
strengthens the idea that the Passion is at hand.[105]

It is also likely that the detailed description of the disciples' objection to the woman's act (if the ''some'' of verse 4 refers to the
disciples) and the subsequent conversation (14.4-6) belong on the wider
circle of the Passion. Once more the disciples fail to grasp the true
meaning of the event, saddening Jesus. As already shown, this motif
touches on the Christology of Passion in a more general way.

3. The third episode of this introductory unit of Mark 14.1-11
brings in Judas' betrayal (14.10-11)[106] and is an outstanding element
impressing the closeness of Christ's sacrificial end.

Mark quite briefly made note of the terrible act of Judas at the
beginning of his Gospel (''Judas Iscariot, who betrayed him,'' 3.19).
In Mark 14.10-11 the Evangelist uses the same basic verb: ''Then
Judas Iscariot, who was one of the twelve, went to the chief priests
in order to betray him to them.''[107] The news is offered dryly,
without comment.[108] Prior knowledge of Judas' treacherous role informs the reader that the moment of betrayal has arrived. This is
further emphasized by the information that ''he sought an opportunity to betray him (i.e. Jesus)'' (14.11).

It would appear that the Evangelist's intention in Mark 14.10-11
is, basically, to present the fast and bitter course of events with Judas
as a contributory factor. It is perhaps for this reason that he also
avoids offering pieces of information or comments, which would
perhaps give his narrative another color. On this point he differs from
the other Synoptics. Matthew plays up the avaricious side of Judas'
act, while Luke points to satanic intervention, both of which draw
attention to the person and motives of Judas.[109] Mark, on the other
hand, does not touch upon motives, and the theme is not so much
Judas and his act, but the betrayal, i.e. the Passion of Christ, a Passion which the note ''And he sought an opportunity to betray him''
(14.11) brings to the threshold of the present.

4. The next pericope, Mark 14.12-16,[110] describes the preparation
for Jesus' Passover meal with his disciples. Conversely, this text hides
ideas of Authority Christology. Jesus appears here as having prior

knowledge of all the details of the dinner arrangement. This is a basic christological element.[111] He shows an undoubtedly supernatural foreknowledge:[112] "Go into the city, and a man carrying a jar of water will meet you: follow him" (14.13). The description of the man and, moreover, the certainty that all is ready ("And he will show you a large upper room furnished and ready," 14.15) suggest a divine knowledge, and this is discernible in Mark's narrative.[113] A verification of this is found later with the material confirming his foreknowledge: "And the disciples set out and went to the city, and found it as he had told them" (14.16).

Along the same lines, the Christology of Authority also seems to be enlisted in the part of the narrative which relates the conversation between the disciples and the householder (14.14-15). The superior authority of Jesus shines through the laconic words and frugal, yet meaningful action.

It is likely that Mark in 14.12-16 wants to remind his readers of the supernatural knowledge and incomparable authority of Christ in view of the impending Passion. It underscores his absolute consciousness and voluntary acceptance of the Passion.[114]

5. The narrative of Mark 14.17-21[115] clearly bears the imprint of Passion Christology. Already, the presence of the term "betray" in the solemn initial pronouncement "Truly, I say to you, one of you will betray me" (14.18), creates an air of sorrow and tension. The same verb is repeated at the end of the brief passage (14.21) to make the wound of the Passion yet deeper.

The tragedy reaches immeasurable proportions with the astounding news that Jesus' betrayal to his enemies will come about through a disciple! This side is punctuated in Mark 14.17-21 by the grievous repetition "one of you" (v. 18) and "one of the twelve" (v. 20), a repetition that maximizes the sorrow with the accompanying detail "one who is eating with me" (v. 18) and "one who is dipping bread into the dish with me" (v. 20). These details suggest the deep communion of love between Jesus and the Twelve[116] making the sorrow of the emergent betrayal more horrible.

The phrase "For the Son of man goes as it is written of him" (14.21) also belongs to Passion Christology. Here "goes"[117] is used with the general meaning of "is betrayed" in the same verse, and of "suffer" and "be killed" in 8.31. It is important that the Messiah's Passion is bound with Scripture ("is written"), i.e. that it takes place within the framework of the Divine Plan (the "must" of Mark 8.31 has a similar theological significance).

Mark 14.21, at the same time, also has vistas of Authority Christology. The Passion was predicted by Scripture and Christ is aware of this fact.[118] He proceeds with knowledge aforethought, voluntarily accepting his sacrificial end. He has absolute authority to offer himself and full understanding of what his offering means.[119] In this instance the ideas of the Passion and Authority are inextricably woven together.

The same is true in the case of announcing the betrayal in Mark 14.17-21. While it bears the seal of Passion, it at the same time connotes Christology of Authority, because it is not simply an announcement, but a prediction.[120] This is due to the supernatural knowledge of Jesus, to his power to foresee the future, a part of which is the betrayal. As laid out in Mark 14.17-21, the betrayal as an event draws attention to the Passion, while as a prediction it underscores the reality of Jesus' divine authority.

6. The subsequent pericope, Mark 14.22-25,[121] focuses on the Last Supper, i.e. the tradition of Holy Eucharist.[122] The text, naturally, expresses aspects of Passion Christology. The narrative is particularly dense, sparsely worded, using language of a somewhat liturgical nature.[123] The main concepts on the part of Passion Christology are the following:

a) The concept of painful death. The mention of body and blood without a doubt implies death. The statement, however, "my blood . . . which is poured out" (14.24) indicates that it deals with a martyrly death, an execution or slaughter. Jesus' Passion is bloody, a martyr's sacrifice dyed in his blood which is plentifully shed.

b) The concept of death for humanity. This important soteriological concept is expressed in the single phrase "This is my blood of the new covenant, which is poured out for many,"[124] (14.24). It should be made clear that here "many" is a semitism and does not mean "many as distinct from the few," but "all as distinct from one."[125] Subsequently, the "for many" is equivalent to saying "for all, for everyone." In this phrase the soteriological dimension of the Passion is revealed. Jesus' death is a sacrifice that is offered for all people. Back in Mark 10.45 the Evangelist mentioned a related concept ("to give his life as a ransom for many"). In Mark 14.24, however, with the image of poured blood, the reality of the sacrificial death for the world's salvation is presented with matchless vividness and power.

c) The concept of a new covenant. Encountered in the phrase "This is my blood of the new covenant" (or, according to another variant, "of the covenant"[126] 14.24) is the fundamental christological perspective that the Passion of Christ becomes the unique foundation upon which the New Covenant is established, i.e. a treaty between God and humanity. The blood of sacrificed animals which sealed the agreement between God and Israel, the Old Covenant, is now replaced by the blood of Jesus, establishing the New Covenant; therefore, the Passion, becoming a basis and guarantee of the New Covenant, inaugurates a new relationship of love, friendship and intimacy between God and his new people.

d) The concept of the Passion's liturgical continuity. In Mark 14.22-25, the sacrificial death of Jesus "for many," with the introduction and use of the "bread" and "cup" of which the disciples partake, becomes a liturgical event.[127] The institution of Holy Eucharist enables Christ's sacrifice to have true continuity within the life of the Church on a liturgical level.[128] By means of Holy Eucharist, which in a liturgical sense begins with Mark 14.22-25, the Passion is actualized essentially and perfectly at every celebration of the Sacrament. It remains an active and immediate event,[129] to which every believing generation can have access both in the present and in the future through this worship.

The text of Mark 14.22-25 is not devoid of indicators of the Christology of Authority. In the statement "This is my blood of the new covenant" (14.24) there exists enormous authority. A new covenant is consecrated in place of an old one, a divine act presupposing the authority of God. The same is true of the solemn declaration at the end of the passage (14.25). Together with impending death, this verse announces the magnificent eschatological reality instituted by the Messiah. The image of drinking "of the fruit of the vine," "new in the kingdom of God" graphically suggests ideas of triumph, joy, and power.[130]

More than anywhere else, Christ's lofty, absolute authority is brilliantly manifested in the institution of Holy Eucharist itself. In Mark 14.22-25 Christ offers his body and blood in communion, a communion which will transfuse into its partakers all the grace and wondrous, unique gifts which have their source in the Passion. The ineffable transformation of the bread and wine of Holy Eucharist into the body and blood of Christ, as well as the offering of this same sacrificed body and blood in communion to the faithful, constitutes a great miracle and an event of divine order, which only God could render.

7. The Christology of Passion predominates the text Mark 14.26-31[131] as well. The narrative proceeds in two stages. The first is dominated by the prophecy of Zechariah: "I will strike the shepherd, and the sheep will be scattered" (14.27).[132] The prophecy's direct application to Jesus immediately produces an image of pain and sorrow. The image is widened to also include the disciples ("sheep"), who will sustain the effects of the blow which the Shepherd-Messiah will receive. The grief of the Passion is manifested more intensely in Jesus' doleful statement: "You will all fall away in this night" (14.27).[133] On the threshold of his terrible sacrifice, Jesus tastes the added pain of his disciples' desertion and dispersion.

The second part of the passage proceeds to augment Christ's deep affliction. The reason is his foreknowledge of Peter's three-fold denial: "Truly, I say to you, this very night, before the cock crows twice, you will deny me three times" (14.30). The leading disciple will not simply forsake Jesus like the others, but will deny him repeatedly. The incident is so shocking that all the Evangelists mention it (Mt 26.33-35, Lk 22.31-34, Jn 13.36-38). It becomes even more shocking with Peter's assurances—and the other disciples': "If I must die with you, I will not deny you. And they all said the same" (14.31). A few hours later, all these promises would be broken and the Messiah will take the ultimate steps of the Passion alone, forsaken by his own. Here the Christology of Passion develops around the parting of ways of Jesus and his disciples, and the reactions of the latter to the oncoming tempest.

The Evangelist, however, does not leave this narrative without the light of Authority Christology. The prediction of the disciples' scattering and Peter's denial, with all its details, presupposes the existence of supernatural knowledge. Jesus is seen as possessing a divine vision with which he can see what will happen in the future.[134]

This foreknowledge, painfully astonishing in the case of Peter's denial, is triumphantly so in the pericope of Mark 14.28: "But after I am raised up, I will go before you to Galilee." Here Christ foretells his resurrection,[135] using the first person.[136] What is still more significant is that the verb denoting resurrection is in the past tense, as if to relate an accomplished fact. The certainty of Christ's resurrection opens the curtain on a scene which heralds his supreme authority.

8. The presentation of the Jesus' prayer and agony in Gethsemane, Mark 14.32-42,[137] constitutes a basic text of Passion Christology. In this text, Mark gives a condensed and concentrated version of that which pervades and reappears throughout his entire Gospel.[138]

a) The first thing that makes an indelible impression on the reader of Mark 14.32-42 is Jesus' suffering, which is unique in its intensity, depth and quality: "And he . . . began to be greatly distressed and troubled. And he said to them, 'My soul is very sorrowful, even to death' " (14.34). The first two verbs are expressive of a most intense experience, dominated by astonishment, awe, affliction, and agony.[139] Jesus' words intimate that his sadness is connected with death, a thing that reveals an extreme state of grief.[140]

The image of unbearable pain becomes even more tragic as the narrative continues: "And going a little farther, he fell on the ground and prayed that, if it were possible, the hour might pass from him. And he said, 'Abba, Father, all things are possible to thee; remove this cup from me' " (14.35-36). "Fell on the ground" immediately generates a feeling of terrible burden. Yet, the repetition of his plea to remove the cup, both in a direct and indirect manner,[141] stresses the critical condition of the plea and the great intensity of Jesus' affliction.

The immeasurable depth and unique intensity of Christ's sorrow are also revealed in the Evangelist's statement, that Jesus twice more repeated his agonized prayer, "saying the same words" (14.39). The repetition of "the same words" resounds like an inexorable hammer-blast to intensify the sense of boundless agony and sorrow.

The description of the type encountered in Mark 14.32-42 is shaped and dominated by the Christology of Passion. Here, Mark is not interested in making a psychological analysis or presenting emotional situations. If he preserves an aspect or any of the intensity of Christ's affliction in this vignette, he does so because he believes in the absolute reality and genuineness of Jesus' Passion as a unique christological reality.[142] The moment Christ's suffering is placed on its proper human basis, any sorrow, any pain, or agnoy is accepted and described in plain and realistic language as is the language of Mark 14.32-42.

b) A second point which captures the attention in the Gethsemane narrative is the attitude of the three leading disciples, Peter, James, and John. Jesus had also chosen them and taken them with him to the miracle of the resurrection of Jairus' daughter (5.37) and to his transfiguration (9.2). Consequently, their selection at Gethsemane signals that events of special significance are to follow,[143] and rightly gives the impression that they are expected to show an attitude of increased responsibility and sensitivity. Instead, however, after the agonizing first phase of his prayer, Christ "came and found them sleeping, and he said to Peter, 'Simon, are you asleep? Could you not watch one hour?' " (14.37). The contrast is striking.[144] Jesus is at the culmination of his agony and affliction, and the three disciples he chose to be with him have fallen into a deep sleep. There is most certainly a shade of tragic irony in the use of the word "hour": Christ prays "that . . . the hour might pass from him" (14.35) and Peter is not able to "watch one hour" (14.37).[145]

The same sorrowful episode will be repeated two more times. In the last, the contrast and the distance will become abysmal: "Are you still sleeping and taking your rest? It is enough; the hour has come; the Son of man is betrayed" (14.41). The disciples welcome the tragic hour of Jesus' betrayal "sleeping and taking . . . rest."

The disciples' attitude here, stressed by Mark in all its painfulness, constitutes yet another aspect of Passion Christology. Christ in Gethsemane, amid the unbearable sorrow of his sacrifice, also must taste the indescribable pain caused by his favorite disciples. He is alone, though his chosen ones are near him!

It should be noted that the pericope of Mark 14.32-42, although thoroughly dominated by aspects of the Messiah's Passion, is not a passage which wails and laments. The narrative breathes a quiet, liturgical magnificence. The great intensity of pain does not alter the dignified tone of the vignette. This is due to the concepts of the Christology of Authority which are permanently present and active,[146] and do not allow a one-sided human perspective or human understanding of the Passion. Beneath the prayer "yet not what I will, but what thou wilt" (14.36) is found an incomparable spiritual strength, an immovable desire and decision on the part of the Son of God to bring about the will of the Father.[147] His words betray a unique power and authority to make such a total offering. The same is also true of the final sentence in the passage: "Rise, let us be going; see, my betrayer is at hand" (14.42). In this sentence Jesus appears to have a full knowledge, control and initiative of movement.

He accepts the Passion and pushes on toward it, because it is his decision and his will.[148]

9. The narrative of the agonized prayer at Gethsemane is followed by the description of Jesus' arrest (14.43-52),[149] a description again saturated with the Christology of Passion. In this case, the reality of the Passion is characteristically disclosed in the actions of the people who are the protagonists in the arrest episode.

First, the chief priests, scribes and elders appear again at this critical moment in the course of events (14.43). This time, however, they do not appear in the role of debaters or planners of plots against the Christ, but as executors of a series of violent acts beginning with his arrest and culminating with his killing. The hatred of the Jewish religious leaders has been converted into brute force.

Second, "a crowd with swords and clubs" (14.43) appears on the scene, sent by the religious leaders to take Jesus. This is the first time in Mark's Gospel that a group of men armed with swords and clubs come against Jesus.

Third, like a tragical protagonist, Judas arrives in the night. The parenthetic information "one of the twelve" implies deep sorrow.[150] The same could be said for the signal (σύσσημον) with which the betrayal would be given: "The one I shall kiss is the man" (14.44). The impression it creates is hideous. It becomes yet more hideous with the detail that Judas did not simply kiss Jesus, but κατεφίλησεν αὐτόν, lit. "kissed him intensely." This kiss must have been immensely painful for Christ.[151]

Fourth, the disciples desert Christ. The terse phrase bares the entire drama before the reader's eyes: "And they all forsook him and fled" (14.50). Even the young man who "followed him, with nothing but a linen cloth about his body . . . left the linen cloth and ran away naked" (14.51-52). The description produces an image of panic flight and utter abandonment.[152] The disciples, the last human group that could assist Jesus, have scattered into the night, leaving him alone in the hands of his deadly enemies.

Thus, every human factor: the Jewish religious leaders, the crowd of servants, Judas, the disciples, the unknown youth, together become factors in Christ's pain and suffering. The duress, the betrayal, the desertion and flight combine to form a tragic picture with the suffering Son of man at its center. In the scene of Jesus' arrest in Gethsemane, the Evangelist masterfully points out the variety of human factors which enter and decisively contribute to Christ's Passion.

The reality of the Passion in the pericope of Mark 14.43-52 must be seen mainly in the event of the Messiah's arrest: "And they laid hands on him and seized him" (14.46). Jesus had predicted his betrayal into the hands of his enemies as a primary element of his Passion (9.31 and 14.41). The prediction has come to pass with this event, and with it, the curtain opens on the last act of this drama.

To the pain of arrest itself is added the hurtful way in which it was carried out, thereby increasing the intensity of the Passion. Mark has considered this aspect in citing Jesus' words: "Have you come out as against a robber, with swords and clubs to capture me?" (14.48). The rude and debasing way in which he was arrested adds more grievous fuel to the Passion.

Against the intensity of the Passion in Mark 14.43-52, concepts of the Christology of Authority are also discernible. The course of events completely verify Jesus' prophetic statements about Judas' betrayal (14.18) and the scattering of the disciples (14.27). These events, then, highlight Christ's supernatural knowledge.[153] Likewise indicative of the suffering Jesus' prerogative is his statement that the events concerning his arrest came about so as to "let the scriptures be fulfilled" (14.49). With this statement, Jesus is placed above the flow of events and interprets them not as the result of human design or human situations, but as elements of the salvation process, directly controlled by God.[154]

Thus is explained Jesus' state during the arrest episode as being one replete with divine peace and dignity. He remains meek and quiet, and only inasmuch as they have already arrested him will he make a quick statement to place the scene in divine perspective. Betrayed and forsaken by his disciples, bound in the hands of boorish servants, the Jesus of Mark 14.43-52 shines with divine excellence.

10. With Jesus' trial before "the chief priests and the elders and the scribes" in Mark 14.53-65,[155] we move further into Christ's Passion, the center of which is his sacrificial death. The deadly arc begins with Jesus' rude presentation before the Sanhedrin, a body possessed with the desire to kill him (14.55) and closes with its irrevocable condemning verdict.[156] The particular points intrinsic of this deadly orbit are the following:

Immediately after his arrest, Jesus is led before the chief priests and Sanhedrin ("the chief priests and the whole council," 14.55). Fatigued by the toil of a horrible day, the agony in Gethsemane, Judas' betrayal, the desertion of the disciples, and his degrading arrest, he is now obliged to face, without respite, a gruesome trial.

He is tried by a body of judges—enemies who have already decided his fate (" . . . sought testimony against Jesus to put him to death," 14.55), and who would go to any lengths to achieve their goal.

Besides the judges, the witnesses are also Christ's open enemies, in that they unhesitatingly resort to false witness: "For many bore false witness against him, and their witness did not agree" (14.56). The oppressive parade of false witnesses is an added source of torment for Jesus.[157] His torment becomes especially acute when their false testimony misrenders in a provocative way Jesus' statement regarding the destruction and re-building of the Temple (14.57-59).[158] At this point, the high priest intervenes, not to censure the false witnesses, but to prevail upon Jesus: "Have you no answer to make? What is it that these men testify against you?" (14.60). The affliction caused by the unscrupulous accusations brought forward is augmented by the unjust stance of the high priest.

The trial has led to an obvious impasse, an impasse which seems insurmountable by reason of Jesus' silence. The high priest decides to ask the ultimate, yet essential question: "Are you the Christ, the Son of the Blessed?" (14.61).[159] Christ's affirmative answer, instead of becoming a topic of thorough investigation or objective discussion, prompts an explosion of indignation from the high priest, to the point where he tears his garments (14.63).[160]

The next tragic step is to immediately characterize Jesus' answer as blasphemy.[161] After this, the sentence of the judges closes the trial: "And they all condemned him as deserving death" (14.64). The final blow has been struck against Jesus, after proceedings which, at every turn, were immensely grievous to him.

In the above analysis of Mark 14.53-65, the emphasis on the Passion's factuality appears graphically. The time of the trial, the place, the main characters, the witnesses, the questions, the motives, the episodes, everything mercilessly and ceaselessly wounds Christ. The climax of all this is most certainly Christ's condemnation to death; however, this does not close the scene. Mark cites the first series of insults and attacks against the condemned Jesus immediately after the decision of the court: spitting, striking, sarcastic remarks, and blows (14.65).[162] The Evangelist's narrative in Mark 14.53-65, is a narrative which with every word, from beginning to end, presents the multifaceted reality of Jesus' Passion in all its ghastliness.

In a pericope such as this one, where the Christology of Passion plays so strong a role, we still have a paramount example of Authority Christology.[163] It is Jesus' answer to the question of the high priest, "Are you the Christ, the Son of the Blessed?": "And Jesus said, 'I am; and you will see the Son of man seated at the right hand of Power, and coming with the clouds of heaven'" (14.62). Here for the first time in Mark's Gospel, Jesus explicitly declares that he is the Messiah, the Son of God.[164] This declaration is absolutely unmistakable: it is said before the highest religio-political council of leaders and teachers among the Jews, and it comes as an answer to a direct question having life or death as its consequences. It therefore has an absolutely solemn character and singular eminence.[165]

The content of this messianic declaration is very significant christologically. It is the first time that the three titles "Son of man," "Son of God," and "Christ" are placed parallel and equal in value.[166] More important than the coexistence and bonding of these christological titles, however, is the coming together in Mark 14.62 of two great christological images: the images of being seated at the right hand and of coming "with the clouds of heaven."

Being seated at the right hand is clearly a position of divine power and lofty authority.[167] The language in Mark 14.62 is obviously influenced by Psalm 109(LXX).1, a text already interpreted messianically by Jesus (12.35-37). The declaration of a christological position of such high lordship and authority, in biblical language, before the Sanhedrin, emphasizes the enormous dimensions of this authority. At the same time, the concept of coming "with the clouds of heaven" reveals perspectives of a magnificent eschatological coming with subsequent divine Judgment. The two concepts together form a very powerful christological network from which Jesus' divine authority emerges with enormous power and wonderful fullness[168] and this in the center of a passage which describes the Passion in such dark colors.[169]

11. The narrative of Peter's denial also belongs within the depiction of Jesus' nocturnal trial and condemnation. The pericope is placed immediately after the trial (14.66-72),[170] while the episode itself occurs concurrently with the trial.

Peter, in the courtyard of the high priest, succumbs to an

incidental[171] pressure which has come over him and denies knowing Jesus, "the Nazarene" (14.68). Provoked a second time, he repeats his denial (14.70), while the third time he goes yet further: "But he began to invoke a curse on himself and to swear, 'I do not know this man of whom you speak'" (14.71). The increasing intensity of his denial is appalling. The fact that Peter denies Christ with an oath at the precise time and place the latter is undergoing the fathomless pain of a ghastly trial makes Peter's denial even more grievous.[172] After Judas' betrayal and the desertion of the disciples, the act of the leading disciple comes as a terrible blow to the suffering Jesus. Without a doubt, Peter's denial touches on the wider circle of Passion Christology and thus made an indelible imprint on the memory of the early Church.[173]

The denial, however, had been foretold by Jesus to the last detail (14.30). Its coming to pass in Mark 14.66-72 is one more reminder of Christ's prophetic power.[174] The confirmation of Jesus' foreknowledge becomes the main factor in Peter's moving repentance ("And Peter remembered how Jesus had said to him . . . ," 14.72). At the climax of the disciple's ultimate fall, the incomparable spiritual might of the Messiah effects a miracle of radical change. Here too, the Christology of Authority is present and active.

12. The first major pericope of the fifteenth chapter, Mark 15.1-15,[175] relates Jesus' trial before Pilate. This pericope, of course, abounds in facts which present, emphasize, analyze or interpret the concept of the Passion.[176] We shall point out the most prominent:

a) "The chief priests, with the elders and scribes, and the whole council" (15.1), i.e. this overtly hostile body which has already condemned the Messiah to death, again comes together to deliberate ("held a consultation"). With little delay, a few hours after the nocturnal trial ("And as soon as it was morning") they came together to make their sentence official and formal,[177] "and they bound Jesus and led him away and delivered him to Pilate," 15.1. The image is characteristic of the Passion. They bind Christ[178] as a common criminal, humiliating him and torturing him bodily. They next deliver him[179] to Pilate, i.e. to the pagan, Roman authority, something which augments the already humiliating situation.

b) His delivery is accompanied by venomous accusations: ("and the chief priests accused him of many things," 15.3). As the passage clearly shows, Pilate does not seem to be impressed by their allegations, moreover, "he perceived that it was out of envy that the chief priests had delivered him up" (15.10). Consequently, their accusations were unfounded; yet, the religious leaders furiously and fanatically support their accusations, even before the official representative of the despised Roman power.[180] Under these conditions the indictment is transformed into a strong factor contributing to Christ's affliction.

c) The episode with Barabbas (15.6-11,15)[181] is also very painful. Pilate, in his attempt to avoid condemning Jesus, offers a choice to the fanatic "crowd." He thinks that, when the mob is called to choose between Jesus and the "robber" (Jn 18.40) Barabbas, they would prefer to release Jesus and let him go free. The opposite occurs, however. The crowd, induced by the chief priests, calls to pardon Barabbas and crucify Jesus. The contrast is tragic[182]—Jesus cannot claim the favor shown to a thief!

d) The Christology of Passion also forcefully accompanies the cry of the crowd, "Crucify him" (15.13). Exactly what factors caused the crowd to do this (15.8, 15.11, 15.15) is not clear. What is clear, however, is that this crowd demands Jesus' execution. In a last attempt, Pilate asks them, "What evil has he done?," indicating that he is not convinced of Jesus' guilt. The question irritates the crowd even more adding fuel to their fury: "But they shouted all the more, 'Crucify him'" (15.14). The adverb "all the more" manifests the intensity of the clamor against Jesus, the fever pitch of their blind animosity.[183] The cry "Crucify him" is flung mercilessly against the Messiah and fills the scene with indescribable pain. Here we have one of the most grievous sides of his affliction.

e) With Pilate's final acquiessence to the plan to execute Christ, the tragic circle of Mark 15.1-15 closes. The Evangelist has condensed all the horror and gloom of this decision into a single verse: "So Pilate, wishing to satisfy the crowd, released for them Barabbas; and having scourged Jesus, he delivered him to be crucified" (15.15). The Roman governor hands Jesus over for ingnominous execution to satisfy the crowd. His decision is not guided by any real or imaginary guilt on Christ's part;[184] he simply bows to the pressure of the chief priests and the crowd. Here a tremendous injustice is committed at the high price of Jesus' life. The tragedy of this decision is also underlined by the fact that, with this same decision, Barabbas is released. The Passion of the innocent Messiah is put on the same level as the freeing of a robber!

Pilate's decision contains yet another element which makes the course of the Passion more excruciating. Before delivering Jesus to the Roman soldiers for crucifixion, he orders him to be scourged with a lash. He could have forgone this scourging. Inasmuch as Pilate yielded to condemn Jesus to death, he had no reason to command a flogging.[185] To this flagrant injustice and a disgraceful punishment of death, however, he adds the torture of scourging. Christ's Passion must reach the maximum of pain, degradation, and injustice with nothing to soften it.

Concepts of the Christology of Authority are constantly being interposed into this classic Passion passage. Their intensity is surely quite subdued, and the manner in which they are given is usually implicit; however, their presence is indeed tangible.

First, many times now, the Messiah's fundamental predictions have come true, thus indicating his supernatural knowledge. In Mark 10.33, Jesus had foretold that the chief priests, after arresting and condemning him to death, would "deliver him to the Gentiles." This comes to pass in Mark 15.1, where Christ is led before Pilate and is delivered to Roman soldiers for execution (15.15).

Secondly, throughout his examination before the Roman govenor, Christ remains silent. Aside from four retortive words, "You have said so" (15.2), nothing issues from his mouth, irregardless of the pressure, threats, and his deep affliction at this monstrous injustice. This fact is overwhelming, and was impressed by Mark in his comment about Pilate: "But Jesus made no further answer, so that Pilate wondered" (15.5).[186] The "wonder" (θαυμάζειν) of a cynical, corrupt and hard person, as this Roman leader was known to be, stands as a testimony to the excellent meaning behind Jesus' silence.[187] Here the magnificence and excellence of Christ is propounded before the Jewish and Roman leaders who try him, and indicates that his path to the Passion is completely his own doing by choice and authority, and is not that of the religious or political powers of his enemies. His silence is transformed into an eloquent herald of his unique power and authority.

Thirdly, to Pilate's question, "Are you the king of the Jews?" (15.2), Christ answers, "You have said so." The question attributes to Jesus a messianic claim with ethno-political nuances. The Roman leader twice more repeats the title "king of the Jews" (vv. 9 and 12), something which shows the significance attached to this title. Christ's answer is neither an unreserved "yes," nor is it a direct denial; rather, it is a conditional affirmation.[188] The "You have said so" along with its accompanying lack of clarity, expresses Jesus' unwillingness to

claim the meaning which the chief priests and Pilate have attached
to the term "king of the Jews." At the same time, however, this "You
have said so," does not directly deny the title "king of the Jews,"
because it may be that he gives it a completely new meaning. What
is important here is the actual acceptance of the title "king,"[189]
which has special significance for the Christology of Authority. Later
on, the Evangelist John will clarify this aspect and will speak about
Jesus as a king, whose kingdom "is not of this world" (Jn 18.36).
The Evangelist Mark prefers to be inprecise which, however, does
not impede projecting the concept of Christ's authority as King-
Messiah, the very hour this Messiah is condemned to death.

13. The pericope Mark 15.16-20[190] describes the scene of Jesus'
vulgar humiliation in all its horrifying cruelty.[191] The Roman
soldiers take Christ, who has been mercilessly scourged, and "clothed
him in a purple cloak, and plaiting a crown of thorns, they put it
on him. And they began to salute him, 'Hail, King of the Jews!'"
(15.17-18). Here, a dreadful parody of a royal greeting is played, using the same title used by Pilate. This indescribable humiliation is
accompanied by bodily tortures (a crown of thorns). The humiliation
and torture are increased from moment to moment: "and they struck
his head with a reed, and spat on him, and they knelt down in homage
to him" (15.19). The humiliation scene, embodying scorn, sarcasm
and violence, palpably expresses one phase of the Messiah's Passion.

Historians refer to incidents in which persons condemned to death,
or unworthy of the title, were given royal honors as an ultimate form
of debasement, as their greatest ridicule.[192] If the Roman soldiers
knew of such practices and made a direct application of the same
to Jesus,[193] then his humiliation becomes yet more terrible because
it subscribes to a more general form of debasement.

With this humiliation, however, the Messiah's prophecy of Mark
10.34 comes to pass ("and deliver him to the Gentiles; and they will
mock him and spit upon him").[194] The soldiers' ridiculing of the
Messiah as an imaginary King becomes a point of verifying and at-
testing the supernatural knowledge of the true King-Messiah.

14. With the Crucifixion narrative in Mark 15.21-32,[195] the Passion of Christ reaches its apex. The description is brief and condensed.
Mark does not need to be analytical here, having given repeated and
continuous aspects, sides, images and projections of the Messiah's

Passion throughout his Gospel. In Mark 15.21-32, the final steps and episodes from the Praetorium to Golgotha are depicted laconically. The dominant element in these episodes is the immense and complex suffering of Jesus.[196]

a) A first point indicative of his suffering is expressed in the information that those responsible for Jesus' crucifixion "compelled a passer-by, Simon of Cyrene . . . to carry his cross" (15.21). The information sheds light on the dramatic physical condition of Christ.[197] In accord with the customs of the times, the one condemned to death by crucifixion had to carry his own cross to the place of execution.[198] Jesus' exemption from such a responsibility indicates that he was in no condition to carry his cross. Exhaustion from the frightful night before, the buffetings, the privation, the scourging had covered his body with grievous wounds. He goes to execution wounded, exhausted, and in unbearable pain.

b) Jesus' refusal to drink the "wine mingled with myrrh" (15.23) reveals a second point of the messianic Passion. As is known, those condemned to death were given wine to which special herbs were added.[199] This wine acted as an analgesic and anaesthetic so that the ones crucified would feel their terrible pains less. Christ does not accept this analgesic drink, i.e. he refuses anything which would dull the terrible pain of crucifixion. He accepts and bears the Passion in all its many-sided pain.

c) A third episode of the Passion's final scene, an episode which produces the deepest sorrow yet, is the taking of Jesus' garments and dividing them among his crucifiers (15.24). Here, torment is by reason of the ultimate humiliation of being exposed naked. The body of the Messiah is exposed naked in the sight of all, a fact indicative of excruciating humiliation. Aside from this, his nakedness entails torments by the sun, wind, insects, inasmuch as Jesus' body bore extensive injury and open wounds.

d) The fourth step is the crucifixion itself, described in language which is of briefest nature, i.e. with one single verb: "and they crucified him" (15.24-25). This one word, unaccompanied by any modifier, directly suggests the absolute ghastliness and finality of the event. In this manner, Mark expresses the idea of suffering, which, at its apex and in its fullness, he cannot describe.[200]

e) The Messiah is crucified, "and with him they crucified two robbers, one on his right and one on his left" (15.27). Here too there is an intense feeling of grief, because Jesus, apart from the others,

undergoes added humiliation by reason of the persons with whom
he is crucified. Christ, who has unique and supernatural authority,
is executed in a common manner together with common criminals.[201] He is made part of a group of thieves and criminals. At the
same time, however, this picture also stresses the essential loneliness
of Jesus.

  f) Yet another side of the pain of the suffering Christ is manifested
in the fact that those before him hurl blasphemies, sarcasms, insults,
and challenges of every sort at him.[202] Mark reserves enough space
in his narrative to relate this fact (15.29-32). The sarcasms and insults come from three categories of people: "those who passed by"
(v. 29), "the chief priests and scribes" (v. 31), and "those who were
crucified with him" (v. 32). Mixed in with these are repetitions of
charges from the false witnesses (vv. 29 and 30), ironic reminders of
miracles (v. 31), demands for signs (v. 32), and sarcastic sneering of
Jesus' messianic identity. Of all the human factors around him, Christ,
in this terrible hour of his crucifixion, hears nothing but words of
humiliation, anger, and inhuman and base remarks, words that show
not only vulgar hardness, but above all a monstrous ignorance of the
singular event of salvation which is being accomplished.

  Step by step and in a masterful way, the entire narrative of Mark
15.21-32 constructs the final stages of the Messiah's drama. The
Evangelist Mark, using the facts about Christ's Passion contained
in early Church tradition, presents the Passion in its wholeness and
in its particulars with unparalleled descriptiveness and conciseness.

  While the narrataive of Mark 15.21-32 reaches its peak in terms
of Passion Christology, it at the same time preserves points of the
Christology of Authority.[203] In this pericope, too, the magnificent
silence of Christ dominates and evokes awe. All those, for whose sake
he is suffering, challenge him; they throw insults, but Jesus is silent.
As in his trial before Pilate, the Messiah's silence here displays his
excellent and incomparable power—his immovable decision to carry
his Passion to the end, so as to save the world.[204]

  The Christology of Authority likewise appears in the connection
of facts about the crucifixion to Old Testament texts. Many interpreters observe that the main purpose of the Evangelist in Mark
15.21-32 is to point out that the crucifixion was in accord with the
Scriptures, specifically mentioning Psalms (LXX) 21, 68 and 108, and
Isaiah 53.[205] Indeed, in the texts mentioned, there are phrases obviously related to the depiction in Mark. Thus the facts of the

crucifixion constitute a verification and fulfillment of Scripture prophecies and teachings and subsequently express the super-worldly power of God who makes the things predicted by the Prophets come to pass.[206] The one suffering and crucified is at the same time the embodiment of the pre-eternal plan of salvation, the sign of God's wondrous power to save mankind.

15. The crucifixion scene is completed in the pericope of Mark 15.33-41.[207] Here the final hours and death of Jesus are described. The sacrificial end reaches its point of no return. The Christology of Passion is indelibly sealed by the event of Christ's death, which sanctions it thus as an absolute element of every Christology.

Jesus' death on the cross is described by Mark in three scenes indicative of the messianic Passion. In the first, the great cry of the Crucified dominates: "'Eloi, Eloi, lama sabachtani?' which means, 'My God, my God, why hast thou forsaken me?'" (15.34). The meaning of this passage is impossible to give by any interpretation or analysis.[208] At any rate, aside from other likely assumptions, the ineffable pain of a sense of remoteness from God is manifested here, an experience of ultimate solitude and forsakenness.[209] This experience, exactly because it is lived within the immediate chronological cycle of the death, acquires an enormous dimension of pain.[210]

The second scene has as its theme the offering of vinegar by someone standing by the dying Christ (15.36). This act appears to be motivated perhaps by a feeling of pity or compassion to momentarily soothe the indescribable hardness of the situation. This positive impression, however, does not last. The offering of vinegar is accompanied by sarcastic remarks on the part of the giver himself:[211] "Wait, let us see whether Elijah will come to take him down" (15.36). This is also the final sentence that the Son of God, nailed to the cross, hears from human lips according to Mark's narrative. The very last words addressed by a human being to Christ in his last moments of earthly life are a blend of sarcasm and provocation.

The third scene, in one verse, recounts the death of Jesus: "And Jesus uttered a loud cry, and breathed his last" (15.37). The Messiah's Passion ends in death, a death which is a public, tangible, irrevocable fact.[212] The sacrifice closes in the final "loud cry," followed by the absolute silence of death. The Christology of Passion has reached its supreme revelation, its perfect expression, and will decisively influence any future attempt to speak genuinely about Jesus.

The finality and ultimateness of death which indicates the climax of Christ's Passion, does not prohibit the Evangelist from including excellent elements of the Christology of Authority in his narrative.

a) First, the unexpected darkness should be mentioned: "And when the sixth hour had come, there was darkness over the whole earth until the ninth hour" (15.33). This highly unusual cosmic phenomenon at midday[213] while Jesus is nailed to a cross, is not commented upon by Mark. It is certain, however, that the Evangelist refers to it because it is a physical sign of a supernatural event.[214] Jesus' Passion causes a visible change in the physical world, a manifestation of wondrous signs.

b) After Jesus "breathed his last," "the curtain of the Temple was torn in two from top to bottom" (15.38). This event is also contained in Mark's narrative as something highly unusual and awe-inspiring. The rending of the veil expresses the presence and activity of a supernatural power bound with the Passion.[215] At the same time it symbolically implies the end of a form of worship and liturgical system having the Temple of Jerusalem at its center.[216] This suggests the supernatural authority of the Messiah.

c) The third element of the Christology of Authority in the pericope of Mark 15.33-41 is the intense cry of Christ before giving up his spirit (15.37). Ancient interpreters have already discerned in this cry a divine power and authority of Christ as King.[217] The fact that the excellent confession of the Centurion (15.39) is connected with this same final expression of Christ on the cross, accurately shows its superhuman character.[218]

d) The confession of the Centurion itself constitutes an important witness of Authority Christology: "And when the Centurion, who stood facing him saw that he thus cried out and breathed his last, he said, 'Truly, this man was the Son of God!' " (15.39). This is an excellent recognition of Christ's divine Person and that in the hour of his terrible death.[219] In this recognition is contained the basic phrase "Son of God" which is a fundamental christological title.[220] It has been observed that the Messiah's Passion is completed with the proclamation "Son of God," a proclamation with which the Gospel of Mark begins (1.1), and which is solemnly repeated at his baptism (1.11). The fundamental phrase recognizing Christ's divine person opens and closes Mark's Gospel. At the hour of humiliation at his baptism and at the peak of his Passion with his sacrificial death on the cross,[221] the same proclamation resounds stating the lofty authority, power, and divinity of Christ: Son of God.

16. With the depiction of the burial (15.42-47)[222] the fifteenth
chapter of the Gospel closes, and with it the Passion narrative. The
related narrative has christological significance because it shows,
verifies, and proclaims the certainty and actuality of Jesus' death.[223]
The entire narrative is oriented in this direction: the request of Joseph,
Pilate's wonder because of Jesus' quick death, the related verification by the Centurion, the delivery of Jesus' dead body to Joseph,
the wrapping in a special shroud, the deposition of the body in a
grave, the massive stone which closes the grave, the women who "saw
where he was laid" (15.47). If the textual variant πτῶμα (corpse) and
not σῶμα (body) in Mark 15.45,[224] is preferred, the concept of certainty in Christ's death is made yet more intense. Thus, the grave
becomes the irrefutable witness and final monument of Christ's
Passion.

THE INVERSION OF THE END: THE RESURRECTION. (16.1-8 and 16.9-20)

1. The certainty of Christ's death, sealed by burial of the dead
body of God's Son, constitutes the line of demarcation, the absolute
end of the Passion. At the close of the fifteenth chapter of Mark's
Gospel, the Christology of Passion has said its last word. This, however,
is not the last word of the Gospel, merely the next-to-the-last. The
last belongs to the sixteenth chapter, which inverts the finality of death,
bringing in the resurrection of Jesus Christ.

The inversion materializes in the pericope Mark 16.1-8.[225] Here
the Evangelist describes the visit to Jesus' tomb of the three faithful
women, Mary Magdalene, Mary the mother of James and Salome.
They come, having "brought spices," "so that they might go and
anoint him," "very early on the first day of the week" (16.1-2).

The first part of the narrative is a natural and outright continuation of the story of Jesus' death and entombment. The Christology
of Passion is present, inasmuch as the narrative's focal point and
the women's destination is the grave where the dead Jesus "was lain."

Suddenly, though, in Mark 16.4, a point is introduced which warns
of an unexpected turn of events. The three women, going to the grave
with their spices, "were saying to one another, 'Who will roll away
the stone for us from the door of the tomb?' " (16.3). When they get

near, however, "looking up, they saw that the stone was rolled back—it was very large" (16.4). The removal of the stone indicates some extraordinary intervention;[226] it shows that something has happened to interrupt or change the course of events anticipated by the three visitors.

Indeed, the verse immediately following (16.5) gives the first impression of the completely unexpected development. The three women enter the tomb, and instead of the dead Jesus, encounter a "young man sitting on the right side, dressed in a white robe."[227] The scene has changed drastically. Jesus' tomb is no longer a place of death, but a place of life and glory. The brilliance of the young man-angel and his wondrous appearance usher in the reality of God's power and magnificence. The unexpected scene fills the three women with awe, astonishment, wonder, and fear (ἐξεθαμβήθησαν, "they were amazed" 16.5).

In this atmosphere loaded with the intense experience of God's phenomenal intervention, the angel addresses the women, announcing the great, unique event: "Do not be amazed; you seek Jesus of Nazareth, who was crucified. He has risen, he is not here; see the place where they laid him" (16.6). The angel's proclamation makes the wondrous reversal a palpable reality. Jesus is no longer a captive of death; "He has risen!" The Passion in its ultimate form, death, is overturned by the resurrection. The tomb of the Son of God, a monument to his Passion, is suddenly transformed into a living testimony of his lofty and invincible power. The Christology of Authority enters triumphantly to say the last word in the Gospel story.

It should be pointed out that, when the angel announces the resurrection, he refers to Christ as "Jesus of Nazareth, who was crucified." This description means to affirm once and for all that the one who is resurrected is the one who was crucified, that the new, supernatural reality of the resurrection is built upon the bitter and painful reality of the Passion. "He has risen' he is not here," a principal message of authority Christology, will be forever accompanied by the term "crucified," the absolute term of Passion Christology, in the very same verse (16.6).[228] This interprets and emphasizes the meaning and significance of the final turn of events, the ultimate victory of the Son of God.

In addition to the announcement of Jesus' resurrection, the angel issues a command to go to Galilee. There the disciples will meet the resurrected Jesus (16.7). The command constitutes a fulfillment ("as he told you," 16.7) of Jesus' promise "But after I am raised up, I will go before you to Galilee" (14.28). Here once again, Christ's supernatural foreknowledge is stressed. This passsage, by reason of its strategic position both in the resurrection narrative and at the end of the Gospel, can be considered a key passage, especially its last words.[229] The "as he told you" can best refer by extension to all his prophecies, and especially to those concerning the Passion and Resurrection (8.31, 9.31, 10.33-34, 9.9, 14.28). The final outcome of events simultaneously shows Jesus' superhuman foreknowledge and his divine authority in light of these events.

The Christology of Authority also defines the final verse of the pericope. The three women leave the grave in a deluge of "trembling and astonishment" (16.8). These feelings betray the experience of events of a divine order, of ineffable, superhuman situations.[230] The first three witnesses of Christ's resurrection are witnesses to an astonishing manifestation of God's power, glory, and authority. Their first reaction to this dazzling manifestation is ecstasy and immeasurable awe.

2. According to basic ancient codices and manuscripts (for example Sinaiticus, B) as well as other textual evidence,[231] the Gospel of Mark ends with Mark 16.8. Such an ending is likely, and, in terms of the christological perspectives of the present study, it does not seem to create any serious problems. Subsequently, we could close the third chapter of this work at this point.

Since, however, the last twelve verses of Mark, the so-called "Longer Ending," i.e. the pericope of Mark 16.9-20, exist in many important codices and manuscripts as well as in Gospel lectionaries and patristic texts,[232] we feel it necessary to include them in the present study.

This pericope, Mark 16.9-20,[233] relates appearances of the resurrected Son of God. The theme, as is immediately apparent, is the Christology of Authority. The first part of the pericope (16.9-14) depicts a series of manifestations of the resurrected Jesus to Mary Magdalene, to two disciples "as they were walking into the country," and to the eleven apostles. Reference to these manifestations is enough in itself to strongly emphasize Christ's divine power and authority, which has triumphed over death.

The same narrative still contains a serious element of Passion Christology: the disbelief of the disciples, especially the eleven. The disciples "would not believe" (16.11) the news that Jesus had risen and lives, which the first witnesses of the resurrection had brought: "they did not believe them" (16.13). Therefore, when the resurrected Jesus appeared to the eleven, "he upbraided them for their unbelief and hardness of heart because they had not believed those who saw him after he had risen" (16.14). The language here is reminiscent of the language of Passion Christology. The disciples appear to have remained at the same level they were at before the resurrection,[234] i.e. continuing in their inability to hear to Jesus, being unable to perceive his true Person and the supernatural truth he reveals.[235]

The second part of the pericope, with which the Gospel closes (16.15-20), is a pure yet complex expression of Authority Christology. With increasing degrees of intensity we follow the ultimate manifestation of the unique and divine power of the Son of God. The main points are the following:

a) The resurrected Jesus without lingering explanations, gives his disciples the unprecedented command: "Go into all the world and preach the gospel to the whole creation" (16.15). For the first time, the entire world, geographically and ethnologically, becomes the immense field of the apostles' missionary activity. The Messiah is no longer a Messiah for the people of Israel alone; the entire inhabited world belongs to him. "All the world" and "the whole creation" become and will remain forever the domain of the gospel of Jesus Christ.[236]

b) The consequences of accepting or rejecting the gospel are absolute and irrevocable: "He who believes and is baptized will be saved; but he who does not believe will be condemned" (16.16). Apostolic preaching in the name of Jesus Christ has the direct effect of salvation. Confronting the gospel is equivalent to a decision for or against God, with redemption or ruin. Christ becomes the focal point and sole criterion of salvation for mankind.[237]

c) Accepting the gospel ushers in an extraordinary series of wondrous phenomena. The resurrected Jesus solemnly proclaims in regard to those who will believe that: "In my name they will cast out demons; they will speak in new tongues; they will pick up serpents, and if they drink any deadly thing, it will not hurt them; they will lay their hands on the sick and they will recover" (16.17-18). Two other times in Mark's Gospel, Christ stated something similar (3.14-15 and 6.7-13). These two cases, however, differ at certain points from Mark 16.17-18. In the latter, the wondrous phenomena accompany "those who believe" generally, and are not restricted only to the twelve apostles. Likewise, the latter, aside from banishing demons and healing the sick, adds speaking in new languages, fail-safe handling of all types of deadly animals (exemplified by "serpents"), and the neutralization of deadly poisons or substances. In comparison to Mark 3.14-15 and 6.7-13, a multifaceted broadening has occurred in Mark 16.17-18. The wondrous phenomena have been diversified on the part of the bearers and receivers of them as well as the variety of forms they take. Christ's supernatural power and authority is presented in an extraordinary plethora of signs, a manifestation exceeding all human limitation.

d) The revelation of the resurrected Son of God's divine authority at its apex materializes in the two final verses (16.19-20). Here, it is solemnly proclaimed that "the Lord Jesus, after he had spoken to them, was taken up into heaven, and sat down at the right hand of God" (16.19). The word "Lord" is used in this instance rather as a christological title, defined by the divine lordship of the risen Jesus.[238] Such use is an indicative example of the Christology of Authority. Yet more indicative is the concept of the ascension "into heaven" and the session "at the right hand of God." Jesus, the "crucified" (16.6) and "risen" (16.9), is taken up into heaven and is seated triumphantly on a divine throne, adorned with the lofty authority, prerogative and power of God.[239] The narrative uses verbs in the past tense (was taken up, sat down) in order to declare the occurrence of these events in an absolutely clear and certain way. The Christology of Authority has said its last word, closing the Gospel with an insurmountable heavenly scene: Jesus enthroned, a Lord with divine power and glory, forever.[240]

After the splendor of the heavenly scene, the Evangelist again turns his attention to the earthly, human realm, informing the reader that the disciples "went forth and preached everywhere, while the Lord worked with them and confirmed the message by the signs that attended it" (16.20).[241] The Christology of Authority already seals human reality. Jesus' people will fill the inhabited world with the indelible mark of his authority which redeems, heals, saves.

Chapter Four

ANATOMY OF THE TWO BASIC
CHRISTOLOGICAL CONCEPTS

In the preceding three chapters, we followed the Markan text step by step, and in every pericope we pointed out the more or less strong presence of the two fundamental christological concepts of Authority and Passion. In this exegetical survey, for methodological reasons, we pointed out the presence and function of these two christological concepts or aspects without entering into a systematic study of their components. The purpose of the preceding analysis was to clearly and fully present the unique position held by the aspects of Authority and Passion of Jesus Christ in Mark's Gospel. We can now go on to explain the specific components in these aspects, their spheres or planes of reference, and the conceptual or situational material with which they are bound.

THE ASPECT OF CHRIST'S AUTHORITY.

1. The first great domain of Jesus' authority in the Gospel of Mark is the demonic world, i.e. authority over evil or unclean spirits. The very first chapter already mentions a decisive struggle between Jesus and Satan ("tempted by Satan," 1.13). The conflict as described alludes to Jesus' lordship over demonic powers. It is typical that on the same occasion, the other side of the world of spirits, i.e. angels, appear to "minister" to the Messiah as his subjects.

A little further on in the same chapter, Christ's authority is presented as one that puts an end to human oppression by demonic powers, that inexorably expels these powers and frees those possessed by evil spirits. The first miracle in the Markan Gospel is one that frees a man from an evil spirit which had possessed him (1.23-28). This action, indicative of the Son of God's invincible might, is repeated a great many times throughout the Gospel text, retelling specific, individual cases, such as that of the Gerasene (5.1-20), the daughter of the syrophoenician woman (7.24-30), or the young man possessed by an unclean, "dumb" spirit (9.17-27). These cases most vividly describe the horrible oppression of human beings by demonic forces, humanity's ruinous torment and its inability to save itself. Thus, Jesus' intervention reveals his unique authority, one that saves from dark, demonic powers which possess, oppress or tyrannize humanity.

Aside from specific references to certain individuals, Mark also preserves general information expressive of this authority in his text: "With authority he commands even the unclean spirits, and they obey him," 1.27; "and cast out many demons," 1.34; "and casting out demons," 1.39.

Characteristic of Jesus' complete, utter authority over demonic forces is the fact that he also grants his disciples this astonishing power to expel evil powers ("and have authority to cast out demons," 3.15; "and gave them authority over unclean spirits," 6.7). This power becomes immediately effective ("and they cast out many demons," 6.13). Christ's might is such that even people who are not his apostles or disciples, by merely using his name, are able to perform exorcisms (9.38).

Christ's lordship in the domain of evil powers is also highlighted by the confessions of the spirits themselves, who recognize the Messiah's divine eminence ("I know who you are, the Holy One of God," 1.24; "What have you to do with me, Jesus, Son of the Most High God?" 5.7) and his authority to punish ("Have you come to destroy us," 1.24). It is equally punctuated by the use of strong imperative phraseology used when Jesus addresses the demons: "Be silent, and come out of him!" (1.25); "Come out of the man, you unclean spirit!" (5.8); "You dumb and deaf spirit, I command you, come out of him and never enter him again" (9.25).

The clearest and most realistic statement of Jesus' decisive victory and triumph in his battle against the demonic comes in the incident of the Beelzebul accusation (3.22-30). The scribes slander Jesus, saying "by the prince of demons he casts out the demons" (3.22), but he answers, "no one can enter a strong man's house and plunder his goods, unless he first binds the strong man; then indeed may he

plunder his house" (3.27). Jesus has the authority to free people from
the oppression of Satan and ruinous demons because he holds Satan
in bondage and submission. This represents a basic element contained
in Christ's authority, an element that has direct and radical effects
on human life.

2. The second great sphere of Christ's authority is the natural
world, his lordship over forces of nature. Mark offers five events indicative of this authority.

Two refer to calming fierce storms or raging seas (4.35-41 and
6.45-52). In these episodes, there is clear and explicit recognition of
the Son of God's lordship: "Who then is this, that even wind and
sea obey him?" (4.41). The disciples confess the great truth that the
Messiah is lord over the powers of nature which are personified in
these passages and are given commands ("Peace! Be still!," 4.39).
It should be pointed out that in these events Jesus' authority operates
benevolently so as to liberate from deadly danger. Christ intervenes
and extricates his disciples from the dread and terror of the heavy
seas and wind. His power is not displayed to dazzle or terrify, but
to save and extricate.

Two other events related by Mark reveal a different side of this
same authority. These are the feeding of the five thousand (6.32-44)
and the feeding of the four thousand (8.1-9). In these two similar
miracles, Christ's authority is presented as the power to stimulate
and activate the forces of nature with the result that they produce
a series of unusual effects on a grand scale. The result is the miraculous increase of food. Here again we should direct our attention to
the fact that Christ's lordship over the world of organic phenomena
and events is benevolent and liberating. In this specific case, people
are freed from hunger and its effects. The manifestation of Christ's
supernatural power is motived by love for people in a state of necessity,
confronting an immediate problem of food.

The fifth event indicative of Christ's supernatural lordship over
nature is the episode with the figtree, which was "withered away to
its roots" (11.12-24). Here, the revelation of messianic might serves
a didactic purpose. The figtree becomes an example of the tremendous possibilities Jesus offers to his people.

3. While basically belonging to the preceding category, for
methodological reasons we will distinguish Christ's authority over

illness. The Evangelist Mark, as we saw in our detailed analysis, stored up a great number of related incidents covering a wide range of infirmities. Here we recall specific healings: Peter's mother-in-law (1.29-31), the leper (1.40-45), the paralytic (2.1-12), the man "who had a withered hand" (3.1-5), the woman with an issue of blood (5.25-34), the man who was deaf and had an impediment in his speech (7.31-37), the blind man of Bethsaida (8.22-26), the blind Bartimaeus (10.46-52). Along with this, the Evangelist often uses general references to declare Jesus' astonishing healing work, such as "he healed many who were sick with various diseases" (1.34), or "he had healed many, so that all who had diseases pressed upon him to touch him" (3.10, cf. 6.2, 6.53-56).

The Messiah's authority in the area of human infirmity is again benevolent. Christ heals, i.e. he acts to liberate the person tormented and held bound by illness. Another terrible enemy, sickness, appears to be under Jesus' control. When he wishes, he can heal, unbind a person. His power is so great as to be transmitted plentifully to his apostles (6.12).

Even when illness has reached the irreversible point of death as in the case of the daughter of Jairus (5.21-43), Christ can perform a resurrection. Mark mentions the event without offering any theological commentary. The simplicity and naturalness with which he presents it, shows that the Evangelist considers death, as well as disease, under Jesus' control. His authority over illness covers its most absolute and endmost effect, death.

4. The next great domain of Christ's lordship is sin. It is interesting that in the Gospel of Mark, we run across only two instances where the term "sin" is used. The first is in the passage describing the baptizing activity of John the Forerunner (1.4-5). The term "sin" in this passage does not have any particular christological meaning. In the second case, however, we encounter a very noteworthy phenomenon. In the episode of the paralytic of Capernaum, Jesus states that "the Son of man has authority on earth to forgive sins" (2.10). The content of this statement is underscored by the scribes' opposition: "Why does this man speak thus? It is blasphemy! Who can forgive sins but God alone?" (2.7). The significance lies principally in the fact that Christ's solemn statement uses the word "authority," that his authority is of a divine order and is expressed as liberating power and action. Moreover, for the paralytic, loosing from sin

becomes visible and tangible because he rises from his bed and walks. Here Christ's authority to release people from sin's oppression is triumphantly certified in its direct effect.

Mark does not return to this theme again, nor does he refer again to the word "sin" until the end of his Gospel. The episode of the paralytic forever sanctions the immovable certainty that Christ is in complete control of the sensitive domain called "sin," that he has the might to relieve humankind of it and its possible consequences.

5. Up to this point we saw diagrammatically the great domains or spheres of Jesus' authority, i.e. the world of demonic powers, nature and its phenomena, sickness, death and sin. On all these levels we invariably encountered processes or actions which freed people from terrible enemies, oppressive situations, dark terrors or incurable afflictions; the Evangelist Mark does not exhaust the Messiah's authority in these domains only. As we mentioned, Christ's activity and teaching in Mark manifests or emphatically suggests still other basic sides of his authority.

One of these is the authority of Jesus to override common religious institutions, to abolish sanctioned expressions of Judaic piety. In the very first steps of his messianic activity, Jesus liberates his disciples from the fasting rules followed by the Pharisees and the disciples of John the Baptist (2.18-22); and when rebuked for his attitude, he gives a basic reply in which he introduces a new criterion for keeping a fast. This criterion is himself! To this he adds certain observations in parabolic form which speak of the need to keep new wine in new skins. Here it is obvious that Jesus' authority acts radically, and while abolishing a Jewish religious institution, he offers new criteria and new frames of theological reference for observing it.

This same radical authority appears in Jesus' debate over cleansings and ritual purity (7.1-14). Here too, we should direct our attention to the fact that it does not merely involve a teaching, but mainly a practice. The Son of God is rebuked again, this time by the Pharisees, not because he teaches the overthrowal of ritual cleansings, but because his disciples do not keep these sanctioned forms of cleansing. The situation appears very advanced. Jesus' disciples already act in a revolutionary manner with regard to what was established, and this owes doubtlessly to the Messiah, who has released them from these obligations. With but one act filled with lofty prerogative, Christ frees his own from the tyranny of Judaic, Pharisaic ordinances of ritual purity and reveals its essence, found in purity of heart.

The most revolutionary act graphically suggesting Jesus' authority in the domain of rules of piety, is his overriding the Sabbath rest. In the pertinent narratives, Mark shows Jesus performing miraculous healings on the Sabbath (1.21-27; 3.1-6) inspite of strong opposition from the Pharisees. He neither suspends his work nor finds any difficulty in doing it, and, as the Pharisees see it, he abolishes the Sabbath rest. Instead of the formal keeping of a religious canon, he brings in the priority of love for a human being found in a state of infirmity, needing salvation.

Christ's authority over the law of the Sabbath is manifested very emphatically in the narrative of the disciples' "going through the grainfields" (2.23-28). In this story, the disciples behave with unprecedented daring, liberated as to the Sabbath rest. Behind freedom of this magnitude and scope is found the supreme authority of Jesus. In this particular episode, Christ bases his argument on the principle of the priority of the value "man" over the value "Sabbath" ("The Sabbath was made for man, not man for the Sabbath," 2.27). In order to leave no further doubt as to the source and justification of the radical position held by the Messiah and his disciples on the subject of the Sabbath, Christ himself states that "so the Son of man is lord even of the Sabbath" (2.28). The phrase declares the unlimited and unconditional lordship of Jesus over a fundamental religious institution. In this case too, his lordship viewed from a human perspective, means liberation, a new interpretation and a new set of criteria.

6. The Jesus of Mark's Gospel has authority to surpass not only religious but also basic "natural" institutions such as family relationships. The incident in Capernaum with Jesus' "mother and his brothers" (3.31-35) is eloquent. His question, "Who are my mother and my brothers?" should not be regarded as a denial of the family relationships but as a surpassing of them, as a changing of their position within the value system of the kingdom of God. Christ has the enormous power to change the meaning of family ties. At the same time, he evidently has the great power to establish a new "family relationship" when he solemnly states, "Whoever does the will of God is my brother and my sister and my mother" (3.35). In essence, Christ's authority in this realm also frees from bonds based on the hard determinism of natural situations and creates relationships built on a foundation of spiritual freedom and individual choice.

7. Christ's authority, unique in its ability to create new relationships, institutions and interhuman roles is handsomely portrayed in the calling, consecration and mission of the apostles. The condensation of the pertinent narratives by Mark more clearly shows its constituent elements. Thus, the initial call occurs at the exclusive initiative of Christ and suggests a magnificent air of divine dignity and a supremacy which summons without accompanying explanation (1.16-20; 2.13-14).

The consecration and mission of the Twelve as described in Mark 6.7-13 and 3.13-19 intensifies this impression of authority. Under the continuous guidance of Jesus, the apostles constitute a human community having novel characteristics. Endowed by the Messiah with unusual competence and astonishing authority, they are sent to carry out the divine work of preaching, expelling demons and healing (6.12-13). After the Passion and Resurrection of Christ they become his continuance and extension. The creation of this circle of apostles with its outgrowth and projection throughout time and space is one of the main features of Jesus' unique authority.

8. There are yet other sides to Christ's authority in Mark. One such side is Jesus' supernatural ability to know people's unspoken or hidden thoughts, and moreover, to perceive the christological and eschatological future.

During the first dispute with his relentless adversaries at the beginning of the Gospel, Christ is shown to have direct knowledge of their hidden thoughts (2.8). The same occurs further on with the thoughts of his disciples (8.16-17). These episodes are revelatory of a power to know inaccessible and deeply hidden spheres. Christ has the authority of a knowledge which even the most gifted human brain cannot have.

This consideration gains more weight when it deals with knowledge of the christological and eschatological future. The Messiah knows and predicts in detail his Passion and Resurrection (8.31; 9.31; 10.32-34), the betrayal of Judas (14.18), the flight of the disciples (14.27), and the denial of Peter (14.29-30). He is remarkably aware of the details of the Last Supper (14.13-16) and the entrance into Jerusalem (11.2-4). Moreover, he knows the different phases, twists, and aftermath of the tribulation about to strike Jerusalem, the Temple, and the inhabitants of Judea. He predicts persecutions, wars, earthquakes, uprisings, unusual heavenly phenomena; and lastly, he reveals the eschatological, glorious coming of the Son of man (13.1-29). All this knowledge is something magnificent and wonderful and manifests a unique authority. This authority of Christ also has a liberating, redeeming quality. The immediate future and the eschatological future are known to the Messiah and by extension, controlled by him. They also become known to believers indirectly, releasing them from the terrible fear brought on by ignorance of future historical events. The wonderful authority of knowledge which the Christ dispenses becomes a unique redemptive power for anyone who believes in him.

9. The Messiah's authority of knowledge mentioned above is expressive of a general authority covering the truth about mankind and its salvation. The Son of God is the holder of this truth, identified with the gospel. He is the only one who has the authority to reveal the truth of the gospel to mankind. This revelation is accomplished primarily by the word, and for this reason Jesus' word is distinguished by a unique authority and absolute lordship. This is already tangible in the first chapter of Mark's text: "they were astonished at his teaching, for he taught as one who had authority, and not as the scribes" (1.22).

We have already encountered innumerable examples of the authority and enormous power of Christ's word: his commands to demons, to forces of nature, to people in a state of infirmity; his proclamations regarding religious institutions, human relationships, liberation from sin; his commands to his apostles, and their endowment with extraordinary gifts; however, here we are dealing with Jesus' word as being revelatory of the truth which saves.

It is worth noting, that in the Gospel of Mark, we do not encounter any of the long didactic pericopes found in Matthew (for example, the Sermon on the Mount), nor any of the extensive theological discourses found in John; nonetheless, Mark is absolutely clear in his presentation of Christ as a unique teacher of gospel truth. The word of the Messiah is the word of God himself. This is immediately apparent in the extensive discursive pericopes of chapters 4 and 13, and is yet more apparent in the characteristic ease with which Jesus refutes deeply rooted religious expressions or practices to alter them completely or substitute them (2.18-22; 2.23-28; 7.1-13 et al.). Very indicative is the example of the dispute over divorce. In this case, Christ's word leads to the basic truth of the subject, entailing a new position.

The authority of truth which characterizes Jesus' word is also quite tangible in the series of dialectic conflicts described in chapters 11 and 12 of Mark's Gospel. In this series of adjoining episodes Jesus is pictured, not merely as an excellent debator who dumbfounds his cunning adversaries, but as the holder of the supreme truth, which triumphs over falsehood, counterfeit and sophistry.

The basic, supreme truth revealed by the Son of God is encountered in his programmatic declaration: "the time is fulfilled, and the kingdom of God is at hand; repent, and believe in the gospel" (1.15). Christ often repeats these fundamental truths of the kingdom of God and the gospel (4.11; 4.26; 4.30; 8.35; 9.1; 9.47; 10.14-15; 10.25; 10.29; 12.34; 13.10; 14.9; 14.25; 15.43). He does not analyze them. For Mark, the whole of Christ's work and teaching constitute the most eloquent commentary and the most convincing presentation of what is contained in the concept "kingdom of God" and "gospel."

Apart from the numerous and diversified examples to which we referred, the Evangelist Mark does not refrain from citing another of Jesus' statements which declares the absolute bond between his words and God's eternal truth: "heaven and earth will pass away, but my words will not pass away" (13.31). This statement establishes once and for all the certainty of identifying Christ's words with the immovable truth of God, which saves humanity. In this domain also the Messiah's authority is one which redeems. It redeems from falsehood and ignorance either as a theoretical condition or as a concrete reality of human existence, and it enters into the sphere of truth as a reality which is at the same time knowledge and life.

10. As appears in our analysis up to this point, the Christology of Authority in Mark is a multifaceted phenomenon which embraces different spheres of reality, relationships and concepts. In these cases, factors are implicated which menace, oppress, pervert or destroy humankind, such as demons, forces of nature, sickness, sin, death, certain religious, family, or community institutions, ignorance, fear of the future, existential or theological falsehood. Against these terrible factors of destruction, oppression and affliction, Jesus Christ arises in his incomparable authority, which functions and acts on whatever level the powers hostile to humankind appear and act. It also functions in two directions at once: toward the powers themselves, which he subjugates or puts into bondage, and toward mankind which he

liberates. Wherever examples of Authority Christology are presented in Mark's Gospel, functions and processes are automatically introduced wherein the Son of God subjugates forces hostile to humankind and redeems humankind from them.

Here we have a Christology propelled not by abstract concepts or static descriptions of its properties, but by dynamic manifestations and direct confrontations. The messianic authority of Christ functions continuously, changing its levels or spheres of activity; it is an energy which is perpetual, many-sided and redemptive for mankind and therefore a saving authority.

It is obvious that this dynamic and multifaceted active authority is one which only God could dispense; therefore Mark does not hesitate to refer to events, phenomena or teachings which presuppose the divine person of Christ. References of this type are of three kinds:

The first kind is constituted by theophanic descriptions such as the baptism (1.9-11) and transfiguration (9.2-8). In preceding chapters we analyzed these pericopes, we specified and evaluated the theophanic material. Here we will simply repeat that in both instances the voice of God the Father "from heaven" (1.11) or "out of the cloud" (9.7) proclaims Jesus to be his "beloved Son" (1.11; 9.7). Mark makes no comment, neither does he interpret these statements. The surrounding material as well as the general context of the passages lead to the opinion that, in these examples, Mark conceives of a sonship that is unique, supernatural, divine. In final analysis, the Son is God, or has a wondrous and direct divine origin, hypostasis and authority.

The second kind of reference is represented by the confessions of Peter (8.27: "You are the Christ") and the Centurion (15.39: "Truly this man was the Son of God"). In these confessions, as we had the opportunity to point out, there exists a pure recognition of Jesus' Messiahship; moreover, they have a rather discernible dimension of divinity, especially in the confession of the Centurion, something really significant.

The third kind comprises those revelations or statements of Christ himself as well as the depiction or announcement of fundamental christological events. The catalog is impressive and contains the eschatological declaration of Jesus in Mark 13 (13.26-27), his reply to the solemn question of the high priest (14.62-64), his dramatic warning to those who would deny him (8.38), his prediction of the resurrection (8.31; 9.9-10; 9.31; 10.34; 14.28), and his resurrection event with all the accompanying phenomena (16.1-8 and 16.9-20). In these

examples the very advanced expressions of Authority Christology un-
cover Jesus' divine Person and proclaim his divinity. By way of sum-
mation we cite:

a) First, we point out the declaration of Jesus' divine Sonship
(14.62-64). We just presented this same view previously in connection with the theophanic scenes of the baptism and transfiguration
(1.11 and 9.7) and the confession of the Centurion (15.39). We refer
to it here because it comes from Christ himself and because it was
stated solemnly at the hour of his trial. When Jesus answers "I am"
to the question of the high priest if he is "the Son of the Blessed,"
he means that he is the Son of God in a unique, essential, divine
way; therefore, he is judged as "deserving death" for "blasphemy"
(14.64). It is exactly this self-revelation of Jesus as the unique Son
of God which authoritatively sheds light on every instance where the
same title is used in Mark's Gospel. It is a title that claims an absolute and literal divine Sonship.

b) The second very important christological statement which should
be mentioned is the one relating Christ's resurrection. The resurrection "after three days" constitutes an inseparable component of three
very representative predictions made by Christ of his Passion (8.31;
9.31; and 10.33-34). Likewise, in a conversation with his disciples after
the transfiguration, Jesus gives guidelines about the time "the Son
of man should have risen from the dead" (9.9); and shortly before
his arrest on the Mount of Olives, he informs them: "after I am raised
up, I will go before you to Galilee" (14.28). Christ's resurrection from
the dead is a constant, clear and repeated fact, regularly appearing
in connection with the passion and death so as to show the Son of
God's authority in its divine nature and essence. This also appears
graphically in Mark 9.9 which comes immediately after the pericope
of the transfiguration and binds the resurrection with the transfiguration. In accord with this passage, the transfiguration, a principal
theophanic event, will be understood correctly only after the resurrection, because obviously, the resurrection is the principal event
revealing the divine nature of Christ with incomparable clarity.

In addition to the above examples where Jesus himself predicts
his resurrection with absolute certainty, we also have chapter 16 of
Mark which the Evangelist devotes to the resurrection event. With
unrivaled inspiration and conciseness of style, Mark 16.1-8 depicts
the astonishing experience of the three women who come to the grave-
tomb of Christ and there, from the heavenly "young man," receive

the singular news that Jesus "has risen"! In Mark 16.9-20 the appearances of the resurrected Jesus to his disciples and his commands to preach the gospel to the world are laconically described. The atmosphere in Mark 16.1-8 and 16.9-20 is one of triumphant power and authority with its focus on the resurrection.

Like the statements of Jesus himself which we have mentioned, Mark 16 presents Christ's resurrection as an event of enormous christological dimensions: the highest expression of Authority Christology, it reveals Jesus' divine person, which destroys death. For Mark's Gospel, Christ's resurrection is a palpable manifestation of his divinity.

c) We conclude with the third chief christological statement: the enthronement of Jesus at the supreme position of authority "on the right hand of God" and his glorious eschatological coming. In his solemn reply to the high priest, Christ declared: "You will see the Son of man seated at the right hand of Power, and coming with the clouds of heaven" (14.62). This declaration combines two dominant ideas of supreme power, in the present and in the eschatological future. After his resurrection, the Son of man and Son of God is elevated to the highest place of honor, power and glory, to a position of actual authority as God. At the same time, he will be the eschatological Judge when he comes to terminate human history and institute the Kingdom of God as the sole, ultimate reality. Variations of these concepts, are also found in Jesus' words as preserved in Mark 13.26-27 and 8.38, as well as in the longer ending of the Markan Gospel (16.19). All these words send the same message, that God is encountered in the person of the resurrected Christ, who has absolute lordship and authority over the present reality, natural as well as supernatural, and over the eschatological future. For Mark, the Son, "seated at the right hand," is Lord and Commander of the present and the future, and is the supreme eschatological Judge. He is God.

As we have often stressed, Mark does not elaborate, neither does he use refined or ingenius interpretative analysis to explain the high christological formulations of the three kinds which we have just presented, and which have a distinct ontological character. His most penetrating commentary is in those citations relating the Christology of Authority as it functions on the human level. His attention seems to be captured by this Christology's significance and operation in the sphere of human life, human life in a state of servitude, perishability, infirmity, sin, or death. For Mark, the Christology of

Authority is being continuously translated into liberation from these conditions.

2. THE ASPECT OF CHRIST'S PASSION

The concept of the Passion of Jesus Christ finds its full and perfect expression in the final chapters of the Gospel of Mark. As we said however, it is presented in several variations from the beginning of the Gospel. A common point among these variations is essentially the negative attitude posed by different groups of people towards Jesus. As we have pointed out, the manner and intensity of this attitude ranges from inability to understand Christ's messianic person and work to a complete rejection of him; from refusing a relationship with him to sentencing him to death. A second common point among these variations is the concept of Jesus' humiliation, his submission to human situations which appear, or indeed are, debasing.

These two points are repeated in perpetual cycles in those Markan pericopes influenced by concepts of Passion Christology, as will be seen in the analytic presentation which follows.

1. Among the texts oriented toward the Passion, a significant position is held by those which mention the chief priests, Pharisees, elders, scribes, and generally, the religious leaders and teachers of the people. From the beginning to the end of Mark's text, these groups project a hostile attitude toward Jesus. This fact is a basic element in the Messiah's Passion. The irreconcilable, unrelenting opposition of the shepherds of the people to the Messiah, who comes specifically to save the people, becomes a steady source of terrible pain.

The hostile attitude of the scribes appears immediately in the first verses of the second chapter. They accuse Jesus for "blasphemy" (2.7) because of the way he speaks to the paralytic. Later on, another censure is brought in, "he is eating with sinners and tax collectors" (2.16). Even before this dispute is closed, a new attack follows, this time on the topic of fasting (2.18-20). The Pharisees immediately join in with the scribes' war against Christ by reason of the Sabbath rest (2.23-28). These four episodes are followed by a fifth, expressive of an intensified enmity and malevolence (3.1-6). At this point Mark ushers in the key-phrase that Jesus "looked around at them (i.e. the Pharisees) with anger, grieved at their hardness of heart . . ." (3.5). The religious teachers' and leaders' hardness of heart occasions deep sorrow for Jesus, constituting a central aspect of his Passion. Along the same lines, Mark offers a second key-phrase: "The Pharisees went out, and immediately held counsel with the Herodians against him, how to destroy him" (3.6). The decision of the religious leaders constitutes the other central aspect of the Passion, the crucial factor of execution.

After Mark 3.5-6, the Evangelist will punctuate the lines of his narrative with reminders of this decision to kill Christ: "The Son of man must suffer many things, and be rejected by the elders . . . and be killed" (8.31), "the Son of man will be delivered to the chief priests . . . and they will condemn him to death" (10.33), "and the chief priests . . . heard it and sought a way to destroy him" (11.18), "And they tried to arrest him" (12.12), "And the chief priests . . . were seeking how to . . .kill him" (14.1). These reminders alternate incessantly with narratives of disputes between the Pharisees-scribes and Christ on different topics, making the cunning of the religious leaders more obvious (3.22-27; 7.1-13; 8.11-13; 10.2-9; 11.27-33; 12.1-12). The Herodians (12.13-17), and finally the Sadducees (12.18-27) are added to the circle of Jesus' assailants.

By the time the Evangelist Mark begins to relate the events in chapters 14 and 15 (the main events of the Passion), he has, in the preceding chapters, already presented and consolidated the following fundamental points:

a) The Jewish religious leadership has decided on the extermination of Jesus since the first moments of his activity. Their hardness of heart and unrelenting hostility constitute the main forces behind this decision.

b) Every faction of the religious leadership participates in the plan to kill Christ (chief priests, scribes, elders, Pharisees, Sadducees, Herodians).

c) These same people continuously seek excuses, debate with Christ, and attack him in various ways. His extermination remains their ultimate purpose.

The points above interpret the dramatic events of chapters 14 and 15. The religious leaders' impatience (14.1), their collaboration with Judas (14.10-11), their sending "a crowd with swords and clubs" (14.43), Jesus' trial at the house of the high priest (14.53 ff.), the sentencing of Christ to death (14.64), spitting on him and striking him (14.65), delivering Jesus to Pilate (15.1-4), working up the crowd to seek his crucifixion (15.13-14), and finally the chief priests' and scribes' ridicule of the crucified Jesus (15.31-32), this entire series of grievous events, having the religious leaders as protagonists, is the natural result and inevitable outcome of all that preceded. Mark's narrative does not leave the slightest doubt that the killing of Jesus is basically the deed of the Jewish spiritual leadership, a deed conceived, planned and pushed on to its culminating point, and is not something that happened on the spur of the moment. The Son of God's Passion is a passion inasmuch as it is bound to a terrible sacrificial end, but it acquires a dimension of fathomless pain in that it is brought about by the shepherds and teachers of the people. It is carried out by all those who represent the God of Israel, his truth, word and will. These people, appointed to recognize the unique One sent by God, the Messiah, and point him out to the people, do not merely do the opposite, but reach the point of murdering the Messiah. The tragedy ends here in the realm of the illogical and unbelievable. The role of the religious leaders in the Passion, as described by Mark, is one which reveals the elements of the paradox, the contradictory, and the painful which nonetheless accompany the process of mankind's salvation.

2. Many of the passages of Mark's Gospel in which the disciples appear, speak or act are in some way texts of Passion Christology. These passages depict Christ's disciples as factors directly or indirectly bound with the Passion in a more general sense, and are worth noting.

To understand this theme correctly, we must remember that Mark presents the disciples as being in an especially privileged position and situation. First, they are chosen and called individually by Jesus Christ to follow him and become his people above all others (1.16-20; 2.13-14; 3.13). Second, they are instituted as his apostles and endowed with special authority to preach the gospel, expel demons and heal infirmities (3.13-19 and 6.7-13), an authority that begins to work immediately (6.30). Third, they follow Christ's activity and teaching at every step, and receive his special and exclusive instruction ("When he was alone" . . . "To you has been given the secret of the kingdom of God," 4.10-11, 33-34). Fourth, certain of the Twelve are called upon to be present at highly unusual (5.35-43), or, more importantly, theophanic events such as the transfiguration (9.2-8).

These same men, holding such eminent positions in quality, variety and magnitude, are shown in Mark's text to have enormous weaknesses and falls, forming a source of deep sorrow for the Messiah, implicating them as being among the primary figures of his Passion on another level. Let us note the most important cases:

a) The Evangelist takes many opportunities to stress that the disciples were unable to comprehend or deeply understand the words or miracles of Christ. This is made crystal clear in the case of the parables (4.13), the loaves (6.52), the cleansings (7.18), the leaven of the Pharisees (8.15-21), the resurrection (9.32), and the children (10.13-14). In the case of Mark 8.15-21 the language Jesus uses is most emphatic: "Do you not yet perceive or understand? Are your hearts hardened? . . . And do you not remember? . . . Do you not yet understand?" In this passage the expression "hardened hearts" stands out because a variation of it is used against the Pharisees (3.5). It is obvious that the disciples' inability to understand constitutes a phenomenon of a spiritual order, approximating them with the Pharisees and scribes. Such a phenomenon, as long as it lasts, is an automatic contributor to the Messiah's Passion.

b) The disciples are censured by Jesus because they do not have faith (4.40; 9.19). The fearsome statement in Mark 9.19, without referring exclusively to them, certainly includes them, showing the unbearable pain they inflict on Jesus with their manner of thinking and attitude.

c) There are instances in which the Twelve, the chief ones among them in particular, are fully incapable of attending to events directly related to the Passion of their Teacher. Thus, in the garden of Gethsemane, the hour of Jesus' immense affliction and agony, the three chief disciples, the ones he took with him to stand by him, are asleep (14.32-42)! And after he awakens them, expressing just and reasonable complaint ("Simon, are you asleep? Could you not watch one hour?" 14.37), they fall asleep once more! Equally remarkable are the cases of the Passion predictions. Jesus announces his impending sacrificial death and they, as if nothing had happened, as if they had not heard one word, argue over their small ambitions (9.33-35) and seats of honor (10.35-45)! Their spiritual distance from Christ is abysmal and the pain this distance inflicts on the Son of God is likewise deep. Jesus' statement, "Are you still sleeping and taking your rest? It is enough; the hour has come; the Son of man is betrayed into the hands of sinners" (14.41), reflects the diametric opposition present at this particular stage in the relationship of Christ to his disciples.

d) Yet more distressing is the flight of the disciples at Christ's arrest in the garden of Gethsemane. This had already been foretold a few hours earlier (14.27); however, the fulfillment of this tragic desertion is a sorrowful affair. Only a little while before, the disciples declared to Jesus that they would not leave him even if remaining with him meant their deaths (14.31); but they retreat all too easily from the opposing forces. Mark's description is shocking in its terseness: "And they all forsook him and fled" (14.50).

e) Incomparably more grievous in connection with the general flight and desertion of the disciples is the triple denial of Peter (14.66-72), especially after his boastful declarations (14.29-31). In our analysis of this same pericope we pointed out the magnitude of the chief disciple's fall and its repercussions for the condemned Jesus. In Mark's narrative, Peter's denial functions parallel to the principal factors of the Passion.

f) A direct contribution to the Passion on the part of the disciples is made by the betrayal of Judas. It was pre-announced very early, when the list of disciples was first presented (3.19: "And Judas Iscariot, who betrayed him"). It is also briefly described in chapter 14 (14.10-11, 18-21, 42, 43-45). The ultimate scene of the betrayal at Gethsemane is matchlessly tragic: "He (Judas) went up to him at once, and said, 'Master!' And he kissed him," 14.45). Here the idea of the disciples' role as contributors to Christ's Passion is given in its greatest intensity. Basically, the betrayal of Judas is not the same as the denial of Peter, the flight of the disciples, or their inability to understand the words, work or actions of Jesus, but in all these cases, there exists a common element—a radical distance from Jesus, an unbridgeable gap. This is a serious element of distress and suffering for the Messiah even if it is not a direct contributor to the Passion in the sense that the betrayal or execution are.

3. This same radical distance from Jesus, which can often intimate levels of hostility, is also encountered among other groups of people in Mark's Gospel.

The most typical are the Nazarenes. The relevant narrative is especially vivid (6.1-6). The people of Nazareth, Jesus' "own country" (6.1), hear him teaching in their synagogue, and at the beginning they are astonished, later on they express a blend of irony and contempt, and finally "They took offense at him" (6.3). Noteworthy is the observation Mark makes, that on this occasion Jesus "could do no mighty work there, except that he laid his hands upon a few sick people and healed them'' (6.5). Here is described a human attitude, a state certainly different from that of the Pharisees or disciples, but still openly hostile, remarkably impenetrable and closed. This attitude, which reaches the point of impeding the expression of Christ's miraculous power, is an obvious source of distress for him. It could be considered as belonging to a general category of opposition to the Son of God and his work, and by extension, a category etiologically bound with the Passion.

Even though different from the Nazarenes, the Gerasenes appear equally decisive in their opposition to Christ. After the miracle of the demoniac and the drowning of the swine, these people ask Jesus to leave their country. Instead of opening themselves to the gospel, after seeing its amazing power, they close the door, they stop the salvation process. Here also the reality of Jesus' Passion emerges, imposed by hard human opposition.

The episode with the father of the demoniac child (9.14-27) also goes to show that the cases of the Nazarenes and Gerasenes constitute elements of the Passion for Mark. In this episode, Christ confronts a state of little faith or unbelief and makes a tremendous declaration: "O faithless generation, how long am I to be with you? How long am I to bear with you?" (9.19). A comparison of this episode with those of the Nazarenes and Gerasenes convinces us of the gravity of the two latter. If, then, in Mark 9.14-27 Christ expresses such an advanced distress mixed with anger, we could only imagine how he could have felt in the cases of the Nazarenes and Gerasenes! In all these episodes, Jesus suffers.

He likewise suffers when he faces the more general lot of people manifesting behavior and manners of thinking analogous with those we just described. Here, we could mention the conversation about the use of parables (4.10-12). The interpretation of this passage is very difficult, but it is certain that Mark 4.10-12 states the fundamental truth that many people cannot or will not see the salvation that the Son of God brings, and this phenomenon veils an opposition to God and an extension of Jesus' affliction and Passion.

4. In the preceding paragraphs, we studied the basic groups of people which constantly reappear to play an active part in Mark's text, and we noted their perceptible connection with the Passion of Jesus Christ. More accurately, we saw how the frame of mind, attitude, and existence of these groups were transformed into factors of the

Messiah's Passion and in a more general sense, sources of deep distress, a principal component of the Passion.

We can now attempt an incision of the Passion itself as it is depicted in its entirety in chapters 14 and 15 of Mark's Gospel. Before these chapters, the most direct references to the Passion were made in the three predictions (8.31, 9.31, 10.33-34) and their particular contexts.

The first obvious element which appears at every stage of the narrative is purely bodily torment, the torture and physical injury of Christ. His Passion itself includes a significant series of events and expressions which constitute bodily torture at various levels and different forms.

The beginning comes with his arrest, which has noticeable signs of violence and brutality ("And they laid hands on him and seized him," 14.46), as if they were arresting a dangerous criminal (14.48). The prognostic statement, "The Son of man will be delivered into the hands of men" (9.31), has a literal meaning. The hands of men which take Jesus in the middle of the night are hard hands which know how to strike, to handle bodily, to drag in a most barbaric manner.

The trial which follows in the house of the high priest likewise has its underlying element of bodily torment. It comes immediately after a long day filled with toil and deep affliction, immediately after the agony at Gethsemane which must have been exhausting for Jesus. It lasts for hours, and when it ends, there follows without respite another trial before Pilate.

These two trials doubtlessly produce bodily torment for Jesus by reason of their time and duration and by reason of the openly hostile atmosphere in which they take place. They, however, contain other material depicting bodily hardship. In the house of the high priest, after the condemning verdict, the guards strike Christ, most likely with rods or sticks, while others slap him hard (" . . . some began to . . . strike him . . . And the guards received him with blows," 14.65). Worse yet is the rude business at his trial before Pilate. The Roman governor, before delivering Jesus for crucifixion, orders his flogging (15.15). This fearsome whipping must have covered the body of Jesus with open sores. Crowning him with thorns and beating him with a reed immediately afterward (15.17-19), complete an image of awful bodily injury.

The effects of all these fearsome tortures appear in Jesus' inability to carry his cross to Golgotha. Compelling Simon of Cyrene to this purpose suggests the advanced state of Christ's exhaustion.

The Passion as bodily suffering finds its highest expression in the crucifixion. As we saw in the interpretation of the related pericope (15.22-37), Mark is especially sparing in his presentation of detailed information. He does not have to enter into dramatic depictions neither does he load his narrative with sentimentalism. The horridness of death by crucifixion is something known. It is a most painful manner of execution, and constitutes one of the most horrible methods devised by human malevolence. That which the Evangelist does point out is that Jesus bore all the bodily pain of crucifixion without using anything that would soothe it, such as the "wine mingled with myrrh" (15.23). He tasted the deepest bodily affliction in it cruelest form undiminished, whole, without the slightest mitigation.

5. The second main component of Christ's Passion is mental torment, ineffable spiritual distress. In this case too, a great river of pain is formed from a multitude of tributaries and innumerable streams. A primary source of suffering here is refusal to accept the gospel message, fierce opposition to the Son of God, and unhesitating rejection of him. In chapters 14 and 15 of the Gospel according to Mark, this rejection is expressed in successive episodes and in a variety of ways so that it quickly reaches its endpoint, the irreversible condemnation to death.

Along with this general idea, other particular concepts are noticeable in Mark's narrative which are bound etiologically with Christ's spiritual distress. In his trial before the chief priests, scribes and elders, as well as in his trial before Pilate, injustice is immediately evident with its ends of wrong verdict. The array of false witnesses (14.55-59), as much more, Christ's silence (14.61), gives us eloquent proof of his denial to accept a trial based on lies and injustice. In the case of Pilate, the situation worsens dramatically. This narrative punctuates the magnitude of injustice, because it shows Pilate as being convinced of Jesus' innocence, and because it compares Jesus with Barabbas. To the question of the Roman governor, "what evil has he done?," the crowd answers with the cry, "Crucify him" (15.14), which shows that in this case, together with injustice, even the concept of legal procedure has disappeared. The terrible climate of injustice both at the house of the high priest and at the Praetorium must have been especially tortuous for Jesus.

The Evangelist Mark has preserved yet another basic source of spiritual anguish for the Messiah. It deals with the insults, mockeries, and sarcastic comments which accompany the Passion at its final stage. Remarks of this type begin immediately after the issuing of the condemning sentence: "And some began to spit on him, and to cover his face, and to strike him, saying to him, 'Prophesy!'" (14.65). A second cycle of even worse remarks comes at the Praetorium with the perpetrators this time being Roman soldiers. The mock ceremonial worship of condemned Christ as King of the Jews combines sarcasm and scorn in deep contempt of the One about to die (15.16-20).

The apex of this horrible mockery is presented at the hour the Son of God is nailed to the cross. The main characters of this terrible scene are "those who passed by" (15.29-30), the chief priests and scribes (15.31), and the robbers "who were crucified with him" (15.32). Here, mockery is transformed into an impudent challenge, because what they seek from the Crucified is that he save himself, coming down from the cross! The sarcasm reaches its highest and inimitable expression when it is presented as an answer to the dramatic cry of Jesus on the cross ("My God, my God, why hast thou forsaken me?" 15.34), and when it becomes the last human word which Christ heard before giving up his spirit!

Yet another source of incomparable mental pain for the Messiah (pain which, as we have repeatedly observed, is a basic constituent of his Passion) is his delivery for execution by the Jews to the Roman rulers. This fact is foretold in the third prediction of the Passion (10.33-34) and is described in Mark 15. The Son of God came to save, first of all, the people of Israel, and his delivery into the hands of this people's conquerors constitutes a tremendous humiliation, in essence, a sacrilege. That this outrage was carried out by the Jewish religious leaders makes matters worse and adds to Christ's suffering as an agent causing spiritual anguish.

6. Beyond physical torture and mental anguish fed by various factors, the core of the Passion, its essence, is found in the fact that it is an offering for humankind and its salvation. At this point we come close to a realm which is unapproachable and defies analysis. It involves the mystery of the Son of God's Passion which brings about redemption for humanity. The Evangelist Mark is very laconic on this subject. The fundamental information he offers us is found primarily in the passages of Mark 10.45 (" . . . the Son of man also came not to be served but to serve, and to give his life as a ransom for many")

and Mark 14.24 ("This is my blood of the new covenant which is poured out for many"). These reveal that the purpose of Christ's coming into the world is to offer his life as a ransom, and to die as a sacrifice on behalf of mankind. This death, this Passion, belongs to God's mysterious plan for the world (8.31, 14.21), and, aside from known elements, it also comprises unknown elements which constitute its impenetrable and inexplorable nucleus.

The latter aspect is also confirmed by two other facts Mark gives us on another level of reference. The first is the prayer and agony of Christ in the garden of Gethsemane (14.32-42). Jesus' pain in the description, given with Mark's usual terseness, is astounding in its intensity and depth. The key-words alone are enough to paint the picture: "distressed," "troubled," "sorrowful," "even to death," "he fell on the ground," "that . . . the hour might pass from him," "remove this cup from me," etc. Such terrible agony is not to be interpreted simply with regard to impending death. It presupposes a death loaded with thoroughly distinctive elements, experiences of processes, which, though bound with mankind's salvation, are impossible to describe or express in any human way. The agony of Gethsemane reveals the ineffable, inexplicable character of Christ's Passion, its inapproachable and forever unknowable side. It reveals also that this Passion, from the aspect of suffering and pain, could never be measured or evaluated by any human criteria of affliction and pain.

The comments above about the agony of Gethsemane also dominate the second fact that Mark offers us: the cry of the crucified Jesus "My God, my God, why hast thou forsaken me?" (15.34). The expression alludes to an ultimate solitude interpreted only by the existence and presence of Passion elements which are beyond the range of human understanding. According to the Markan text, the essence of the Passion as the martyrly end of a painful path, has sides which theological language describes with the term "mystery of salvation," sides which are not susceptible to descriptions in any linguistic form.

7. The final, supreme and absolute event of the Passion is the death of Jesus, his sacrificial end on the cross. For Mark's Gospel, the Son of God's death is the underlying and principal point toward which all the lines of text converge.

a) As we saw, Mark, at the beginning of his Gospel, is already speaking about the plans of the Pharisees and Herodians against Jesus "how to destroy him" (3.6). The verb "destroy" (ἀπολέσωσιν) immediately brings in the concept of killing. The same verb will be repeated later on in similar passages: "And the chief priests and the scribes heard it and sought a way to destroy him" (11.18). Three chapters later the terminology will become implacably more clear: "And the chief priests and the scribes were seeking how to arrest him by stealth and kill him" (14.1). Ἀποκτείνωσιν means simply to murder him. Violent death is the certain terminus.

b) The same verb is used by Jesus in the three very significant predictions of his Passion: ἀποκτανθῆναι (8.31), ἀποκτενοῦσιν, ἀποκτανθείς (9.31), and ἀποκτενοῦσιν (10.34). The three-fold, constant repetition from the mouth of Christ officially and irrevocably confirms his execution as the end of his Passion.

c) Jesus' death is also hinted at or referred to clearly in other pericopes of Mark's Gospel. Here we can refer to the description of John's execution by Herod (6.17-29). As we explained in the related interpretation, the incident is a precursory indicator of Jesus' death. The discussion of Christ with James and John (10.35-40) can likewise be brought to mind as a clear allusion to his sacrificial end. Much clearer is the parable of the vineyard (12.1-12), in which the characteristic verb ἀποκτείνω is notably used, and where the victim of the murderous enterprise is "one other," the "beloved son" (v. 6). We should yet mention the incident of the myrrh (14.3-9), which, with its reminder of "entombment," draws an advanced picture of death. Finally, the unique depiction at the Last Supper, "this is my blood of the new covenant, which is poured out for many" (14.24), announces a sacrificial termination of life.

d) The foremost text which describes the death of Jesus with fullest clarity and certainty is, as we pointed out, the second part of the fifteenth chapter of Mark's Gospel (15.22-47). This narrative is dotted with terms which express the concept of death at different levels: "And they crucified him" (v. 24), "they crucified him" (v. 25), "breathed his last" (v. 37), "he thus breathed his last" (v. 39), "asked for the body of Jesus" (v. 43), "if he were already dead" (v. 44), "whether he was already dead" (v. 44), "he granted the body (corpse) to Joseph (v. 45), "laid him in a tomb" (v. 46). The pericope projects the absolute sureness of Christ's death with crystal clarity. What he had announced about himself, what the religious leaders of the Jews had planned, what different events had underlined, becomes a reality: Jesus is dead, nailed to a cross; his death is proven, real and complete. He is dead and ends up in the tomb, the ultimate place of the dead. Jesus' death and burial place a permanent and absolute seal on the Passion, giving it a final and immutable form. Thus, they become the heart and the demarcation line of Passion Christology.

8. Jesus' death, as the main event and predominant component of his Passion, reveal his human person, his indubitable human identity. The Christology of Passion in Mark, ending in the death of Christ, suggests the truth that Christ is genuine, complete, perfect and truly human in a way which leaves no room for doubt. He is subordinated to human situations of humility and affliction, the permanent and supreme expression of which is death.

At the beginning of his Gospel, Mark made references to the above truth. The baptism of Jesus (1.9-11) as well as his temptation in the wilderness (1.12-13), are examples which demonstrate his participation in human situations of humility and hardship.

Likewise indicative are the incidents with Jesus' sleeping on the boat (4.38), the request of his relatives (3.31-32), the visit to his homeland (6.1-6), his agony in Gethsemane (14.32-42), and his inability to carry his cross to Golgotha due to fatigue (15.21). In all these cases, and especially at the trials of Christ before the chief priests and Pilate (14.55-65, 15.1-15) and his crucifixion (15.22-37), Mark allows different sides of Jesus the man to appear with lucidness and vigor, sides which relate to pain, toil, rejection, agony, injustice, i.e. with genuine expressions of human existence in its worldly captivity.

The human person of Christ makes his Passion real and multifaceted, while on the other side, his Passion, with death at its end, makes the human person of Jesus an immediate reality. In final analysis, the Christology of Passion in Mark simultaneously and indivisibly proclaims the truth of the human person of Jesus and the truth of his Passion. The reciprocity and indivisibility of these two truths reveals and announces a singular, saving and superb message for humankind in its worldly situation.

Chapter Five

AUTHORITY AND PASSION: THE SUPERB CHRISTOLOGICAL REALITY

As we saw in the last chapter, the components of the two basic christological concepts in Mark reveal the Evangelist's astonishing theological depth along with strong anthropological concerns. In addition to these elements, however, the presence, coexistence, relationship and interdependence of Christ's Authority with his Passion in Mark's Gospel is an excellent christological achievement indeed. This phenomenon is worth studying, if only in general terms.

1. That which characterizes Mark's presentation could be named *concurrent view.* The careful reader of the second Gospel will notice that its author sees Jesus Christ in light of both his Authority and his Passion at every major point of the text. As we read it, the text leaves no doubt about this. There is certainly a difference in emphasis, or in the magnitude and clarity of the two opposing images due to the focus; but in every case, the two principal concepts stay on the same visual level.

Concurrent view, considered from another side, is the view of Christ as a divine and a human Being. In describing the various incidents in his Gospel, Mark stays with these two christological images, concurrently but distinctly presenting Jesus' divine and human natures. It should be pointed out, however, that these images are primarily and basically images, and therefore become ideas, concepts or theological truths only through interpretation.

Jesus moves, acts, speaks, and heals; he is baptized, transfigured, rejected, betrayed, and crucified. These acts, his activity, sufferings and words continuously convey facts which reveal, describe and portray Jesus' absolutely divine and perfectly human hypostasis in a perpetual alternation. Concurrent view commences with images of Authority and Passion, but develops into a view of the divine and human natures of Christ. From the first verse of his Gospel to the last, Mark imbeds expressions and manifestations of Christ's two natures one after the other, in mutual dependence and on the same line of vision.

Concurrent view does not allow one-sided development or unchecked dominance of either of the two main christological aspects. Authority does not become an easy triumph nor does Passion degenerate into incurable pessimism. On the other hand, as our text shows, the Evangelist does not busy himself with how the two basic christological concepts coexist, neither does he attempt to explain how Jesus can at the same time be a divine and a human Being. He simply describes real, powerful manifestations of these two natures in events, words and actions. The great achievement of Mark and the tradition he preserves is a concurrent view of Christ as authoritative God and suffering man. These two christological realities coexist intact and unadulterated from the beginning of the Gospel text to its end, and coexist in alternating expressions of life and function as tangible, visible and immediate facts.

2. Concurrent view of the two christological concepts in Mark is a phenomenon which is neither exhausted on purely narrative elements nor on the particular pericopes which compose the second Gospel. The phenomenon is so intense and basic that it may have defined and formed the selection, use and function of the second Gospel's main christological names-titles. An eloquent example of this is the christological title-appellation, "Son of man." In preceding chapters we had the opportunity to comment on this briefly, but here it would be advantageous to look at the subject more analytically. It is not our intention to delve into the entire subject regarding the term "Son of man," about which innumerable works have been written. Our purpose here is to examine the term in association with the phenomenon we named concurrent view of the Messiah's Authority and Passion, or Jesus' divine and human Person.

Before we go on to examine specific passages, we should point out that the term "Son of man" itself suggests the concept of concurrent view, because, over any other likely interpretation, the word man comprising an inseparable component of the title "Son of man" unavoidably operates as a reminder of Jesus' human side, while the eloquent relationship of the title with texts of the Old Testament (e.g. Dan 7.13) makes it revelatory of his supernatural, divine side. With this general introductory observation, we can go on to discuss the specific texts. These passages are numerous and can be classified into four categories:

a) To the first belong Mark 2.10 and 2.28. These passages express the direct authority of the Messiah in two very significant areas: remitting sins ("the Son of man has authority on earth to forgive sins," 2.10), and overruling the Sabbath rest (2.28: "so the Son of man is lord even of the sabbath"). Authority in both cases is divine, as was shown in our interpretation of the related pericopes in the first chapter of this book. The Messiah, as Bearer of this authority, is called "Son of man." The appellation is doubtless reminiscent of Jesus' human side; therefore, in these two instances which reveal the Messiah's divine power and authority, he is referred to by a title which somehow reminds us of his human hypostasis. We should yet point out that the proclamation of authority in both Mark 2.10 and 2.28 occurs in an atmosphere hostile to Jesus due to the Pharisees and scribes, i.e. it is an atmosphere that generally touches the domain of the Passion. We therefore have a perfect concurrent view of Authority and Passion, and in this context the term "Son of man" is used and functions, being strategically placed in the middle of a statement of divine rule and lordship, but one revealed in a climate of Passion. Thus, the appellation "Son of man" becomes a decisive factor enabling a concurrent view.

b) The second group includes Mark 8.31, 9.31, and 10.33-34, the well-known predictions of Christ's sufferings. An analytic examination of these texts and their related material ascertains that they deal with clear cases of suffering, constantly naming Jesus with the term "Son of man." The verbs describing the Passion are intense and eloquent: "suffer," "be rejected," "be killed" (8.31); "be delivered," "will kill him," "is killed" (9.31); "be delivered," "will condemn to death," "deliver him to the Gentiles," "will mock him," "spit upon him," "scourge him," "kill him" (10.33-34). The one who will undergo all this is the "Son of man." Here, the term in its human shade seems to be absolutely appropriate, in full harmony with the pericopes' Passion contents. It draws a clear and striking picture of the suffering and dying human Jesus.

The three Passion predictions terminate with a resurrection statement ("after three days he will rise," 9.31 and 10.34; "after three days rise again," 8.31). The image of divine authority has undergone no eclipse: the divine person of Christ again appears concurrently with his human, humiliated person. The Messiah's name in his supernatural resurrection remains the same: the "Son of man," a name which, with its mysterious divine shades can exquisitely convey Jesus' divine hypostasis. Thus, in Mark 8.31, 9.31 and 10.33-34, the term "Son of man" is again amid depictions offering an excellent possibility for a concurrent view of the two principal christological concepts, wisely harmonized together.

c) In the third group are Mark 9.12, 10.45, 14.21, and 14.41. Here the term "Son of man" is encountered in texts which seem to refer decisively to the Passion. The sentences are characteristic: "the Son of man goes," "the Son of man is betrayed" (14.21), "the Son of man is betrayed" (14.41), "it is written of the Son of man, that he should suffer many things" (9.12), "the Son of man also came . . . to give his life" (10.45).

In these cases also, the appellation "Son of man," as observed in the preceding category (8.31, 9.31, 10.33-34), is in special harmony and conceptual homogenuity with the Passion contents of those passages. At the same time, however, the implicit supernatural dimension of the appellation does not allow the image of authority to disappear from view. Furthermore, this image is also suggested by the surrounding material of the passages of the group under examination. Thus, we observe that Mark 9.12 comes hardly three verses after 9.9 which announces the Son of man's resurrection. In Mark 10.45, Jesus states that the Son of man came "to give his life as a ransom for many." This text decidedly reduces the Passion to the will and decision of the Son of man, and exudes divine magnificence and eminence. The same is true of the other two passages, Mark 14.21 and 14.41.

Consequently, in the four sayings of this group, i.e. Mark 9.12, 10.45, 14.21, and 14.41, the term "Son of man" functions simultaneously as an indicator of Jesus' Authority and Passion, and is as sagaciously harmonized with the basic sense of the passages, the Passion, as it is with their context, divine magnificence and power.

d) In the fourth group we find one of the most significant and characteristic uses of the term "Son of man." It concerns Mark 8.38, 13.26, and 14.62. In Mark 8.38 the disciples are warned that whoever "is ashamed" of Christ and his words in the present, "of him will the Son of man also be ashamed, when he comes in the glory of his Father with the holy angels." The final image is one of eschatological authority, judgment and glory, underlined by the utmost phrasal brevity. The name used for this glorious, almighty and divine eschatological Being, however, is "Son of man," automatically recalling the human hypostasis of this eschatological Judge. Furthermore, Mark 8.38 is the last of a series of statements bound with concepts of suffering and is introduced with a most significant statement: "If any man would come after me, let him deny himself and take up his cross and follow me" (8.34). It is obvious that Mark 8.38, together with its broader context (8.34-38), once again offers a concurrent view of Authority and Passion in the generation and formation of which the term "Son of man" plays a leading role.

Mark 13.26 belongs to the long eschatological discourse of Jesus which composes the thirteenth chapter of the Gospel of Mark: "And then they will see the Son of man coming in the clouds with great power and glory." This declaration in its immediate context (13.24-27) is a very strong text of Authority Christology. In a radical transformation of the natural and spiritual worlds, the almighty eschatological Lord will appear to "gather his elect from the four winds, from the ends of the earth to the ends of heaven." This supreme eschatological Lord, who will close and seal history, is here again called the "Son of man." The reader is thus reminded of the human side of this heavenly Lord and the Passion concepts bound with this side. Passion concepts are also in the pericopes which precede Mark 13.24-27. Therefore, they are not actually brought in for the first time in Mark 13.26, but are again placed within a view dominated by a christological image of great power. Thus, concurrent christological view is once more accomplished and the term "Son of man" is a decisive factor in its creation.

Perhaps the most significant text in this group is Mark 14.62. Here Jesus, at the crucial point in his trial, answers the question of the high priest as to whether he is the Christ, saying, "I am," adding, "and you will see the Son of man seated at the right hand of power, and coming with the clouds of heaven." The reference is eschatological and the situations described are ones of absolute divine authority and lordship. Christ's statement about his session at the right hand and his glorious coming is equivalent to a declaration of divinity.

This very solemn and singular statement, however, comes in a trial which is humiliating for Jesus, one which will end in his death sentence. In the course of proceedings which are utterly humiliating, debasing and death-bent, there is a fresh opening revealing perspectives of absolute power and divine authority in an eschatological fulfillment. The case is a typical concurrent view of Authority and Passion, of divine and human elements in Christ. It cannot be fortuitous that the christological appellation in this very significant case is "Son of man," which exquisitely binds the suffering of a death sentence and the brilliance of eschatological authority, assuring the comfortable coexistence of manifestations of the divine and human natures of Christ.

The presence of the term "Son of man" in the passages we examined, a presence in absolute harmony with the phenomenon of concurrent view, we believe showed the christological significance and function this term has for Mark and the tradition from which he drew. While utilized in texts which reveal the magnitude of Christ's superhuman authority, it is also used in others which express the magnitude of his human Passion or in cases which combine these two sides. This may owe to the fact that the title-appellation "Son of man" itself is linguistically and conceptually reminiscent and descriptive of Christ's divine side as it is of his human side. We therefore have an especially powerful title, capable of depicting aspects of Passion and Authority Christology, a term which reveals and conceals, which can be loaded with both the christological maximum and the christological minimum. It may very well be that Mark and his tradition used the term in the very significant passages we looked at exactly because, as a depictive term, "Son of man" becomes an excellent agent for a concurrent view of the two christological realities, a phenomenon which constantly seems to accompany Mark's christological thinking.

3. The study of one other fundamental christological title in Mark serves to substantiate the above view: the title "Son of God." Here also, we should note first that this term, both in its basic form or in its variations, reveals or intimates the divine authority, Sonship or hypostasis of Christ. It is very characteristic that it is used, or functions in the Gospel of Mark in direct and organic relation to the phenomenon we named concurrent view, as demonstrated by the particular texts. These texts are worth studying more closely.

a) There are two instances in which the title "Son of God" is used as a frank confession of Jesus' divine power and lordship: In Mark 3.11

"whenever the unclean spirits beheld him, they fell down before him and cried out, 'You are the Son of God.'" Also, in Mark 5.6-7 the Gerasene demoniac, "when he saw Jesus from afar, he ran and worshiped him; and crying out with a loud voice, he said, 'What have you to do with me, Jesus, Son of the Most High God?'"

In the passages above, acknowledgement of divine authority is perfectly clear; furthermore, it is accompanied and verified by tangible proofs, astonishing healings and exorcisms (3.9-10 and 5.8-13). It is not by accident, however, that recognition of Jesus' divine authority comes from unclean spirits, i.e. inexorable adverse powers, from implacable enemies, whose work the Messiah has come to destroy. The fact reveals a discernible shade of indignity or humiliation for Jesus, when we remember that the worst accusation against him was that "by the prince of demons he casts out the demons" (3.22, cf. 3.29-30). Consequently, in Mark 3.11 and 5.7, the mighty christological title of power and divinity, "Son of God," is found in a contiguity and conceptual sequence which safeguards a concurrent view of the other christological side, humiliation and Passion.

b) Likewise, a variation of the basic christological title under study is used by Christ's adversaries. In Mark 14.61, the high priest asks, "Are you the Christ, the Son of the Blessed?" In this case too, observations can be made similar to those in the preceding paragraph. This very significant christological title is sanctioned in Jesus' answer, "I am," and in the unique christological statement of authority and lordship which follows (14.62). The high priest's tone, however, is clearly hostile and ironic, and Christ's death sentence immediately afterward serves to project the Passion concept. Thus, the christological image of Authority drawn in Mark 14.61-62 by the title "Son of the Blessed" with the accompanying answer of Christ, coexists with the Passion image created by the tone of the high priest's question and the death sentence.

c) Also of fundamental significance for our subject is the confession of the Centurion at Golgotha: "Truly this man was the Son of God!" (15.39). In the analysis we made of this particular chapter, it became obvious that the confession of the Roman officer was equivalent to an admission of Christ's divinity. The following, however, are very characteristic of this fact: First, the expression "this man" has been preserved in the confession of recognition, an expression-indicator of the human side of Jesus. Second, the confession of the Centurion comes after the crucified Jesus "breathed his last" (15.39), i.e. after the Passion had ended in its final irrevocable form, death. Therefore, in Mark 15.39, the title "Son of God," an incontestable title of high christology, is presented during an event which obviously describes the Passion, i.e. it functions as an agent of concurrent view.

d) In two other significant events, i.e. Jesus' baptism and transfiguration, a title related to "Son of God" is encountered, and is worthy of comment along the same lines as our immediately preceding paragraphs. It concerns the expression "my beloved Son," which is stated by God the Father in regard to Jesus, either in second person ("Thou art my beloved Son; with thee I am well pleased," 1.11) or in the third ("This is my beloved Son; listen to him," 9.7). Here before us is an especially developed picture of Mark's Authority Christology. The title "my beloved Son" is introduced with the emphatic "Thou art" or "This is," as a direct word from God himself, and is stated within the framework of unparalleled theophanic scenes, the baptism (1.9-11) and transfiguration (9.2-8). The essential contribution of this title to the consolidation of the concept of Christ's authority and divine sonship is obvious.

The brief pericope of the baptism, however, begins with the information that Jesus "was baptized by John in the Jordan" (1.9). In the analysis of this pericope, we showed that this information intimates a humiliating situation for Jesus, a submission to human circumstances. The same is also true of the information concerning the Messiah's temptation in the wilderness immediately following the baptism (1.12-13), and again in regard to the theophanic transfiguration. The footnote, "And suddenly looking around they (the disciples) no longer saw any one of them, but Jesus only" (9.8), is immediately appended to the statement of divine sonship. Abruptly the supernatural light of the transfiguration is gone, Moses and Elijah disappear, and the disciples are again with Jesus as in their everyday relationship. Moreover, the transfiguration comes after a series of strong texts of Passion Christology (8.31-38). Thus, in the transfiguration as well as the baptism, the principal statements of divine sonship and authority are framed by material revealing Christ's human hypostasis and passion. It is clear that in Mark 1.11 and 9.7, the loftily christological title-appellation "my beloved Son" is mentioned in units which automatically suggest the double christological image, i.e. a concurrent view of the Son of God's divine and human sides.

The general conclusion rendered by the above study of the term "Son of God" and its variations in Mark are analogous with the one obtained from the study of the term "Son of man." The very important title, "Son of God," likewise functions decisively in units of fundamental christological significance, creating or holding the image of the Messiah's divine authority and hypostasis on the same visual level as the image of his Passion and human hypostasis, intimated by other material in the text.

It should be repeated once more that the study of the two representative titles or appellations "Son of man" and "Son of God," has not been done for the sake of the titles in themselves, as we have already clarified. By reason of their principal significance to Mark, we viewed them as examples revelatory and expressive of what we called concurrent view. This christological phenomenon is absolutely essential to Mark, being one that ceaselessly sends out a strong, vivid impression-message, persistently stressing in its many variations the need to constantly keep the image of Jesus, Son of God and God, and the image of Jesus the man, humiliated and suffering unto the cross, within the same spectrum.

4. Concurrent view of the christological concepts of Authority and Passion has most likely determined and shaped the particular pericopes and the use and function of christological titles in the Gospel of Mark. It may have also dictated the more general division and architecture of the text and the emphasis and interdependence of the two christological concepts in the major sections of the Gospel. This has already been presented or indicated in the preceding pages. Let us briefly review the pertinent data.

The majority of interpreters agree that the Gospel according to Mark can be divided into three parts: a. Mark 1.1-8.26; b. Mark 8.27-10.52; c. Mark 11.1-16.20. Variations on this divison exist, but in its main lines it is acceptable and exegetically legitimate. As the reader can see, the present work proceeded in an analysis of the text on the basis of the above three-fold division. What have we observed in the three major parts?

Our remarks, which are also outlined in the titles of the first three chapters of this book, are the following: In the first part, Mark 1.1-8.26, which relates the public activity of Christ centered in Galilee, the christological concept of Authority appears emphatically over the Passion concept. One's attention is focused on the manifestations of the

Messiah's divine power and hypostasis, while statements which generally hint at his Passion are described on a secondary level. In the second unit, Mark 8.27-10.52, describing the principal christological statements and events concerning Jesus' journey-ascent with his disciples from Galilee to Jerusalem, the two main christological concepts are mutually balanced. The Evangelist gives the same general stress and lucidity to the images of Christ's Authority and Passion. In the third part, Mark 11.1-16.20, which depicts the events in Jerusalem from Jesus' entrance into the city up to his crucifixion and resurrection, the priority belongs to the christological reality of the Passion. The narrative more or less adheres to images of Jesus' Passion which capture the attention, while also keeping manifestations of his divine hypostasis and power in the same field of view.

The tradition Mark draws upon must have had significant material describing Christ's public activity before his final entrance into Jerusalem. The narrative and discursive units of this material were expected to bear the strong seal of Authority Christology, a fact observable in the major section Mark 1.1-8.26. Likewise, the same tradition must have also contained the principal material of the Passion narratives culminating in the Crucifixion. This material, as expected, was dominated by Passion Christology, as preserved in the third major section, Mark 11.1-16.20. Mark, then, in two major sections (1.1-8.26 and 11.1-16.20) has correspondingly kept the two christological emphases of his sources, i.e. Authority and Passion. The parataxis and succession of these two major sections of the narrative, however, immediately emphasizes the format "Authority and Passion" on a general scale, as the format of the basic and total structure of Mark's Gospel.

The same format also dominates each of the two major sections down to the individual pericopes which compose them, i.e. in the substructure and the various components of these sections. It may be here that we encounter the excellent achievement of Mark. While keeping the appropriate christological emphasis of the two major sections, Mark 1.1-8.26 and Mark 11.1-16.20, he at the same time sagaciously preserved in each of them the opposite christological aspect. Thus, the christological format, "Authority and Passion," is active and visible on a minor scale as well as on a major one, in the entirety of the second Gospel as in the two major units and their innumerable individual pericopes.

The other major section of Mark's Gospel, i.e. Mark 8.27-10.52, is in absolute harmony with the above format. As we have mentioned

several times, there is an alternation in emphasis on the two christological concepts in this section. Authority and Passion, Christ's divinity and humanity alternate ceaselessly and remain in the forefront
concurrently, with equal emphasis and distinction of lines. Thus, the
transition from a major section with its emphasis on Authority
Christology (1.1-8.26) to another emphasizing Passion Christology
(11.1-16.20), occurs in an excellent manner via a third section (8.27-
10.52), where the two aspects are presented as balanced. This transition, this connection, is masterful. The harmonization of the three
major sections in Mark's Gospel in the christological format of
"Authority and Passion," is perfect both on a major scale and on
a minor one.

The section Mark 8.27-10.52, exactly at the center of the Gospel
story, is an excellent indicator of the tenacious adherence Mark and
his sources had to the christological unity of "Authority and Passion," the concurrent view of the divine and human natures of Jesus.
Mark 8.27-10.52 inseparably binds Mark 1.1-8.26 and Mark 11.1-16.20.
It interprets them and, at the same time, becomes with them the inspired Gospel text, which in its general outline, in its entirety, in its
major sections and in its innumerable pericopes ceaselessly, and concurrently proclaims the supernatural dominion and the grievous Passion of the God-Man, Jesus.

5. The three major sections Mark 1.1-8.26, 8.27-10.52, and
11.1-16.20, within or beyond the concurrent view, offer yet other significant christological aspects referring to the concepts of the
Messiah's Authority and Passion or relate them to areas vital to human
life and existence. They are worth pointing out very briefly as they
appear in the aforementioned sections.

a) In Mark 1.1-8.26 the emphasis is, of course, on the Christology
of Authority. This section decidedly covers only the public activity
of Jesus on earth. Here, before the cross and resurrection, the Messiah
appears in successive events with the power, lordship and authority
of God. He is basically presented as having that divine authority he
has after his resurrection, ascension and session at the right hand
of God, described in the ancient christological confessions of faith
(e.g., Eph 1.20-23, Phil 2.6-11, Heb 1.3-4). Eight full chapters, i.e. half
the Gospel is employed to present this side. Christ's earthly life
becomes the great herald of his divine authority, which is revealed
in its fullness after the resurrection. This has the effect of emphasizing

the inseparable relationship and full christological unity of the period before the resurrection with the period after it. The immeasurable worth of this unity is obvious. Likewise obvious is the intense stress placed on the unique significance of Christ's earthly life. Mark 1.1-8.26 becomes a fundamentally corrective and critical text lending clarity to all those theological tendencies that would not correctly view the enormous significance of the "earthly" Jesus' history.

It should be pointed out again that the content of the Messiah's authority in Mark 1.1-8.26 is connected with a great number of grave human problems, and has the redemption and liberation of humankind as its constant focal point. Such divine authority is richly manifested, unhampered and tangible in the course of Christ's public activity in Mark 1.1-8.26. Its description not only emphatically suggests Jesus' divine authority as homologous and uniform both before and after the resurrection; it also suggests its specific multidimensional and materialized elements, elements which refer to pressing, huge and formidable human problems, as we saw analytically in the fourth chapter of this book. The Christology of Authority here has been directly and organically bound with the human being in its worldly captivity; thus, along with a christological focal point, it has acquired an anthropological one. The other fixed aspect of Jesus' authority in Mark 1.1-8.26 is the liberation, the redemption of humankind. The Christology of Authority at each step becomes a tangible Christology of redemption for human existence from its fearsome enemies: illness, sin, falsehood, the devil, and death.

In the same section, Mark 1.1-8.26, another significant side of this christological continuity and unity is offered, this time based on the Passion aspect. Indeed, this section already presents the Messiah, at the beginning of his activity, as being accompanied by the shadow of his Passion. The Passion is not localized or restricted to the events of the final week in Jerusalem, ending on Golgotha; it is extended retrospectively, completely covering Jesus' earthly life. Just as the concept of Authority organically and indivisibly binds the period before and after the resurrection, so too, the Passion binds Christ's public activity to his crucifixion with the same infrangible unity. The Passion is not the terrible reality which is suddenly thrust at the end of a long course, but a reality which marks this course at every step, at every stage. Therefore, it is also a completely indispensible key for a correct christological interpretation of the events in the Messiah's public life, as described in Mark 1.1-8.26.

b) In the second major section, i.e. Mark 8.27-10.52, we can perceive the presence of christological concepts and interconnections similar to those in Mark 1.1-8.26 above. The manifestations of divine power and sublime prerogative of the "earthly" Jesus follow the form and content already discussed in the first major section. As such, the uniform image of Christ's authority before and after the resurrection is maintained clear and intact. The same is also true of the perspective of Authority Christology as one which redeems mankind from destructive situations. Similar observations can also be made in regard to the christological concept of the Passion in Mark 8.27-10.52 when compared to Mark 1.1-8.26.

We have repeatedly stressed, that in Mark 8.27-10.52, there is a palpable emphasis on the Christology of Passion compared to that in the first section of the Markan Gospel. Moreover, in this section, the effects of Christ's Passion on his disciples and followers have been emphasized in a special way. The interdependence and bond of these two vital levels of reference has been made in a well-planned arrangement of the material in Mark 8.27-10.52, which is impossible to pass over unobserved. Indeed, the three most significant points in this section, i.e. the three predictions of the Passion (8.31, 9.31, and 10.33-34), are strategically placed, and function as constant indicators pointing to the Messiah's unavoidable end. Each prediction is accompanied by an episode which reports the disciples' inability to understand Jesus, or moreover, their objection to the way of sacrifice he has chosen (8.32-33, 9.32-34, 10.35-37). Following this episode in each of the three cases is one of Christ's teachings which directly or indirectly bind the Passion with its consequences for his disciples. Christ speaks openly and frankly about his disciples' cross and death (8.34-38), about dismemberment (9.43-50), and about service unto the sacrifice of one's own life (10.38-45). An enormous step has taken place here. The Passion, the cross, the offering of life is not only a christological perspective; it is also an anthropological one. The genuine disciples of Jesus must follow him on the road to the cross and sacrifice. Mark, at the very center of his Gospel, has treasured these statements of Christ which, along with his own Passion and in intrinsic and full dependence upon it, forever sanction the suffering of his disciples as a supreme, irreplaceable expression of genuiness and truth. The Christology of Passion is translated into the supreme criterion, an absolute guideline of life for all those who truly want to follow the Son of God.

c) As we have often pointed out, the christological aspects of the Passion have reached their extreme expression in the last major section of Mark's Gospel, Mark 11.1-16.20: the disciples' difficulty in understanding has become desertion, denial and betrayal; the opposition of the religious leaders has become violent action, slander and condemnation; the general menace and the foretelling of tribulations have become hard bodily pain, cruel torture, and fathomless mental and spiritual distress; the predictions of the Passion have become terrible death by crucifixion followed by burial.

This pragmatic, almost cruel language in Mark 11.1-16.20, especially chapters 14 and 15, establishes the reality of the Passion in an absolute manner: extreme, many-faceted pain and cruel death. Such a reality does not allow room for romanticized stylizations or Docetic christological inventions of the type found later in different Gnostic systems. Here the Christology of Passion on a purely theoretical level sets up a forever impassable and immovable barrier against any attempt to docetize, while on a practical level it gives the Church the genuine, eternal standard and criterion of christological realism.

At the same time, the cruel reality of the Passion fully reveals the perfect human hypostasis of Jesus. In Mark 14 and 15 the Christology of Passion makes its supreme statement in regard to the human Jesus; a statement which cannot be neglected without wounding the Gospel message in its heart.

This statement, by reason of its nature and content, is not limited only to the strictly cordoned christological domain; it also passes into the realm of anthropology. Christ sought from those who would follow him that they take up their cross, a cross of affliction, sacrifice and death (8.34-38, 10.38-45). After the Passion, after his crucifixion, it is clear and certain exactly what this means, what magnitude and what type of suffering it presupposes. From the moment that Jesus, as full and perfect man, experienced the Passion, up to its ultimate crowning form, sacrificial death, the cross of mankind, the cross of each person, is no longer that which it was before Christ. More accurately, Jesus' people have a new perspective, a new possibility for confronting even the gravest afflictions, the bitterest deaths; they have it in the Christology of Passion itself, notably in its crowning expression.

They have it, however, at a degree and in a kind unique and incomparable, in an absolute form and state within the Christology of Authority, notably within its main expression, the resurrection of

Christ. In the major section Mark 11.1-16.20, specifically at its end in Mark 16, the Lord's resurrection as an event constitutes the overcoming of pain, impasse, death, of borderline human situations. Here, the Christology of Authority, as a Christology of liberation, offers its supreme and greatest gift: redemption from death, from captivity to corruption, failure, demonic powers, and the devil. With the Son of God's resurrection and its limitless possible consequences, not only has the Christology of Authority reached its zenith, but anthropology as well. The anthropological perspectives of the Christology of Authority are now opened without measure or limit. The human being has attained the supreme gift of true life and genuine freedom.

In Mark 11.1-16.20, the Christology of Passion made its supreme proclamation in regard to Jesus' human hypostasis. In the conclusion of this same major section, the Christology of Authority also makes its supreme declaration in regard to Jesus' divine hypostasis. In the marvelous, magnificent light of the resurrection, Christ is revealed, the Son of God and God. This chief christological confession, this truth of Christ's divinity, is and will remain the basis for believing in him.

6. Emphasis on the christological reality of Jesus' Authority and Passion, which we verified on every page of Mark's Gospel, could perhaps be interpreted also as a basic reference to two immediate topics in the life of the Church to which the inspired Evangelist addresses himself.

The first is the danger of distorting or corrupting the true faith in Jesus Christ. It may very well be that Mark writes his Gospel, presupposing church communities that are confronting serious problems of genuineness and completeness of true christological faith. For this reason, it is perfectly clear that the "gospel of Jesus Christ, the Son of God" (1.1), reveals and preaches one and only one christological faith, having the Authority and Passion of Christ as basic and irreplaceable components.

The second topic is persecution and more generally, situations hostile to Christ and his people. It is safe to surmise that Mark has direct knowledge of situations of this type, as we observed at different points in our analysis of his text. It is for this reason, perhaps, that he also places so much emphasis on the christological reality of Jesus' Passion and Authority. For the church communities to which the Evangelist addresses himself, the Passion of Jesus Christ is a unique and supreme point of reference and orientation in times of persecution and affliction. His authority, on the other hand, is the guarantee of ultimate victory over persecutions of every shape and form.

7. The title given this chapter, "Authority and Passion: the Superb Christological Reality," is based on the analysis which was undertaken in the last chapter as much as in this one. In his Gospel, Mark succeeded in giving us excellent images revealing the divine authority of Jesus and his complex Passion, his divine and human Person in continuous variation and concurrent view. The images were given in an astonishing variety of combinations, emphases and interconnections, accompanied by a continuously allusory, or clearly theological commentary. The achievement of presenting the two basic christological aspects, Authority and Passion, the divine and human, is very great; however, it is even greater if we consider that Mark managed to preserve the two aspects integrally, genuinely and fully in his Gospel. Without making any attempt to interpret the coexistence of the lofty Authority and the horrible Passion, he acted with clarity, to paint us an incomparably faithful picture of Jesus Christ: God and man, absolute Lord of life and death, but dead upon the cross; Son of God, unique and beloved in the brilliant light of the transfiguration, but a scorned and dishonored carpenter in his own country, Nazareth. From beginning to end, in Mark's Gospel the two christological sides retain their integrity without having one diminished, overshadowed or absorbed by the other. On this point, the Evangelist has kept the unique and invaluable double, or concurrent christological view of ancient tradition. The enormous significance of this achievement appeared in later centuries when heresies, perverting or destroying the concurrent view which preserves the wholeness and genuineness of the two basic christological aspects, diminished either the divine or the human hypostasis of Christ.

Mark gives us the superb christological reality of the coexistence and inseparable connection between the two natures of Christ, concurrently preserving their integrity. This has an incalculable effect on purely theoretical topics of christology, but it also has a direct effect on one's frame of mind or attitude in regard to faith in Jesus Christ. The Gospel according to Mark does not allow a triumphant mentality which focuses exclusively on the Christology of Authority while neglecting or diminishing the Passion. On the other hand, the same Gospel does not adopt a frame of mind which puts such an overpowering emphasis on the Christology of Passion and the cross, that the reality of Christ's Authority is diminished. Concurrent view, simultaneous adherence to the absolutely divine and perfectly human hypostasis of Jesus, to the coexistence of Authority and Passion, is the great message of Mark. It is the genuine and sole criterion of any true Christology.

Abbreviations

1. COMMENTARIES (IN CHRONOLOGICAL ORDER)

Victor   Victor, presbyter of Antioch, Σύντομος Ἑρμηνεία εἰς τὸ κατὰ Μᾶρκον εὐαγγέλιον, in J. Cramer, *Catenae in Evangelia,* Volume 1 (Oxford, 1844).

Theophylact   Theophylact of Bulgaria, Ἑρμηνεία εἰς τὸ κατὰ Μᾶρκον εὐαγγέλιον, PG 123.491-682.

Zigabenos   Euthymios Zigabenos, Ἑρμηνεία τοῦ κατὰ Μᾶρκον εὐαγγελίου, PG 129.765-852.

Damalas   Damalas, N. M., Ἑρμηνεία εἰς τὴν Καινὴν Διαθήκην, Vols. 2 and 3 (Athens, 1892).

Swete   Swete, H. B. *The Gospel according to Mark* (London, 1927[2]).

Lagrange   Lagrange, M. J., *Évangile selon Saint Marc* (Paris, 1929,[5] repr. Gabalda 1966).

Lohmeyer   Lohmeyer, E., *Das Evangelium des Markus* (Göttingen, 1967[17]).

Klostermann   Klostermann, E. *Das Markus-Evangelium* (Tübingen, 1971[5]).

Trembelas   Trembelas, P. N., Ὑπόμνημα εἰς τὸ κατὰ Μᾶρκον Εὐαγγέλιον (Athens, 1951).

Taylor   Taylor, V., *The Gospel according to St. Mark* (London, 1963[5]).

Nineham	Nineham, D. E., *The Gospel of St. Mark* (Harmondsworth, 1963).
Haenchen	Haenchen, E., *Der Weg Jesu* (Berlin, 1968²).
Schweizer	Schweizer, E., *The Good News according to Mark* (London, 1978⁴). English trans. of *Das Evangelium nach Markus* (Göttingen, 1967).
Lane	Lane, W. L., *The Gospel according to Mark* (Grand Rapids, 1974, repr. 1979).
Pesch	Pesch, R., *Das Markusevangelium*, I und II Teil (Freiburg, 1976-1977).
Achtemeier	Achtemeier, P. J., *Invitation to Mark* (Garden City, 1978).
Gnilka	Gnilka, J., *Das Evangelium nach Markus*, I-II Teilb. (Zürich, 1978-1979).
Schmithals	Schmithals, W., *Das Evangelium nach Markus*, I und II (Gütersloh, 1979).
Montague	Montague, G. T., *Mark: Good News for Hard Times* (Ann Arbor, 1981).

2. TEXTS AND GENERAL WORKS

Bauer	Bauer, W., Arndt, W. F., Gingrich, F. W., *A Greek-English Lexicon of the New Testament* (Chicago, 1964⁸).
Billerbeck	Strack H., Billerbeck P., *Kommentar zum Neuen Testament aus Talmud und Midrash*, 4 Bd. (Munich, 1922-1928).
GCS.	*Die griechischen christlichen Schriftsteller der ersten drei Jahrhunderte*, Leipzig.
PG	Migne, *Patrologiae Cursus, series Graeca*.
Nestle-Aland	Nestle, E.-Aland, K., *Novum Testamentum Graece*, 26. neu bearbeitete Auflage (Stuttgart, 1979)
TDNT	Kittel, G., Friedrich, G., *Theological Dictionary of the New Testament* (Grand Rapids, 1964-1974).

3. PERIODICALS

ALW	*Archiv für Liturgiewissenschaft*
AsSeign	*Assemblées du Seigneur*
BA	*Biblical Archeologist*
BibLeb	*Bibel und Leben*
BJRL	*Bulletin of the John Rylands University Library*
BLit	*Bibel und Liturgie*
BO	*Bibbia e Oriente*
BSac	*Bibliotheca Sacra*
BR	*Biblical Research*
BT	*Bible Today*
BTB	*Biblical Theology Bulletin*
BZ	*Biblische Zeitschrift*
CBQ	*Catholic Biblical Quarterly*
CCER	*Cahiers du Cercle Ernest Renan*
CurTM	*Currents in Theology and Mission*
CV	*Communio Viatorum*
ΔBM	*Δελτίο Βιβλικῶν Μελετῶν*
DR	*Downside Review*
DT	*Divus Thomas*
EC	*Ephemerides Carmeliticae*
EE	*Der Evangelische Erzieher*
ΕΕΘΣΠΘ	*Ἐπιστημονικὴ Ἐπετηρὶς τῆς Θεολογικῆς Σχολῆς τοῦ Πανεπιστημίου Θεσσαλονίκης*
EQ	*Evangelical Quarterly*
ER	*Ecumenical Review*
EstBib	*Estudios Biblicos*
ETL	*Ephemerides Theologicae Lovanienses*
ETR	*Études Théologiques et Religieuses*
EvT	*Evangelische Theologie*
ExpTim	*Expository Times*
GL	*Geist und Leben*
HTR	*Harvard Theological Review*
IBS	*Irish Biblical Studies*
JAAR	*Journal of the American Academy of Religion*
JBL	*Journal of Biblical Literature*
JETS	*Journal of the Evangelical Theological Society*
JSNT	*Journal for the Study of the New Testament*
JSS	*Journal of Semitic Studies*

JTSA	*Journal of Theology for Southern Africa*
JTS	*Journal of Theological Studies*
KG	*Katholische Gedanke*
LinguB	*Linguistica Biblica*
LV	*Lumière et Vie*
NB	*New Blackfriars*
NovT	*Novum Testamentum*
NRT	*Nouvelle Revue Théologique*
NTS	*New Testament Studies*
RB	*Revue Biblique*
REG	*Revue des Études Grècques*
RevQ	*Revue de Qumran*
RevScRel	*Revue des Sciences Religieuses*
RivB	*Rivista Biblica*
RQ	*Restoration Quarterly*
RSR	*Recherches de Science Religieuse*
RT	*Revue Thomiste*
RTL	*Revue Théologique de Louvain*
SB	*Studia Biblica*
SBFLA	*Studii Biblici Franciscani Liber Annuus*
SE	*Studia Evangelica*
SNTU	*Studien zum Neuen Testament und seiner Umwelt*
ST	*Studia Theologica*
TPQ	*Theologisch-Praktische Quartalschrift*
TToday	*Theology Today*
TTZ	*Trierer Theologische Zeitschrift*
TynBul	*Tyndale Bulletin*
US	*Una Sancta*
VD	*Verbum Domini*
VT	*Vetus Testamentum*
WD	*Wort und Dienst*
ZDPV	*Zeitschrift des Deutschen Palästina-Vereins*
ZKT	*Zeitschrift für Katholische Theologie*
ZNW	*Zeitschrift für die Neutestamentliche Wissenschaft*

CHAPTER ONE
THE MANIFESTATION OF AUTHORITY
AND THE PRELUDE TO THE PASSION (MARK 1.1-8.26)

1. For a select bibliography on Mk 1.1, see W. Marxsen, *Mark the Evangelist* (Nashville, 1969) 117-50; W. Feneberg, *Der Markusprolog: Studien zur Form-bestimmung des Evangeliums* (Munich, 1974); P. Lamarche, *Révélation de Dieu chez Marc* (Paris, 1976) 29-46; M. Bouttier, "Commencement, force et fin de l'évangile," *ETR* 51 (1976) 465-93; G. Arnold, "Mk. 1.1 und Eröffnungswendungen in griechischen und lateinischen Schriften," *ZNW* 68 (1977) 123-27; P. Pokorny, "Anfang des Evangeliums," *Die Kirche des Anfangs*, Festschr. H. Schürmann, ed. R. Schnackenburg (Freiburg, 1978) 115-32; A. Feuillet, "Le commencement de l'économie chrétienne d'après He. 2.3-4, Mc. 1.1 et Ac. 1.2," *NTS* 24 (1978) 163-74; C. R. Kazmierski, *Jesus the Son of God* (Würzburg, 1979) 1-26; and A. Globe, "The Caesarean Omission of the Phrase 'Son of God' in Mk. 1.1," *HTR* 75 (1982) 209-18.

2. "The opening verse is Mark's confessio fidei," notes R. P. Martin, *Mark Evangelist and Theologian* (Exeter, 1972) 127. The confession becomes even stronger if the phrase "Son of God" belongs to the original text of the Gospel of Mark, a case defended again recently by A. Globe, "The Caesarean Omission," 218.

3. The phrase "Ἰησοῦ Χριστοῦ" is rather a genitive objective. Cf. Lagrange 2-3, Taylor 152, Pesch 1, 75, Gnilka 1, 43. One, however, should take into account the contention by W. Marxsen, *Mark the Evangelist* 146-50, that the phrase is both an objective and a subjective genitive and that Christ preaches a Gospel which preaches Christ.

4. See W. H. Kelber, *Mark's Story of Jesus* (Philadelphia, 1979) 16-17: "Before Jesus himself speaks in the Gospel story and before he is designated by the heavenly voice, Mark has introduced him to the reader as a figure of extraordinary authority." Cf. M. Bouttier, "Commencement," 465-67; P. Lamarche, *Révélation de Dieu*, 42-43. If the introductory sentence is related to the immediately following pericope Mk 1.2-8, then the excellence of the Messiah is emphasized through the Old Testament. Such a suggestion was already offered by Origen, *Commentary on John*, Tom. 1, 13, GCS Origen Vol. 4, 18.

5. For a select bibliography on Mk 1.2-8, see W. Marxsen, *Mark the Evangelist* (1969) 30-53; J. D. G. Dunn, "Spirit and Fire Baptism," *NovT* 14 (1972) 81-92; J. C. Meagher, *Clumsy Construction in Mark's Gospel* (Toronto, 1979) 35-39; K. R. Snodgrass, "Streams of Tradition emerging from Is. 40,1-5 and their adaptation in the New Testament," *JSNT* 8 (1980) 24-45; and H. J. Steichele, *Der leidende Sohn Gottes* (Regensburg, 1980) 41-80.

6. Cf. J. M. Robinson, *The Problem of History in Mark* (London, 1971[4]) 26, Marxsen, *Mark the Evangelist* (1969) 42-43, 33.

7. Cf. Lohmeyer 18: "The mightier, the Lord of an immeasurable excellence . . . This one is the divine Lord, that one (i.e. John the Baptist) remains the prophetic man." See also H. C. Kee, *Community of the New Age* (Philadelphia, 1977) 119-20, who thinks that the comparison mighty-mightier is ultimately a reference to the opposition between Christ and Satan. Cf. Photios of Constantinople (*Amphilochia*, Quest. 216, PG 101.980): "I count, he says (i.e. John the Baptist) that he (i.e. the Messiah) is superior in magnitude and office beyond what the difference between Master and slave describes, and even beyond any possible difference or distance which indicates superiority."

8. Origen paraphrases the passage Mk 1.8 in the following way: "He (Christ) will flood you in abundance with the graces of the Spirit. My own baptism does not offer a spiritual grace . . . But he will offer the remission of your sins and also he will give the Spirit in profusion" (*Commentary on Matthew*, Fragm. 49 (Catenae) GCS, Origen Vol. 12, 35). Cf. Victor 268: "The baptism by John through repentance purified in preparation for sanctification, whereas the baptism by Christ through grace sanctified to perfection." For an extensive presentation and discussion of various interpretations on Mk 1.8, see J. D. G. Dunn, "Spirit and Fire Baptism."

9. Chrysostom observes here: "Why Christ did not preach to them from the very beginning? Why was there any need of John the Baptist, when the witness of the works was proclaiming him (i.e. Christ)? This happened so that we learn his eminence: Like the Father so Christ too has his prophets" (*Homilies on Matthew*, Homily 14, PG 57.218). Cf. Damalas 2, 303, Lane 48, 53, R. H. Lightfoot, *The Gospel Message of St. Mark* (Oxford, 1950) 18.

10. For a select bibliography on Mk 1.9-11, see L. E. Keck, "The Spirit and the Dove," *NTS* 17 (1970) 41-67; G. Richter, "Zu den Tauferzählungen Mk. 1,9-11 und John 1,32-34," *ZNW* 65 (1974) 43-56; L. Hartman, "Taufe, Geist und Sohnschaft," *Jesus in der Verkündingung der Kirche*, ed. A. Fuchs (SNTU 1, 1976) 89-109; S. Gero, "The Spirit as a Dove at the Baptism of Jesus," *NovT* 18 (1976) 17-35; C. R. Kazmierski, *Jesus the Son* (1979) 27-72; H. J. Steichelle, *Der leidende Sohn* (1980) 109-60; P. Garnet, "The Baptism of Jesus and the Son of Man Idea," *JSNT* 9 (1980) 49-65; R. E. H. Uprichard, "The Baptism of Jesus," *IBS* 3 (1981) 187-202.

11. W.Wrede, *The Messianic Secret* (Cambridge, 1971) 73 uses here phrases like "supernatural dimension," "supernatural nature of Jesus."

12. Cf. *Syriac Apocalypse Baruch* 22.1, *Testament of Levi* 2.6, *Testament of Juda* 24.2. The important element here is that Jesus, and only him, sees "the heavens opened" not as an apocalyptic vision but as an immediate sight and reality. Cf. Lohmeyer 23.

13. For the theophanic meaning of the appearance of the dove in the baptism of Jesus see S. Gero, "The Spirit as a Dove," 17-19. For the christological meaning of the pertinent archaic traditions see L. Keck, "The Spirit and the Dove," 63-67, G. Richter, "Zu der Tauferzählungen" 43-53, 56. For the basic christological significance of the term spirit in the baptism of Jesus in connection with the preaching of John (1.8) and the temptation in the wilderness (1.12) see J. M. Robinson, *The Problem of History* (1971) 29-32.

14. "The importance of Mk 1.11 cannot be exaggerated," observes Taylor 162, who analyzes the formula of the recognition. Cf. H. Weinacht, *Die Menschwerdung des Sohnes Gottes im Markusevangelium* (Tübingen, 1972) 51-53; I. H. Marshall, "Son of God or Servant of Yahweh?" *NTS* 15 (1969) 326-36; Lane 57-58; Pesch I, 93; Gnilka 1, 52-54; Schmithals 1, 85-86; R. Lightfoot, *The Gospel Message* (1950) 32.

15. Origen emphasizes here not only the general theophanic element but the revelation of the Trinity: "In the river Jordan the Trinity has been revealed to humankind. If the Father was the one who bore witness, and the Son was the object of the witness, and the Holy Spirit was the one who pointed to the event, then how (can one say that) the divinity is not Trinity?", *Commentary on Matthew*, Fragment 58 (Catenae), GCS Origen Vol. 12, 38.

16. Cf. the relevant observation by Chrysostom: "The Master comes to be baptized with his servants, the Judge with the defendants. But do not worry! It is in these humiliating circumstances that his eminence shines through. If he condescended to be carried in a virgin womb for such a long time, and to be born with our nature, and to be slapped and crucified and to suffer all other things that he suffered, then why are you amazed at the fact that he also condescended to be baptized and to come to the servant with the other people? The astonishing thing is that he being God willed to become man; all the rest follow by logical sequence," *Homilies on Matthew*, Homily 12, PG 57.201-02. Cf. R. E. H. Uprichard, "The Baptism of Jesus," 192-96, 199-200, who offers suggestions relating the humiliation of the baptism with the idea of the Servant-Messiah and his death.

17. At any event, the humiliation which is manifested in the baptism of Jesus is less pronounced than the authority and divine eminence which are expressed in the heavenly voice and the descent of the Spirit. Cf. H. Weinacht, *Die Menschwerdung* (1972) 49-53.

18. For a select bibliography on Mk 1.12-13, see E. Best, *The Temptation and the Passion* (Cambridge, 1965); J. A. Kirk, "The Messianic Role of Jesus and the Temptation Narrative," *EQ* 44 (1972) 11-29; P. Pokorny, "The Temptation Stories and their Intention," *NTS* 20 (1974) 115-27; H. Mahnke, *Die Versuchungsgeschichte im Rahmen der synoptischen Evangelien* (Frankfurt, 1978) 17-50; W. D. Carroll, "The Jesus of Mark's Gospel," *BT* 103 (1979) 2105-12; C. Bonnet, "Le désert. Sa signification dans l'Évangile de Marc," *Hokhma* 13 (1980) 20-34.

162   *Authority and Passion*

19. W. Wrede, *The Messianic Secret* (1971) 74, offers here the more general observation that Jesus meets and confronts Satan "bodily in a way possible only for somebody who is not 'man' but is a supernatural being."

20. It is noteworthy that Luke does not mention serving angels (Lk 4.1-13) whereas in Matthew the angels appear after the end of the battle (Mt 4.11). Cf. Damalas 2, 339, Lohmeyer 28.

21. Both old (e.g. Zigabenos 7) and contemporary (e.g. P. Pokorny, "The Temptation Stories," 118, 120-22, H. Mahnke, *Die Versuchungsgeschichte* 28-37) exegetes, have drawn attention to the relationship between the present description and the description of the life and fall of Adam in Eden (Gen 1.26-3.7). The comparison underlines the superiority of Jesus. For a pertinent discussion and a special bibliography see Pesch 1, 94-100, Gnilka 1, 58-60.

22. For a select bibliography on Mk 1.14-15, see A. Ambrozic, *The Hidden Kingdom* (Washington, 1972) 3-31; E. Graesser, "Zum Verständnis der Gottesherrschaft," *ZNW* 65 (1974) 3-26; W. Kelber, *The Kingdom in Mark* (Philadelphia, 1974) 3-15; G. Dautzenberg, "Zur Stellung des Markusevangeliums in der Geschichte der urchristlichen Theologie," *Kairos* 18 (1976) 282-91; W. Egger, *Frohbotschaft und Lehre* (Frankfurt, 1976) 43-63; B. D. Chilton, *God in Strength* (Lins, 1979) 27-96; J. Schlosser, *Le règne de Dieu dans les dits de Jésus* (Paris, 1980) 92-109; V. K. Robbins, "Mark 1,14-20," *NTS* 28 (1982) 220-36.

23. Cf. A. Ambrozic, *The Hidden Kingdom* (1972) 21-25; W. Kelber, *The Kingdom in Mark* (1974) 9-15.

24. Only Mark among the Evangelists uses the phrase, "believe in the gospel." W. Marxsen, *Mark the Evangelist* (1969) 135, in analyzing Mk 1.14-15 on the basis of the tradition of the early Church to which Mark belongs, justifiably observes that "believe in the gospel is identical to believe in Christ Jesus."

25. Lohmeyer 30, rightly observes that here Jesus "claims for himself a knowledge and a word which belongs only to God . . . His word is either a blasphemy for the Jewish ears or God's own word and voice for the early Christian ears." Cf. Lane 65-66.

26. Mk 9.31, 10.33, 14.10, 14.21, 15.15. W. Marxsen, *Mark the Evangelist* (1969) 38-43; Gnilka 1, 65; Schmithals 1, 96; Montague 18; C. F. Evans, *The Beginning of the Gospel* (London, 1968) 16; and other scholars, consider Mk 1.14 as an indisputable reference to the passion of the Messiah.

27. For a select bibliography on Mk 1.16-20, see R. Pesch, "Berufung und Sendung, Nachfolge und Mission," *ZKT* 91 (1969) 1-31; J. Brière, "Jésus agit par ses disciples," *AsSeign* 34 (1973) 32-46; J. C. Meagher, *Clumsy Construction in Mark's Gospel* (1979) 43-44; J. D. M. Derrett, "Esan gar halieis," *NovT* 22 (1980) 108-37; E. Best, *Following Jesus: Discipleship in the Gospel of Mark* (Sheffield, 1981) 166-75; and V. K. Robbins, "Mark 1,14-20," *NTS* 28 (1982) 220-36.

28. The scene of the call of the first four dicsiples contained more descriptive elements as it is suggested by the narrative in Luke (Lk 5.1-11). The descriptive condensation in Mark emphasizes the high significance of the words of Jesus. The predominance of Jesus in the present pericope is absolute.

29. For a select bibliography on Mk 1.21-28, see R. H. Stein, "The Redaktionsgeschichtlich Investigation of a Markan Seam," *ZNW* 61 (1970) 70-94; J. Brière, "Le cri et le secret," *AsSeign* 35 (1973) 34-46; L. Schenke, *Die Wundererzählungen des Markusevangeliums* (Stuttgart, 1974) 95-108; A. M. Ambrozic, "New Teaching with Power," *Word and Spirit,* Festschr. D. M. Stanley, ed. J. Plevnik (Willowdale, 1975) 113-49; and P. Guillemette, "Un enseignement nouveau plein d'autorité," *NovT* 22 (1980) 222-47.

30. See the special discussion in Schmithals 1, 118. Cf. W. Wrede, *The Messianic Secret* (1971) 79; R. Martin, *Mark* (1972) 131-32.

31. See 1 Enoch 69.27-28. Cf. R. Lightfoot, *The Gospel Message* (1950) 21.

32. An insightful analysis of the pertinent Markan data which depict an impressive image of Jesus' supreme authority over the evil spirits, see in J. M. Robinson, *The Problem of History* (1971) 33-42.

33. See the pertinent discussion in Taylor 174. Cf. Gnilka 1, 80-81, and Victor 275-76: "Holy was also each of the prophets; but here Mark does not mean one of the prophets; here he proclaims the one coming from the One. For the usage of the definite article (ὁ ἅγιος) signifies the one who is distinguished from all others and superior." Similiarly Zigabenos 10: ". . . Only God is holy in essence and in nature. This is why Mark said 'the holy' (i.e. he used the definite article) instead of saying 'the one holy in essence and in nature.'"

34. The Israelites had some idea of healing of demoniacs and of exorcisms, but here the process is unusual. There is no exorcistic language, no special phraseology, no ceremonial movements typical of an exorcism. This explains the extraordinary wonder of the people (Mk 1.27) which is typical of theophanic narratives. Cf. Lohmeyer 38; Taylor 176.

35. This will be verified in the continuation of the narrative in Mark 2. Cf. R. C. Tannehill, "The Gospel of Mark as narrative Christology," *Semeia* 16 (1979) 65-66.

36. P. Achtemeier, "He taught them many things," *CBQ* 42 (1980) 478-79, rightly observes that Mark's purpose in Mk 1.21-28 is to show that the authority and power of Jesus expressed in his teaching is the same with that revealed in his casting out of the evil spirits. Cf. Lagrange 24; Trembelas 40-41.

37. For a select bibliography on Mk 1.29-31, see G. Gaide, "De l'admiration à la foi," *AsSeign* 36 (1974) 39-48; D. A. Koch, *Die Bedeutung der Wundererzählungen für die Christologie des Markusevangeliums* (Berlin, 1975) 134-36; P. Lamarche, *Révélation de Dieu* (1976) 49-60; M. G. Steinhauser, "Healing Stories in the Gospels," *Liturgy* 25 (1980) 27-30.

38. As Schmithals 1, 127 notes, "Jesus has authority not only on exceptional cases, but on the daily basic situation of human beings (e.g. disease).

39. The phrase "they told him of her" (Mk 1.30) is mainly a piece of information used perhaps by the disciples as an explanation for the absence of Peter's mother-in-law from the reception of Jesus at Peter's house.

40. P. Larmarche, *Révélation de Dieu* (1976) 53-55, on the basis of the verb ἤγειρεν of Mk 1.29-31, sees here also a prefiguration of the resurrection, and not only the healing that the Messiah offers.

41. For a select bibliography on Mk 1.32-34, see T. W. Kowalski, "Les sources pré-synoptiques de Marc 1,32-34," *RSR* 60 (1972) 541-73; T. Snoy, "Les miracles dans l'évangile de Marc," *RTL* 4 (1973) 59-72; W. Egger, *Frohbotschaft und Lehre* (1976) 64-72; and J. C. Meagher, *Clumsy Construction in Mark's Gospel* (1979) 47-50.

42. The difference between "all" (πάντες) and "many" (πολλοί) of Mk 1.32-34, is rather the result of Semitic linguistic influence and, therefore, does not introduce a substantial distinction. Cf. Victor 278 ("By many . . . he means all according to the practice of the Scripture . . . "), Theophylact 505; Zigabenos 13; Damalas 2.625.

43. The injunction for silence in connection with miracles, constitutes a phenomenon repeated frequently in Mark. This phenomenon has become a topic of lengthy discussions especially after the publication of the influential book by W. Wrede, *Das Messiasgeheimnis in den Evangelien* (Göttingen, 1901); English trans. J. G. G. Greig under the title *The Messianic Secret* (Cambridge, 1971). In spite of the serious weaknesses of Wrede's theory about the "Messianic Secret," his analysis and several of his observations are insightful.

44. For a select bibliography on Mk 1.35-39, see M. Wichelhaus, "Am ersten Tage der Woche," *NovT* 11 (1969) 45-66; D. O. Wretlind, "Jesus' Philosophy of Ministry," *JETS* 20 (1974) 321-23; W. Egger, *Frohbotschaft und Lehre* (1976) 73-78; W. Kirchschläger, "Jesu Gebetsverhalten als Paradigma zu Mk. 1,35," *Kairos* 20 (1978) 303-10; and J. C. Meagher, *Clumsy Constructon in Mark's Gospel* (1979) 50-51.

45. The expression "throughout all Galilee" is considered a major step in the description of the activities of Jesus. Cf. Achtemeier 43.

46. For a select bibliography on Mk 1.40-45, see A. Paul, "La guérison d'un lépreux," *NRT* 92 (1970) 592-604; L. Schenke, *Die Wundererzählungen* (1974) 130-45; B. Standaert, *L'Évangile selon Marc; Composition et genre littéraire* (Brugge, 1978) 126-34; W. D. Carroll, "The Jesus of Mark's Gospel," *BT* (1979) 2105-12; C. H. Cave, "The Leper: Mark 1,40-45," *NTS* (1979) 245-50; M. E. Boismard, "La guérison du lépreux," *Salmanticensis* 28 (1981) 283-91; and V. Fusco, "Il segreto messianico nell'episodio del leproso," *RivB* 29 (1981) 273-313.

47. As Montague 29 notes, Mark relates the story in such a way as to indicate that this is not just an expression of mercy but another victorious act of Jesus against the powers of evil and death. Victor 281-82 notes that Jesus touches the leper in spite of the relevant prohibition by the Mosaic Law in order to show that he is God and that "he is Lord over his own law." Cf. Theophylact 509.

48. B. Standaert, *L'Évangile selon Marc* (1978) 129-30. Not only the command but also the gesture of Jesus ("he stretched out his hand and touched him") constitutes a sign of "divine or kingly majesty" (Lohmeyer 46).

49. Chrysostom comments here: "Jesus charges the former leper to say nothing to anyone, thus teaching the overcoming of boasting and ambition. He knew, however, that the leper would not be persuaded and that he would proclaim the benefactor" (*Homilies on Matthew,* Homily 25, PG 57.329).

50. For a select bibliography on Mk 2.1-12, see L. S. Hay, "The Son of Man in Mk. 2,10 and 2,28," *JBL* 89 (1970) 69-75; I. Maisch, *Die Heilung des Gelähmten* (Stuttgart, 1971); D. Dormeyer, "Narrative Analyse von Mk. 2,1-12," *LinguB* 31 (1974) 68-88; W. Thissen, *Erzählung der Befreiung* (Würzburg, 1976) 47-53; J. Calloud, "Toward a Structural Analysis of the Gospel of Mark," *Semeia* 16 (1979) 141-60; J. Dewey, *Markan Public Debate* (Chico, 1980) 66-78; H. J. Klauck, "Die Frage der Sündenvergebung in der Pericope von der Heilung des Galähmten," *BZ* 25 (1981) 223-48; G. Hallbäck, "Materialistische Exegese und structurale Analyse," *LinguB* 50 (1982) 7-32; C. Tuckett, "The Present Son of Man," *JSNT* 14 (1982) 58-81.

51. Cf. T. Weeden, *Mark: Traditions in Conflict* (Philadelphia, 1971) 22.

52. Cf. T. L. Budesheim, "Jesus and the Disciples in Conflict with Judaism," *ZNW* 62 (1971) 192-93; J. Dewey, *Markan Public Debate* (1980) 76-79.

53. In another section we will discuss the conceptual components of the term "the Son of man." Presently we only remark that here Jesus, by the term "Son of man," means himself. A first image of the christological dimensions of the term is given by Victor 286: "Why did he say that the son of man has authority on earth to forgive sins? In order to show that he has brought down to the human nature the authority of the divinity because of the indivisible unity (between them)."

54. The scribes in this instance express a fundamental idea based on the Old Testament: Ex 34.6-7; Ps 102 (LXX).3; Is 43.25. Jesus declares that he has the authority meant by the above mentioned passages. Cf. Lohmeyer 54; Achtemeier 49; Lane 98; A. J. B. Higgins, *Jesus and the Son of Man* (Philadelphia, 1964) 27; and M. D. Hooker, *The Son of Man in Mark* (London, 1967) 89-92.

55. The comments by Chrysostom are characteristic: "Here Jesus shows another great sign of his divinity and of his equality in honor with the Father. They (i.e. the Scribes) said that only God has the authority to forgive sins. Jesus, however, does not only forgive sins, but before that he does something else which belongs only to God, namely he makes public what people had hidden in their hearts," *Homilies on Matthew,* Homily 29, PG 57.359. Cf. Theophylact 512; Zigabenos 18; Damalas 2, 692; and Trembelas 48.

56. Cf. Mk 3.21. See also Taylor 198.

57. Pesch 1, 157; Gnilka 1, 101-02; Schmithals 1. 154.

58. For a select bibliography on Mk 2.13-14, see J. Donaldson, "Called to Follow," *BTB* (1975) 67-77; P. Lamarche, "L'appel de Lévi," *Christus* 23 (1976) 107-18; W. Thissen, *Erzählung der Befreiung* (1976) 54-62; J. Dewey, *Markan Public Debate* (1980) 79-87; E. Best, *Following Jesus* (1981) 175-79; F. J. Moloney, "The Vocation of the Disciples in the Gospel of Mark," *Salesianum* 43 (1981) 487-516.

59. The story of the call of Levi has been highly condensed, not because of its continuous repetition during the phase of the oral tradition (Taylor 199), but rather because of the predominance of its central idea which is the authority of the Messiah.

60. Various interpreters have rightly observed that the response of Levi is more advanced and has more drastic consequences than the response of the first four disciples (Swete40; Taylor 203). Cf. Victor 288: "Levi without any delay, leaving everything, followed Jesus, thus making his election joyful through a sharp faith."

61. A characteristic passage from Lucian is worth citing here. In this passage there is a report that in Mino's tribunal in Hades "adulterers, and panders, and tax-collectors, and flatterers, and slanderers" . . . "were brought bound with a long chain" (*Necyomantia* 11). See more in *TNDT* 8, 88-105.

62. The phrase "many tax-collectors and sinners were sitting with Jesus" is indicative of a big dinner and of an atmosphere not determined by formality.

63. Attention should be drawn to the fact that the tax-collectors were considered not simply "sinners" but also "impure" according to the Law, because of their frequent contacts and business with the pagans. Hence for the pious Jews there were no margins of social contacts of the type of dinner with the tax-collectors.

64. The first part of the passage is proverbial in nature. Similar examples from the ancient Greek literature, see in Swete 42; Lagrange 44-45. For the relationship between the first and the second part of the passage, see Pesch 1, 166-68; Schmithals 1, 171-74.

65. For a select bibliography on Mk 2.18-22, see A. Kee, "The Question about Fasting," *NovT* 11 (1969) 161-73; F. Hahn, "Die Bildeworte vom neuen Flicken und vom jungen Wein," *EvT* 31 (1971) 357-75; J. A. Ziesler, "The Removal of the Bridegroom," *NTS* 19 (1973) 190-94; P. Trudinger, "The Word on the Generation Gap," *BTB* 5 (1975) 311-15; W. Thissen, *Erzählung der Befreiung* (1976) 63-69; J. Dewey, *Markan Public Debate* (1980) 88-93; and P. J. Maartens, "Mk. 2,18-22: An Exercisse in Theoretically-founded Exegesis," *Scriptura* (Stellenbosch, S. Africa) 2, (1980) 1-54.

66. The text does not clarify the exact nature of fasting. Besides, this is not the real problem here. Hence the Evangelist does not need to go into details.

67. J. Ziesler, "The Removal of the Bridegroom," 192-94, argues that in Mk 2.18-22 the main point is the rejection by Jesus of the pharisaic fasting tradition.

68. Most scholars agree that in Mk 2.19-20 the word bridegroom (νυμ-φίος) has a messianic meaning. See the pertinent discussion in Taylor 210-11. Pesch 1, 173 thinks that the messianic idea is related more to the wedding as a symbol of the messianic time of salvation. Cf. also Schmithals 1, 176-77 and Montague 38.

69. Cf. Pesch 1, 173.

70. Taylor 212-13. Cf. Damalas 2, 721; Schweizer 69; and Achtemeier 53.

71. For a select bibliography on Mk 2.23-28, see E. Délébêque, "Les épis égrenés dans les Synoptiques," *REG* (Paris) 88 (1975) 133-42; B. Jay, "Jésus et le sabbat," *ETR* 50 (1975) 65-68; W. Thissen, *Erzählung der Befreiung* (1976) 70-73; A. J. Hultgren, *Jesus and His Adversaries* (Minneapolis, 1979) 111-14; L. Schottroff-W. Stegemann, *Der Gott der kleinen Leute*

(Munich, 1979) 58-70; J. Dewey, *Markan Public Debate* (1980) 94-99; and F. Neirynck, *Evangelica.* Collected Essays, ed. F. van Segbroeck (Leuven, 1982) 637-80.

72. The accusation is related to an Old Testament injunction which prohibited plowing and harvesting on Sabbath (Ex 34.21).

73. The relative comment by R. Simeon b. Menasya on Ex 31.14, "the Sabbath has been given to you, not you to the Sabbath" (Billerbeck 2,5) may have been likely influenced by the New Testament, since Menasya lived at the end of the second century A.D. Cf. Swete 49; Taylor 218-19; Pesch 1, 184-85; and Schmithals 1, 186-89.

74. The observation by Lohmeyer 66, is indicative: "With the word lord (κύριος) it is implied that the commandment about the Sabbath acquires its value and its validity primarily through the son of man. He can sanction it or reject it." Cf. A. Hultgren, *Jesus and His Adversaries* (1979) 111-14, J. Dewey, *Markan Public Debate* (1980) 98-99; M. Hooker, *The Son of Man* (1967) 99-102; C. F. Evans, *The Beginning of the Gospel* (1968) 65.

75. Victor 292 notes characteristically: "The Pharisees say that "it is not lawful" (οὐκ ἔξεστιν). And they say this to the one who has all authority and who grants it to his own people. And they do not know that the law has no authority over the lawgiver." Cf. Damalas 2.865-866, R. Martin, *Mark* (1972) 132, and Achtemeier 54, who remarks: "In this context, however, the verses point to the importance of Jesus. He as Son of Man is (like God!) Lord of the Sabbath. The story is clear evidence of Mark's high Christology."

76. This idea cannot be supported with certainty, because we do not know the subjects of the verbs ἔρχονται and λέγουσιν (came and said) in the passage Mk 2.18.

77. For a select bibliography on Mk 3.1-6, se L. Schenke, *Die Wundererzählungen* (1974) 161-72; W. J. Bennett, Jr., "The Herodians of Mark's Gospel," *NovT* 17 (1975) 9-14; C. Dietzfelbinger, "Vom Sinn der Sabbatheilungen Jesu," *EvT* 38 (1978) 281-98; A. J. Hultgren, *Jesus and His Adversaries* (1979) 82-84; J. Dewey, *Markan Public Debate* (1980) 100-06.

78. E.g. Lohmeyer 69-70.

79. It is worth noting that in the parallel narratives of Mt 12.9-14 and Lk 6.6-11 we do not encounter the same sharpness in language. Cf. J. Dewey, *Markan Public Debate* (1980) 103-05.

80. The word εὐθὺς here is not the conjunctive-paratactic term used frequently by Mark, but an adverb of time which means "immediately." See Blass-Debrunner-Funk, *A Greek Grammer of the New Testament* (Chicago, 1961) 55.

81. The Herodians were not a religious group. The name has been used in order to designate supporters or friends of Herod. Perhaps they are the same group called by Josephus "οἱ τὰ Ἡρώδου φρονοῦντες" (the ones who take Herod's side), *Jewish Antiquities* 14, 450, Loeb, Josephus 7, 680. Regardless of their real identity, the important item here is the alliance between Herodians and Pharisees as W. J. Bennett, "The Herodians of Mark's Gospel," 13-14, points out.

82. The phrase "συμβούλιον ἐδίδουν" is a hapax legomenon and corresponds to the phrase "συμβούλιον ποιήσαντες" (Mk 15.1) which means to hold a consultation. See Bauer 778.

83. See the entry of this word in Bauer 94. Cf. also Chrysostom (*Homilies on Matthew*, Homily 39, PG 57.434): "When he (i.e. Jesus) stretched out and cured the withered hand of the sick man in the synagogue, then they (the Pharisees) became so enraged that they decided his (Jesus') slaughter and execution."

84. In Matthew the corresponding incident occurs in the twelfth chapter (Mt 12.9-14). In Luke it occurs in the sixth chapter (Lk 6.6-11) but without any mentioning of a decision to kill Jesus.

85. P. M. Beernaert, "Jésus controversé," *NRT* 95 (1973) 129-49, analyzes the essence of the conflicts, their extreme nature, and their outcome in Mk 3.6, on the basis of the christological presuppositions of Mark.

86. See the pertinent discussion in Lagrange 60, who points out the finality of the decision made by the Pharisees and Herodians.

87. For a select bibliography on Mk 3.7-12, see L. E. Keck, "Mark 3,7-12 and Mark's Christology," *JBL* 84 (1965) 341-58; T. A. Burkill, "Mark 3,7-12 and the Alleged Dualism in the Evangelist's Miracle Material,' *JBL* 87 (1968) 409-17; W. Egger, "Die Verborgenheit in Mk. 3,7-12," *Biblica* 50 (1969) 466-90; T. Snoy, "Les miracles dans l'évangile de Marc," *RTL* 4 (1973) 73-95; and C. R. Kazmierski, *Jesus the Son of God* (1979) 73-104.

88. We have already drawn attention to this characteristic type of information in the pericopes Mk 1.32-34, Mk 2.1-12 et. al. Cf. W. Egger, "Die Verborgenheit in Mk 3,7-12" 478-81, W. Kelber, *Mark's Story of Jesus* (1979) 25-26.

89. Cf. Schweizer 79: "The very fact that the boat was standing in readiness illustrates Jesus' dynamic power which sets everything in motion."

90. Cf. Schweizer 79, Gnilka 1, 134.

91. E.g. Mk 5.7; 14.61; 15.35. Cf. also Mk 1.11; 9.7. See Taylor 228, Schweizer 80.

92. T. Snoy, "Les miracles," 85-86, proposes another explanation: Jesus "strictly orders the unclean spirits not to make him known," because he wants to remain "incognito," because he is opposing the wide publicity related to his wondrous works. This paradoxical double view ("double éclairage paradoxal," p. 86) corresponds to the bifocal scheme Christology of Passion — Christology of Authority.

93. For a select bibliography on Mk 3.13-19, see G. Schmahl, "Die Berufung der Zwölf im Markusevangelium," *TTZ* 81 (1972) 203-13; J. Donaldson, "Called to Follow," *BTB* 5 (1975) 67-77; S. J. Anthonysamy, "The Gospel of Mark and the Universal Mission," *Biblebhashyam* 6 (1980) 81-96; M. F. Kirby, "Mark's Prerequisite for Being an Apostle," *BT* 18 (1980) 77-81; R. Buth, "ΒΟΝΕΡΕΓΕΜ and Popular Etymology," *JSNT* 10 (1981) 29-33; and E. Best, *Following Jesus* (1981) 180-89.

94. The text of the present pericope is characterized by textual problems. The various solutions to these problems do not affect drastically the christological data of the pericope.

95. E.g. 1 Sam 12.6; 1 Kgs 12.31 et. al. The verb used here in the Septuagint text is precisely the verb ποιεῖν.

96. H. C. Kee, *Community of the New Age* (1977) 88, rightly remarks that "The continuity between the prophetic-charismatic ministry of Jesus and that of the disciples is stressed in Mark." Behind such an underlining, one could discern the concept of authority Christology at work.

97. For a select bibliography on Mk 3.20-30, see L. Cope, "The Beelzebul Controversy, Mk. 3,19-30 and Parallels," *SBL Meeting 1971*, I, 251-56; R. Holst, "Reexamining Mk. 3,28f. and its Parallels," *ZNW* 63 (1972) 122-24; H. Wansbrough, "Mark 3,21 — Was Jesus Out of His Mind?", *NTS* 18 (1972) 233-35; D. Wenham, "The Meaning of Mark 3,21," *NTS* 21 (1975) 295-300; M. E. Boring, "The Unforgivable Sin Logion Mk. 3,28-29," *NovT* 18 (1976) 258-79; H. Kruse, "Das Reich Satans," *Biblica* 58 (1977) 29-61; A. J. Hultgren, *Jesus and His Adversaries* (1979) 100-05; and A. Fuchs, *Die Entwicklung der Beelzebul-kontroverse bei den Synoptikern* (Linz, 1980).

98. See Swete 63; Lagrange 69-70; Taylor 236; and Gnilka 1, 148.

99. Zigabenos 26: "Some people possessed by envy said that he (i.e. Jesus) became insane, because he gave himself completely to the work of healing. They interpreted philanthropy as insanity." Cf. Photios (*Amphilochia*, Quest. 50, PG 101.377-81): "Some people . . . understand the verb ἐξέστη in its ordinary meaning, i.e. he was beside himself and carried away from the established order." See also Damalas 2, 908; Trembelas 63; Lagrange 70-71; and Lane 139.

100. The novel interpretation by H. Wansbrough, "Mk 3:21 — Was Jesus Out of His Mind?" 233-35, that the verb ἐξέστη refers to the crowd, not to Jesus, supported also by D. Wenham, "The meaning of Mark 3:21," 296-300, is not persuasive to the point of taking precedence over the traditional interpretation. Cf. E. Best, "Mark 3.20,21,31-35," *NTS* 22 (1976) 309-14.

101. For the names Beelzebul, Satan, see *TDNT* 1, 605-06, Vol. 7, 151-65.

102. This is the way in which H. Kee, *Community of the New Age* (1977) 108, sees the present pericope.

103. The introductory phrase "truly, I say to you" (ἀμὴν λέγω ὑμῖν) emphasizes the importance of the statement that follows. Cf. Mk 8.12; 9.1; 13.30.

104. The condemnation is particularly underlined, because it constitutes the only exception to the universality of salvation which the immediately preceding verse proclaims (Mk 3.28).

105. Photios (*Amphilochia*, Quest. 214, PG 101.972) comments here: "For those who took offense of the Lord Jesus because of his more human elements, there is a rather easy forgiveness and change through the higher and greater ones. But for those who abandoned the spiritual and supernatural and divine ones, the correction is absolutely difficult and impossible. This is why there is no possibility for forgiveness for their wrongdoings." Cf. Trembelas 65-67; Schweizer 87; Pesch 1, 217-18, 220; Achtemeier 64; and Gnilka 1, 154-55.

106. For a select bibliography on Mk 3.31-35, see J. D. Crossan, "Mark and the Relatives of Jesus," *NovT* 15 (1973) 81-113; J. Lambrecht, "The Relatives of Jesus in Mark," *NovT* 16 (1974) 241-58; E. Best, "Mk. 3,20-21 and 31-35," *NTS* 22 (1976) 309-19; B. Buby, "A Christology of Relationship in Mark," *BTB* 10 (1980) 149-54.

107. Extensive discussion and presentation of the material related to the "brothers" of Jesus, see in Lagrange 79-93. Cf. also Taylor 247-49.

108. J. D. Crossan, "Mark and the Relatives of Jesus," 96-98, emphasized too much and isolated the opposition to the relatives of Jesus revealed in Mk 3.31-35. J. Lambrecht, "The Relatives of Jesus in Mark" 255-58, more persuasively, has shown that Mark in 3.31-35 besides the opposition to the relatives is chiefly interested in the new relationship established by the Messiah. Cf. also H. Kee, *Community of the New Age* (1977) 109-10.

109. This is the reason why ancient exegetes tried to mitigate the sharpness of the passage Mk 3.31-34. Chrysostom, for instance, writes: "You can see that the reproof was becoming to him (i.e. Jesus) and helpful to her (his Mother). In addition it was mild in tone. For he did not say, 'go tell the mother that you are not my mother,' but he turned to the fellows who conveyed the information and said, 'who is my mother?' This way he added something else. What was that? It was the truth that they should not, relying on the bond of kin, neglect the cultivation of virtue. If she (i.e. the mother) was not helped by being his mother unless she was a person of virtue, all the more no one else could be saved through kinship (to Jesus). For there is but one and only nobility, the nobility of doing the will of God. This nobility is better and more substantial than the other (acquired by kinship)" (*Homilies on Matthew*, Hom. 44, PG 57.465-66). Cf. Victor 300: "When Jesus said what he said, he was not rebuking his mother and brothers." Theophylact 528 disagrees with the above interpretation.

110. Cf. J. Lambrecht, "The Relatives of Jesus in Mark," 257-58, Achtemeier 65-66.

111. For a select bibliography on Mk 4.1-34, see D. Wenham, "The Synoptic Problem Revisited: Some New Suggestions about the Composition of Mark 4,1-34," *TynBul* 23 (1972) 3-38; H. Räisänen, *Die Parabeltheorie im Markusevangelium* (Helsinki, 1973); B. Englezakis, "Markan Parable," ΔBM 2 (1974) 349-57; W. Kelber, *The Kingdom in Mark* (Philadelphia, 1974) 25-43; P. Merendino, "Gleichnisse und Wortligurgie. Zu Mk. 4,1-34," *Archiv für Liturgiewissenschaft* 16 (1974) 7-31; É. Trocmé, "Why Parables? A Study of Mark 4," *BJRL* 59 (1977) 458-71; B. Standaert, L'Évangile selon Marc (1978) 201-18; V. Fusco, *Parola e regno* (Morcelliana, 1980); and C. C. Marcheselli, "Le parabole del Vangelo di Marco," *RivB* 29 (1981) 405-15.

112. For a select bibliography on Mk 4.1-20, see J. W. Bowker, "Mystery and Parable: Mk. 4,1-20," *JTS* 25 (1974) 300-17; P. Lampe, "Die markinische Deutung des Gleichnisses vom Sämann," *ZNW* 65 (1974) 140-50; A. N. Wilder, "The Parable of the Sower (Mk. 4,3-9)," *Semeia* 2 (1974) 134-51; C. E. Carlston, *The Parables of the Triple Tradition* (Philadelphia, 1975) 137-49; E. E. Lemcio, "External Evidence for the Structure and Function of Mk. 4,1-20, 7,14-23 and 8,14-21," *JTS* 29 (1978) 323-38; T. J. Weeden,

"Recovering the Parabolic Intent in the Parable of the Sower," *JAAR* 47 (1979) 97-120; V. Fusco, *Parola e regno* (1980) 223-78; and P. B. Payne, "The Seeming Inconsistency of the Interpretation of the Parable of the Sower," *NTS* 26 (1980) 564-68.

113. Chrysostom, in interpreting the parallel Matthean passage, places more emphasis on the responsibility of the hearers: "Some people say that he (i.e. Jesus) should open the eyes of those who do not see. Yes! He should, if blindness were a condition due to natural circumstances. But here blindness is a voluntary and self-chosen condition. This is the reason why Jesus did not simply say 'they don't see,' but 'they see and they don't see'; so blindness is the result of their wickedness," (*Homilies on Matthew*, Homily 45, PG 58.473). Cf. V. Kesich, *The Gospel Image of Christ* (New York, 1972) 108-09. Very interesting, christologically, is the interpretation by Cyril of Alexandria: "Christ spoke in parables in order to show that he was the one about whom David, prophetically speaking, said, 'I will open my mouth in parables' (Ps 77 [LXX]). Another prophet also said (Is 32.1-2 [LXX]), 'Behold, a righteous king will reign, and princes will rule with justice, and the man will be concealing his words,' " *Commentary on Matthew*, 40, PG 72.412.

114, Mk 4.11-12 has caused long discussions, and more particularly verse 12 which is considered a "crux interpretum." Cf. A. Ambrozic, *The Hidden Kingdom* (1972) 46-106; K. Haaker, "Erwägungen zu Mark 4:11," *NovT* 14 (1972) 219-25; M. Hubaut, "Le mystère révélé dans les paraboles (Mk 4:11-12)," *RTL* 5 (1974) 454-61; J. C. Meagher *Clumsy Construction* (1979) 83-142; F. C. Synge, "A Plea for the Outsiders," *JTSA* 30 (1980) 53-58; F. Kermode, *The Genesis of Secrecy* (Cambridge, 1980³) 28-33; and C. A. Evans, "The Function of Isaiah 6:9-10 in Mark and John," *NovT* 24 (1982) 124-38.

115. Cf. W. Wrede, *The Messianic Secret* (1971) 106: "The disciples' lack of understanding acts as a foil to Jesus' eminence and greatness."

116. See Schmithals 1, 233. Cf. A. Ambrozic, *The Hidden Kingdom* (1972) 71-72.

117. We should, however, not let pass unnoticed the phrase "when tribulation or persecution arises" (Mk 4.17), a phrase which implies actualized hostility.

118. For a number of exegetes this is not one of the two main points but the main point of the parabole. Cf. Taylor 250-51; and R. Lightfoot, *The Gospel Message* (1950) 40.

119. This is the concluding point of the analysis by C. Carlston, *The Parables of the Triple Tradition* (1975) 137, 146-48, who sees in Mk 4.1-20 clear intentions of a word of comfort and encouragement rather than of moral admonition.

120. For a select bibliography on Mk 4.26-29, see W. G. Doty, "An Interpretation: Parable of the Weeds and the Wheat," *Interpretation* 25 (1971) 185-93; R. Stuhlmann, "Beobachtungen und Überlegungen zu Mk. 4,26-29," *NTS* 19 (1973) 153-62; C. E. Carlston, *The Parables of the Triple Tradition* (1975) 202-10; and V. Fusco, *Parola e regno* (1980) 341-64.

121. This condensed power is in the final analysis revelatory of the amazing energy and might of God. See the pertinent discussion in R. Stuhlmann, "Beobachtungen und Überlegungen zu Mk. 4,26-29," 154-59. Cf., however, also C. Carlston, *The Parables of the Triple Tradition* (1975) 208-10, for the need to pay attention to the eschatological priority in interpreting the parable.

122. For a select bibliography on Mk 4.30-32, see H.K. McArthur, "The Parable of the Mustard Seed," *CBQ* 33 (1971) 198-210; R. W. Funk, "The Looking-Glass Tree Is for the Birds," *Interpretation* 27 (1973) 3-9; A. Casalegno, "La parabola del granello di senape," *RivB* 26 (1978) 139-61; and V. Fusco, *Parola e regno* (1980) 365-80.

123. R. Funk, "The Looking-Glass Tree is for the Birds" 7-9, by studying Mk 4.30-32 alongside the passage Ezek 17.22-24, argues that the contrast is deeper and more complex than the one expressed by the pair "the smallest of all . . . the greatest of all," with result the emphasis on the hidden dynamism of the kingdom of God. Cf. C. Carlston, *The Parables of the Triple Tradition* (1975) 159-62.

124. This idea is central in those two parables, regardless of the general meaning that they may have. At the same time, nonetheless, the very same idea suggests also the difficulty and the affliction which accompany the growth of the kingdom of God. Cf. W. Kelber, *The Kingdom in Mark* (1974) 41-43.

125. For a select bibliography on Mk 4.35-41, see L. Schenke, *Die Wundererzählungen* (1974) 1-94; T. M. Suriano, "Who then is This?" *BT* 79 (1979) 449-56; P. Lamarche, *Révélation de Dieu* (1976) 61-77; B. Standaert, *L'Évangile selon Marc* (1978) 135-39; G. M. Soares Prabhu, "And There Was a Great Calm," *Biblebhashyam* 5 (1979) 295-308; V. Fusco, *Parola e regno* (1980) 307-40; K. M. Fischer and U. C. von Wahlde, "The Miracles of Mk. 4,35-5,43," *BTB* 11 (1981) 13-16.

126. Pesch 1, 267-81, regards the event described in Mk 4.35-41 as one of the outstanding New Testament manifestations of the supernatural-miraculous energy of Jesus, and analyzes it in connection with the so-called "Christology of the divine man." Cf. B. Standaert, *L'Évangile selon Marc* (1978) 136-37, and P. Lamarche, *Révélation de Dieu* (1976) 66.

127. The exegetes have already pointed out that the term διεγερθείς (Mk 4.39) has the meaning "that Jesus awoke, not that he stood up" (Taylor 275). Cf. Swete 90; Lagrange 124; and Bauer 193.

128. We could mention, for instance, the call of the disciples (Mk 1.17), the healing of the demoniac (Mk 1.25), the cure of the paralytic (Mk 2.11), and the call of Levi (Mk 2.14).

129. This is the meaning that the verb φοβοῦμαι has also in other passages of Mark, like Mk 5.15; 10.32; 16.8. Cf. Trembelas 86; and Gnilka 1, 197.

130. This seems to be the meaning of the question of the disciples, and not the lack of faith and understanding as W. Kelber, *The Kingdom in Mark* (1974) 49-50, claims.

131. Dan 7.3ff. Cf. Rev 13.1: "And I saw a beast rising out of the sea, with ten horns and seven heads." Cf. P. Lamarche, *Révélation de Dieu* (1976) 64-66.

132. Pesch 1, 269-74, offers detailed data related to the alleged similarity. Schmithals 1, 256, on the contrary, does not see any substantial similarity.

133. Achtemeier 78: "Jesus here does what the Old Testament knew God alone could do (see Ps 89.9; 107.28-29). God's power is now at work in Jesus." Lane 178: "In the account of the subduing of the sea we are told that Jesus is the living Lord. What is true of the God of Israel is true of him." Cf. Ps 105 (LXX).9; Ps 88 (LXX).10; Job 38.8-11; and Jer 5.22. Cf. also the interesting observation by Severian of Gabala: "Christ says to the sea, 'be silent, be still,' and it became still, and the creature knew the creator. He spoke to the sea and it became still; he spoke to the wind and it became silent. If it had not obeyed him then he had not created it (*Homilies on the Creation of the World*, Homily 3, 6, PG 56.455).

134. Chrysostom, in commenting on the parallel Matthean passage, offers the following analysis of the event of the rebuke: "Christ rebuked them (i.e. the disciples) not because they called him man, but because he expected, having taught them through the signs, that they would recognize the wrong idea. Whence did they consider him man? From the sight, from the sleep, from the need to use the boat. This is the reason why they found themselves at an impasse and they asked 'Who then is this?' The sleep and the appearance showed a man; the sea and the calm, however, displayed a God" (*Homilies on Matthew*, Homily 28, PG 57.352).

135. For a select bibliography on Mk 5.1-20, see C. Argenti, "A Meditation on Mk. 5,1-20," *ER* 23 (1971) 398-408; P. Lamarche, *Révélation de Dieu* (1976) 79-103; F. Annen, *Heil für die Heiden* (Frankfurt, 1976); H. Harsch, "Psychologische Interpretation biblischer Texte," *US* 32 (1977) 39-45; J. D. M. Derrett, "Legend and Event: the Gerasene Demoniac," *SB* 2 (1978) 63-73.

136. Cf. Lohmeyer 99: "Jesus here is the divine mighty Lord, in the presence of whom anything that is impure disappears and the demons are subjugated. For him there are no limits."

137. The description in the parallel narratives of Matthew (8.28) and Luke (8.27-29) does not have the same dread realism. For characteristic details in Mark's narrative see Swete 92-94; Pesch 1, 285-86; Gnilka 1, 205; and P. Lamarche, *Révélation de Dieu* (1976) 84.

138. Cyril of Alexandria notes; "The divine nature of the only Begotten (i.e. Son of God) was burning them (i.e. the demons). This is the reason why they said to him 'you came . . . to torment us' " (*Commentary on Matthew*, Comment on Mt 8.29, PG 72.392). Cf. Trembelas 89-90; and Haenchen 193.

139. Chrysostom, in interpreting the parallel passage in Matthew notes: "If someone asks why Christ did what the demons demanded by letting them enter into the herd of swine, we will answer that Christ acted the way he did not because he was persuaded by them, but because he was taking care of many things. First, because he wanted to teach the people liberated from the evil oppressors (i.e. the demons), the magnitude of the catastrophic power of their plotters. Secondly, in order to send a message to all that the demons do not dare to harm even the swine, unless he permits it. Thirdly, in order to let the people know that they could have suffered even worst (than the loss of swine), if even in their mischief they did not have the benefit

of the providence of God in abundance" (*Homilies on Matthew,* Homily 28, PG 57.354).

140. Cf. Taylor 283-84. We should not forget that the events take place in the country of the Gerasenes, namely in an area Gentile rather than Jewish. The unusual nature of the divine intervention is related to the opening of the saving activity of the Messiah toward the Gentiles. Cf. W. Kelber, *Mark's Story of Jesus* (1979) 32.

141. In the parallel narrative of Luke, it is stated overtly that the Gerasenes asked Jesus to depart from them "for they were seized with great fear" (Lk 8.37). Contrary to what Taylor 284 suggests, Luke rightly ascribes the Gerasenes' demand to fear. Cf. Swete 98; and Klostermann 50.

142. The switching from "the Lord" (i.e. God) to "Jesus" in Mk 5.19-20, seems to be the result of a process based on the concept of the divine authority of Jesus (cf. Schweizer 113), and not a case of usage of ancient christological titles, as Taylor believes (Taylor 285). Cf. Zigabenos 39; and P. Lamarche, *Révélation de Dieu* (1976) 91.

143. For a select bibliography on Mk 5.21-43, see L. Schenke, *Die Wunderezählungen* (1974) 196-216; J. T. Cummings, "The Tassel of his Cloak," *SB* (1978), 2 (1980) 47-61; M. G. Steinhauser, "Healing Stories in the Gospels," *Liturgy* 25 (1980) 27-30; M. J. S. Schierling, *Woman, Cult and Miracle Recital: Mk. 5,24-34* (Ph.D. Dissertation, St. Louis University, 1980); J. Moiser, "She Was Twelve Years Old," *IBS* 3 (1981) 179-86.

144. Relevant discussion see in Schmithals 1, 283-86. Cf. F. Kermode, *The Genesis of Secrecy* (1980) 131-33.

145. See Damalas 2, 741, Lohmeyer 102; Taylor 291; Nineham 157; Gnilka 1, 215-16; and Montague 68.

146. Luke adds to the phrase "and they laughed at him," the explanation "knowing that she was dead" (Lk 8.53). See the pertinent remarks by Theophylact 545, and by Zigabenos 43: "Jesus wanted to be laughed at, so that the loud wailing, and the mockery, and the rest would be a clear proof that the girl was dead."

147. Only Mark has preserved Jesus' command in its original Aramaic language. Its Greek rendering appears in a slight variant which underlines the authority of Jesus. Cf. Damalas 2, 746.

148. Cf. Nineham 159-61.

149. This interpretation explains the mentioning of the three disciples, better perhaps than the one proposed by Schweizer 119 and related to the Messianic secret.

150. For a select bibliography on Mk 6.1-6, see E. Grässer, "Jesus in Nazareth," *NTS* 16 (1969) 1-23; H. K. McArthur, "Son of Mary," *NovT* 15 (1973) 38-58; C. Perrot, "Jésus à Nazaret," *AsSeign* 45 (1974) 40-49; B. Mayer, "Überlieferungs — und redaktions — geschichtliche Überlegungen zu Mk. 6,1-6a," *BZ* 22 (1978) 187-98.

151. The contrast is strong and deliberate, and it belongs to the narrative technique of Mark. Cf. Achtemeier 89, R. Martin, *Mark* (1972) 117: "his (i.e. Jesus') rejection at Nazareth (in Mk 6.1-6) is so written as to bring out the sense of pathos."

152. Origen notes characteristically: "It is likely that through them (i.e. the questions of the Nazarenes) a wonderment is manifested about Jesus being not human but something more divine . . . and that he has nothing comparable to his relatives, nor that he has come to such degree of wisdom and power through training and education," *Commentary on Matthew,* Tom. 10, 17, GCS Origen Vol. 10, 22. Cf. Trembelas 101.

153. The corresponding passage in Matthew has "the carpenter's son" (Mt 13.55), namely, a much milder expression, whereas Luke in his parallel does not mention anything about a carpenter (Lk 4.16-30).

154. Cf. Taylor 299-300; Nineham 166. There is also the theory that the phrase "the son of Mary" has been used because Joseph had passed away long ago, Schweizer 124; Montague 71. J. M. Robinson, *The Problem of History in Mark* (1971) 81, thinks that the omission of Joseph is deliberate, and that it is the result of Mark's christological presupposition according to which Jesus, being the Son of God, could not be called son of Joseph. See relevant discussion in H. McArthur, "Son of Mary," 47-58.

155. Concerning the relatives of Jesus mentioned here, see Lagrange 79-93, Taylor 247-49; Pesch 1, 322-25; and Schmithals 1, 301.

156. Taylor 301 discerns here mainly the concept of being offended. Pesch 1, 319 prefers the concept of showing disbelief or unbelief. See word in Bauer 760.

157. Is 53.2-3 according to the Septuagint text. For a concise discussion of the term ἄτιμος in Mk 6.4, see Pesch 1, 320.

158. Lk 4.29, "And they rose up and put him out of the city, and led him to the brow of the hill on which their city was built, that they might throw him down headlong."

159. In this instance Matthew uses again a milder terminology (Mt 13.58), in comparison with the Markan one.

160. Cf. Origen, *Commentary on Matthew,* Tom. 10, 19, GCS Origen Vol. 10, 25; Victor 322.

161. For a select bibliography on Mk 6.7-13, see G. Testa, "Studio di Mc. 6,6^b-13 secondo il metodo della storia della tradizione," *DT* 75 (1972) 177-91; J. Delorme, "La mission des Douze en Galilée," *AsSeign* 46 (1974) 43-50; J. Donaldson, "Called to Follow," *BTB* 5 (1975) 67-77; S. J. Anthonysamy, "The Gospel of Mark and the Universal Mission," *Biblebhashyam* 6 (1980) 81-96.

162. Beyond the sentence, "they went out and preached that men should repent," no other information is offered concerning the contents of the preaching. This perhaps is an indication that the center of attention is to be found in the event of the preaching rather than in its contents.

163. The terminology is the same (cf. Mk 1.34; 3.10; 6.5). The difference lies in the fact that the twelve use olive oil during the healing process, something that Jesus does not.

164. "What Jesus does here only God can do. God only can grant the power of his word and of his miracles to human beings," observes Lohmeyer 113-14. Cf. the relevant remarks by R. Martin, *Mark* (1972) 132.

165. The emphasis here lies on the initiative of Jesus, which demonstrates his divine authority, and not on the apostles. This perhaps explains a phenomenon encountered in the pericopes that follow, namely the "insignificance" of the apostles, a phenomenon which J. Wellhausen, *Das Evangelium Marci* (Berlin, 1909²) 44, has difficulty in explaining. See Nineham 167-68.

166. The mission is characterized by the intensity of something extremely urgent (see Taylor 304). Nonetheless, the demands of the Messiah seem to be quite advanced for the still weak apostles.

167. The text in the parallel pericope of Matthew is eloquent in its warning concerning the eschatological and soteriological consequences: "Truly I say to you, it shall be more tolerable on the day of judgement for the land of Sodom and Gomorrah than for that town" (Mt 10.15).

168. For a select bibliography on Mk 6.14-29, see I. De La Potterie, "Mors Johannis Baptistae," *VerbDom* 44 (1966) 142-51; J. Gnilka, "Das Martyrium Johannes des Täufers, *Orientierung an Jesus,* Fest. J. Schmid (Freiburg, 1973) 78-92; B. Standaert, *L'Évangile selon Marc* (1978) 68-82; F. Kermode, *The Genesis of Secrecy* (Cambridge, MA, 1980) 128-33; and F. Manns, "Marc 6,21-29 à la lumière des dernières fouilles de Machéronte," *SBFLA* 31 (1981) 287-90.

169. Recently, the literary critic F. Kermode, *The Genesis of Secrecy* (1980) 128-33, has expressed unusual but interesting ideas concerning the interpretation of this narrative.

170. Cf. Pesch 1, 338-39; Gnilka 1, 252.

171. It is indicative that the narrative in Mark extends to 302 words, versus 170 words in Matthew and only 52 in Luke, in the parallel pericopes (Mt 14.1-12; Lk 9.7-9).

172. See Nineham 173; Schweizer 132; Pesch 1, 334. An extensive analysis of the dramatic elements which connect the killing of John with the passion of Jesus, see in B. Standaert, *L'Évangile selon Marc* (1978) 70-82.

173. For details in the inter-relationship between Jesus, John, and Elijah on account of miraculous events, see Swete 120-21; Haenchen 235-37.

174. Many exegetes see in the unit Mk 6.30-44 two pericopes, namely Mk 6.30-33 and Mk 6.34-44.

175. For a select bibliography on Mk 6.30-44, see G. Ory, "Des pains, des poissons et des hommes," *CCER* 18 (1971) 21-28; J. M. van Cangh, "La multiplication des pains dans l'Evangile de Marc," *L'Évangile selon Marc,* ed. M. Sabbe (Gembloux, 1974) 309-46; L. Williamson, Jr., "An Exposition of Mark 6,32-44," *Interpretation* 30 (1976) 169-73; J. Delorme, "L'intégration des petites unités littéraires dans l'évangile de Marc du point de vue de la sémiotique structurale," *NTS* 25 (1979) 469-80; C. Bonnet, "Le désert. Sa signification dans l'évangile de Marc," *Hokhma* 13 (1980) 20-34; R. M. Fowler, *Loaves and Fishes* (Chico, CA., 1981) 5-42, 68-148; and S. Masuda, "The Good News of the Miracle of the Bread," *NTS* 28 (1982) 191-219.

176. The manifestation of the divine power of Jesus seems to constitute the focal point of both Mk 6.30-44 and Mk 6.45-52 which follows immediately. The argument by R. Fowler, *Loaves and Fishes* (1981) 80-81, 95-96, 99, that in these pericopes the central point is the conflict between Jesus and his disciples, does not appear strongly supported by the text.

177. Some exegetes discern in the word ἔρημος an allusion to the life of ancient Israel in the wilderness and her miraculous feeding there by God, whose place Jesus takes in Mk 6.35-44. Cf. Lane 226, 232-33, H. C. Kee, *Community of the New Age* (1977) 111-12, S. Masuda, "The Good News of the Miracle of Bread," 206-07.

178. The question is a mixture of wonder and reserved irony. One denarius "was a workman's average daily wage" (Bauer 179).

179. The mentioning of the fish in Mk 6.30-44 has been done in a special way which emphasizes the Messiahship of Jesus, according to J. M. van Cangh, "Le thème des poissons dans les récits évangéliques de la multiplication des pains," *RB* 78 (1971) 71-83.

180. For the relationship between this sentence and Old Testament texts, see Lagrange 167 and Pesch 1, 350. Lohmeyer 125 and Gnilka 1, 259 note that here the term ἐσπλαγχνίσθη is more than an expression of human sympathy. Cf. TDNT 7,554.

181. Cf. Origen, *Commentary on Matthew*, Tom. 10, 25, GCS Origen Vol. 10, 34, Masuda, "The Good News of the Miracle of the Bread," 201-03, 210-14. Chrysostom does not relate here the terminology to the Eucharist. He offers, however, the following interesting christological observation: "Why Jesus 'looked up to heaven and blessed?' Because it was needed that he should be believed as being from the Father and as being equal to the Father . . . The equality was shown in the fact that he did everything with authority; his being from the Father, on the other hand, could not be demonstrated otherwise, but if he did everything with great humility, and if he related everything that he performed to the Father . . . Then in order to avoid the impression that there is a conflict between the two attitudes, he looks up to heaven in the cases of minor miracles whereas in the cases of major deeds he does everything with authority. When he forgave sins, and opened paradise, and abolished the old law, and raised many dead, and calmed the sea . . . , deeds that only God can do, he did not seem to pray; when, on the other hand, he multiplied the loaves, which was much less than the above mentioned achievements, then he looked up to heaven" *Homilies on Matthew,* Homily 49, PG 58.498.

182. This is a valid assumption even if one prefers the idea that Mk 6.30-44 is chiefly a prefiguration of the eschatological Messianic banquet. Cf. J. Karavidopoulos, "The Beginnings of Ecclesiology in the Gospel of Mark," *ΕΕΘΣΠΘ* 17 (1972) 82-86 (in Greek).

183. For a select bibliography on Mk 6.45-52, see Q. Quesnell, *The Mind of Mark* (Rome, 1969); G. D. Fee, "Some Dissenting Notes on 7 Q 5 = Mk. 6,52-53," *JBL* 92 (1973) 109-12; T. Snoy, "Marc 6,48.. et il voulait les depasser," *L'Évangile selon Marc,* ed. M. Sabbe (Gembloux, 1974) 347-63;

H. Ritt, "Der Seewandel Jesu," *BZ* 23 (1979) 71-84; J. D. M. Derrett, "Why and How Jesus Walked on the Sea," *NovT* 23 (1981) 330-48; and J. P. Heil, *Jesus Walking on the Sea* (Rome, 1981).

184. Pesch 1, 358 thinks that in Mk 6.45-52 the rescue motif has been diminished in comparison to Mk 4.35-41, and that the narrative is dominated by theophanic elements. Already Lohmeyer 133-34 had considered the appearance of Jesus in Mk 6.45-52 purely theophanic and he had related it to Ex 33.18ff. Cf. Gnilka 1, 268-70; Schmithals 1, 332, 335; and Montague 83-84.

185. Origen, on the basis of the Markan text, indicates the fact that Jesus was not on the boat, and that his absence was deliberate in order to ultimately emphasize his unique power, *Commentary on Matthew*, Tom. 11, 5, GCS Origen Vol. 10, 42.

186. A detailed presentation of the relevant data see in H. Ritt, "Der Seewandel Jesu," 74-82.

187. Pesch 1, 360; Achtemeier 104.

188. Cf. Schweizer 142; Pesch 1, 364; Gnilka 1, 271.

189. For a select bibliography on Mk 6.53-56, see T. Snoy, "Les miracles dans l'évangile de Marc," *RTL* 3 (1972) 449-66, 4 (1973) 58-101; W. Egger, *Frohbotschaft und Lehre* (1976) 134-42; and J. T. Cummings, "The Tassel of his Cloak," *SB* 1978, 2, 47-61.

190. Cf. Schweizer 143.

191. For a select bibliography on Mk 7.1-23, see N. J. McEleney, "Authenticating Criteria and Mk. 7,1-23," *CBQ* 34 (1974) 431-60; K. Berger, *Die Gesetzauslegung Jesu*, Teil I: Markus und Parallelen (Neukirchen, 1972) 461ff.; H. Huebner, "Mark 7,1-23 und das Jüdischhellenistische Gesetzesverständnis," *NTS* 22 (1976) 319-45; J. Lambrecht, "Jesus and the Law: An Investigation of Mk. 7,1-23," *ETL* 53 (1977) 24-82; A. J. Hultgren, *Jesus and His Adversaries* (1979) 115-18; D. Lührmann, " . . . womit er alle Speisen für rein erklärte," *Wort und Dienst* (Bielefeld) 16 (1981) 71-92; and Y. Ronen, "Mark 7,1-23, Traditions of the Elders," *Immanuel* 12 (1981) 44-54.

192. See the discussion on this specific topic in Taylor 334, 338-39; Nineham 188-91; Schweizer 145-47; and Gnilka 1, 279-80.

193. Cf. Schweizer 147; Schmithals 1, 344; and Montague 87-88.

194. E. Trocmé argues that here Mark displays some anti-intellectualistic tendencies and attacks the theological ideas of the scribes without having anything to put in their place, *The Formation of the Gospel according to Mark* (London, 1975) 98-99. Such an argument misses the main point of the pericope which is the incomparable authority of Jesus.

195. See Klostermann 69; Lagrange 188-89; Schmithals 1, 342-44. Victor 335 notes here: "From this point on the new law begins, a law according to the spirit which does not require bodily purifications nor food distinctions but virtue of mind" . . . for there is no bodily impurity in man."

196. Cf. J. Lambrecht, "Jesus and the Law," 78-79; H. Huebner, "Mark 7:1-23," 345.

197. For a select bibliography on Mk 7.24-30, see W. Storch, "Zur Perikope von der Syrophönizierin," *BZ* 14 (1970) 256-57; T. A. Burkill, *New Light on the Earliest Gospel* (1972) 48-120; J. D. M. Derrett, "Law in the New Testament," *NovT* 15 (1973) 161-86; A. Dermience, "Tradition et rédaction dans la péricope de la Syrophénicienne," *RTL* 8 (1977) 15-29; S. J. Anthonysamy, "The Gospel of Mark and the Universal Mission," *Biblebhashyam* 6 (1980) 81-96; E. A. Russell, "The Canaanite Woman and the Gospel," *SB* 1978, 2 (1980) 263-300; and F. J. Steinmetz, "Jesus bei den Heiden," *Geist und Leben* 55 (1982) 177-84.

198. The woman is presented in terms of religion as "Greek," i.e. Gentile, and in terms of ethnicity as "Syrophoenician," i.e. as a Phoenician coming from Syria.

199. For T. A. Burkill, *New Light* (1972) 70, Mark's purpose in the pericope of the Syrophoenician woman is precisely the projection of this idea.

200. Origen notes: "According to Mark, 'Jesus arose and came to the region of Tyre,' the distress of nations, so that the people of that region could be saved through faith, if they get out of it," *Commentary on Matthew,* Tom. 11, 16, GCS Origen Vol. 10, 60. Cf. A. Dermience, "Tradition et rédaction," 26-29.

201. The addressing word "Lord" (κύριε) used by the Syrophoenician woman should not pass unnoticed (Mk 7.28). If, as T. A. Burkill, *New Light* (1972) 89-91, argues, the address is equal to a recognition of the divine Lordship of Christ, then Mk 7.24-30 reveals one more aspect of the Christology of authority. Cf. G. Schille, *Offen für alle Mensche* (Stuttgart, 1974) 21-22.

202. Scholars have pointed out that outside of the Gospel we do not encounter cases of a healing from a distance. See Taylor 348, Nineham 198.

203. For a select bibliography on Mk 7.31-37, see I. Rabinowitz, "Ephphatha: Certainly Hebrew, Not Aramaic." *JSS* 16 (1971) 151-56; S. Morag, "Ephphatha: Certainly Hebrew, Not Aramaic?" *JSS* 17 (1972) 198-202; L. Schenke, *Die Wundererzählungen* (1974) 269-80; and G. Lang, "Über Sidon mitten ins Gebiet der Decapolis," *ZDPV* 84 (1978) 145-60.

204. See, however, the comment by Zigabenos 58: Jesus "could cure the deaf man by using other methods as well; he acted, nonetheless, the way he did so that we know that every and all parts of his holy body were replete with divine power." Cf. Victor 339.

205. Cf. Trembelas 135 and Schweizer 154.

206. An additional evidence for the connection between Is 35.5-6 and Mk 7.31-37 is the word μογιλάλος which occurs only in these two passages of Isaiah and Mark within the entire Old Testament (Septuagint) and New Testament.

207. Gen 1.31: "And God saw everything that he had made, and behold it was very good." Cf. Swete 162; Pesch 1, 398. Schmithals 1, 359, although he sees the connection between Mk 7.37 and Gen 1.31, considers the phrase "he has done all things well" of Mk 7.37 as a chorus epilogue (Chorschluss) of Jesus' messianic activity in Galilee.

208. As Taylor 357 observes, here "the narrator's intention is to relate one of the greatest of the mighty acts of Jesus." Cf. also Schweizer 157:

180 Authority and Passion

Authority and Passion

"The story was told first as a miracle-story designed to extol the unlimited divine power of Jesus."

209. For a select bibliography on Mk 8.1-10, see E. S. English, "A Neglected Miracle," *BSac* 126 (1969) 300-05; J. M. van Cangh, "La multiplication des pains dans l'évangile de Marc," *L'Évangile selon Marc*, ed. M. Sabbe (1974) 309-46; D. A. Koch, *Die Bedeutung der Wundererzählungen* (Berlin, 1975) 104-09; R. M. Fowler, *Loaves and Fishes* (1981) 5-57, 91-148; and S. Masuda, "The Good News of the Miracle of the Bread," *NTS* 28 (1982) 191-219.

210. Exegetical questions related to the similarities between the two pericopes, Mk 6.35-44 and 8.1-10, are beyond the scope of the present study. We only note that the similarities (Schmithals 1, 363-65) do not eliminate the fact of "important differences" (Montague 95) and of the autonomy of the story in Mk 8.1-10. See detailed discussion in R. Fowler, *Loaves and Fishes* (1981) 5-89.

211. Victor 341 offers here an interesting christological comment: "The readiness of the authority was so great! The thanksgiving was offered to God as if it was coming from man; the energy in the given case was manifested as if it was coming from God."

212. Montague 95 rightly observes that "the eucharistic overtones of the passage are even stronger here than before." Cf. S. Masuda, "The Good News," 201-03, 210-14.

213. For a select bibliography on Mk 8.11-13, see O. Linton, "The Demand for a Sign from Heaven," *ST* 19 (1965) 112-29; D. Merli, "Il segno di Giona," *BO* 14 (1972) 61-77; T. Snoy, "Les miracles dans l'évangile de Marc," *RTL* 3 (1972) 449-66; D. A. Koch, *Die Bedeutug der Wundererzählungen* (1975) 155-59.

214. The verb πειράζω has been used in the case of the conflict with Satan (Mk 1.13), and in two other episodes relating clashes with the Pharisees (Mk 10.2 and 12.15).

215. For the meaning of the term σημεῖον and its relationship to the term δύναμις (power, miraculous deed) in Mark, see *TDNT* 7, 234-36, Gnilka 1, 306-07. Interesting suggestions for the meaning of the word σημεῖον in Mk 8.11-13, see in O. Linton, "The Demand for a Sign," 112-29, T. Snoy, "Les miracles," 456-64, and W. Kelber, *The Kingdom in Mark* (1974) 61, 63.

216. Victor 342 comments here: "It is understandable that Jesus sighed deeply when he spoke (to the Pharisees). At this point he was thinking what he has come to accomplish, namely, to die for them and to suffer the ultimate passion, whereas they were causing whatever they were causing against themselves." Cf. Damalas 3.63-64.

217. For a select bibiography on Mk 8.14-21, see A. Negoita and C. Daniel, "L'énigme du levain," *NovT* 9 (1967) 306-14; D. J. Hawkin, "The Incomprehension of the Disciples in the Markan Redaction," *JBL* 91 (1972) 491-500; F. McCombie, "Jesus and the Leaven of Salvation," *New Blackfriars* 59 (1978) 450-62; J. C. Meagher, *Clumsy Construction* (1979) 74-81; and N. A. Beck, "Reclaiming a Biblical Text," *CBQ* (1981) 49-56.

218. N. Beck, "Reclaiming a Biblical Text," 51-56, argues that in this case the center of attention is not the spiritual blindness of the disciples.

His analysis and his argumentation, however, are not persuasive.

219. The terminology here seems to have been influenced by Jeremiah (Jer 5.21) and by Ezekiel (Ezek 12.2).

220. See Lagrange 210-11. In the parallel pericope of Matthew the rebuke does not have the same sharpness (Mt 16.8-11). Chrysostom succinctly notes: "Do you see the magnitude of indignation? We do not seem to have any other case in which he (i.e. Jesus) rebuked them in such a way" (*Homilies on Matthew,* Homily 53, PG 58.529).

221. If the hypothesis by A. Negoita and C. Daniel, "L'énigma du levain," 310-14, referring to the term ζύμη in Mk 8.15 is correct, then the spiritual blindness of the disciples appears to be even bigger. The blindness and the hardness of the hearts of the disciples, nonetheless, is not of the kind that would justify the contention by W. Kelber, *Mark's Story of Jesus* (1979) 42, that in the whole section Mk 4.35-8.21 the real opponents of Jesus are the disciples.

222. See C. Focant, "L'incompréhension des disciples dans le deuxième Évangile," *RB* 82 (1975) 167-69. The accusations against the disciples are grave, but they don't seem to verify the conclusions of T. Weeden, *Mark: Traditions in Conflict* (1971) 50-51, that "Mark is assiduously involved in a vendetta against the disciples," and that "he is intent on totally discrediting them." See also W. Wrede, *The Messianic Secret* (1971) 106 who states emphatically that "if anyone for a moment entertained the idea that Mark is ill-disposed towards the disciples, he would soon dismiss it again. In the Evangelist's mind it is actually no dishonor to the disciples."

223. Characteristic for our case is the Logion from *Papyrus Oxyrhynchus* 1 (lines 18-22. Hennecke-Schneemelcher, *New Testament Apocrypha,* Vol. 1, 106-07): "My soul feels pain for the sons of men, because they are blind in their heart and do not s[ee] ... " Cf. also Chrysostom who notes: "What is happening to the disciples? They are still bound to the earthly. He (Jesus) did innumerable things to bring to memory that miracle (i.e. the miracle of the multiplication of the loaves). He did it by asking questions, by giving answers, by having them help him, by having them take up the baskets. Yet, they were still behaving in a manner which was far from perfection," *Homilies on Matthew,* Homily 53, PG 58.526.

224. For a select bibliography on Mk 8.22-26, see G. Walker, "The Blind Recover Their Sight," *ExpTim* 87 (1975) 23; G. M. Lee, "Mark 8,24 and 15,8," *NovT* 20 (1978) 74; B. Standaert, *L'Évangile selon Marc* (1978) 112-17; E. S. Johnson, "Mark 8,22-26: The Blind Man from Bethsaida," *NTS* 25 (1979) 370-83; J. D. M. Derrett, "Trees Walking, Prophecy, and Christology," *ST* 35 (1981) 33-54; and E. Best, *Following Jesus* (1981) 134-45.

225. Cf. Haenchen 291; E. Johnson, "Mark 8:22-26," 379-80, 383.

226. Mark is the only Evangelist who includes the present miracle in his Gospel.

227. Detailed presentation of this topic see in B. Standaert, *L'Évangile selon Marc* (1978) 114-18.

228. See Taylor 370; Schweizer 164; Pesch 1, 421; Schmithals 1, 372; Montague 97-98; and E. Johnson, "Mk 8:22-26," 380.

182   *Authority and Passion*

CHAPTER TWO
BALANCE WITHIN ALTERNATING CONCEPTS
OF AUTHORITY AND PASSION (MARK 8.27-10.52)

1. For a select bibliography on Mk 8.27-30, see M. Horstmann, *Studien zur markinischen Christologie* (Münster, 1969) 8-33; A. Denaux, "La confession de Pierre et la première annonce de la Passion," *AsSeign* 55 (1974) 31-39; D. C. Duling, "Interpreting the Markan Hodology," *Nexus* 17 (1974) 2-122; R. Pesch, "Das Messiasbekenntnis des Petrus," *BZ* 17 (1973) 178-95, 18 (1974) 20-31; and E. Best, *Following Jesus* (Sheffield, 1981) 19-54.
2. Cf. Victor 346.
3. Cf. Klostermann 80, Pesch 2, 32 and Gnilka 2, 14.
4. See M. Horstmann, *Studien* (1969) 17-18; H. Riesenfeld, *The Gospel Tradition* (Philadelphia, 1970) 67-68; and R. Lightfoot, *The Gospel Message* (1950) 33-34.
5. Origen notes: "The Jews, because of the veil on their hearts, had the wrong idea about Jesus. But Peter . . . confessed him as being the Christ. Peter's confession, "you are the Christ," was already great in view of the ignorance of the Jews that Jesus was the Christ. But even greater was the fact that Peter knew Jesus not only as the Christ but as the Son of the living God," *Commentary on Matthew*, Tom. 12, 9, GCS Origen Vol. 10, 82.
6. Cf. M. Horstmann, *Studien* (1969) 18-20.
7. Victor 346, sees in Jesus' injunction in Mk 8.30 his desire to strengthen and cleanse the faith of the disciples.
8. For a select bibliography on Mk 8.31-33, see A. Feuillet, "Les trois grandes prophèties de la Passion et de la Résurrection des évangiles synoptiques," *RT* 67 (1967) 533-60; C. J. Reedy, "Mk. 8,31-11,10 and the Gospel Ending: A Redaction Study," *CBQ* 34 (1972) 188-97; N. Perrin, "Towards an Interpretation of the Gospel of Mark," *Christology and a Modern Pilgrimage*, ed. H. D. Betz (SBL, 1973²) 14-30; M. Vellanickal, "Suffering in the Life and Teaching of Jesus," *Jeevadhara* 4 (1974) 144-61; W. J. Bennett, Jr., "The Son of Man must . . . ," *NovT* 17 (1975) 113-29; J. F. O'Grady, "The Passion in Mark," *BTB* 10 (1980) 83-87; and C. Walters, Jr., *I Mark, a Personal Encounter* (Atlanta, 1980) 122-24.
9. See the insightful comment by Gregory of Nyssa: "This (i.e. the death) has been ordained by him (i.e. Jesus) who has ordained the passion for himself according to his authority. He did not say that the son of man will suffer this and that, the way we speak when we announce something about to happen; but he determines something necessary to happen on account of an ineffable cause by his word when he said "the son of man must (δεῖ)," *On Holy Easter*, Sermon 1, PG 46.621.
10. The verb δεῖ occurs in the cases of the coming of Elijah the Prophet (Mk 9.11), of the eschatological afflictions (Mk 13.7), and of the preaching of the Gospel to all nations (Mk 13.10), cases indicative of the process of actualization of a soteriological-eschatological divine plan. See W. J. Bennett, Jr., "The Son of Man Must . . . " 128-29. Cf. Trembelas 147 and

N. Perrin, "Towards an Interpretation," 15, 21, 28-29.

11. See M. Hooker, *The Son of Man* (1967) 103-16.

12. Mk 12.10; Mt 21.42; Lk 9.22, 17.25, 20.17. See Bauer 90.

13. See, for instance, Mt 23.37; Lk 11.47-49, 13.34; Acts 7.52.

14. See Mt 24.9; Lk 12.4; Jn 16.2.

15. See Jn 5.18; 7.1, 7.19, 8.37, 40, 11.53, 12.10, 18.2; Acts 3.15. For the connections between the term ἀποκτείνω, as well as other martyrological elements of the passion predictions in Mk 8.31, and the Old Testament, see Pesch 2, 49-51; Gnilka 2, 15-16; and N. Perrin, "Towards an Interpretation," 26.

16. Lohmeyer 167 comments here: "The certainty that the son of man is precisely human being means that his destiny is the passion and death. The certainty that he is also precisely divine being means that death and passion are not and cannot be the last event but the first step to a divine life."

17. As. W. Wrede, *The Messianic Secret* (1971), observes, "the proclamation of the resurrection is indissolubly linked with that of the suffering and dying . . . To suppress it is to change the evangelist's meaning.

18. In the parallel passage, Matthew has preserved the words of Peter, "God forbid, Lord! This shall never happen to you" (Mt 16.22) which show the contents of the rebuke.

19. The rebuke by Jesus is of christological and not of anthropological nature as B. A. E. Osborn ("Peter stumbling block and Satan," *NovT* 15 [1973] 187-90) has tried to show. Cf. T. Weeden's observation that "Mark accentuates the suffering role of Jesus through the motif of the disciple's misconception of messiahship," *Traditions in Conflict* (1971) 52.

20. Matthew adds here the phrase, "you are a hindrance to me" (Mt 16.23) which increases the tension. See Origen, *Commentary on Matthew*, Tom. 12, 23, GCS Origen Vol. 10, 120-21. Damalas 3.90.

21. Chrysostom comments: "Jesus did not say, 'Satan has spoken through you,' but 'Get behind me, Satan!' because it was Satan's desire that Christ should not suffer. This is the reason why Christ rebuked him so sternly, since he knew that Peter and the other disciples were afraid of the passion and they would not easily accept it. So he reveals what was in Peter's mind, saying, 'you are not on the side of God, but of men' . . . You think that suffering is inappropriate for me. But I am saying to you that the idea that I should not suffer comes from the mind of Satan," *Homilies on Matthew*, Homily 54, PG 58.536-37. Cf. Theophylact 576: "The Lord shows that his passion will be for the salvation (of humankind), and that only Satan does not want Christ to suffer and die, so that humanity will not be saved."

22. As W. Wrede remarks, "Jesus did not merely have to suffer; he has to will to suffer," *The Messianic Secret* (1971) 89.

23. For a select bibliography on Mk 8.34-9.1, see M. Horstmann, *Studien zur markinischen Christologie* (1969) 34-71; G. Schwartz, "Aparnesastho heauton," *NovT* 17 (1975) 109-12; E. Best, "An Early Sayings Collection," *NovT* 18 (1976) 1-16; M. Künzi, *Das Naherwartungslogion Markus 9,1* par. (Tübingen, 1977); B. D. Chilton, *God in Strength* (1979) 251-74; W. A. Beardslee, "Saving One's Life by Losing it,' *JAAR* 47 (1979) 57-72; K. Brower,

"Mk 9,1: Seeing the Kingdom in Power," *JSNT* 6 (1980) 17-41; J. Schlosser, *Le règne de Dieu* (1980) 323-50; B. Lindars, "Jesus as Advocate: A Contribution to the Christology Debate," *BJRL* 62 (1980) 476-97; E. Nardoni, "A Redactional Interpretation of Mk 9,1," *CBQ* 43 (1981) 365-84; J. J. Kilgallen, "Mk 9,1, the Conclusion of a Pericope," *Biblica* 63 (1982) 81-83.

24. See Pesch 2, 60; Gnilka 2, 23, 27; and Schmithals 1, 391. The last one, however, proposes some other possible interpretations.

25. Cf. Klostermann 84 and Nineham 227-28.

26. See Victor 349: "You must, therefore, be lined up for a constant death."

27. R. Tannehill, "The Gospel of Mark as narrative Christology," *Semeia* 16 (1979) 73-74, has already pointed out that in Mk 8.34-38 the language used was "almost the same language" which "was used in the call of the first disciples." It is obvious that this is a language of supreme authority.

28. As W. Marxsen, *Mark the Evangelist* (1969) 127-29, has shown the phrase καὶ τοῦ εὐαγγελίου can be equivalent to the phrase ἕνεκεν ἐμοῦ, but in all possibility it is mainly a phrase interpretative and emphatic of the ἕνεκεν ἐμοῦ.

29. For the significance of the passage Mk 8.38 in the early Christian tradition see Haenchen 298-99.

30. In Mk 8.38, "the Son of man" is most likely Jesus. Cf. Mt 16.27; Victor 351; M. Hooker, *The Son of Man* (1967) 121; and Taylor 382-84. The last author, however, insists also on the difference between the two titles-names. Gnilka 2, 26-28, on the contrary, argues that in Mk 8.38 the identity Jesus-Son of man attracts in addition also the title Son of God. Cf. Schmithals 1, 395; Lane 310-11; and M. Horstmann, *Studien* (1969) 40-41, 50-54.

31. For the particular relationship between the christological motifs of the passion, the resurrection, the cross, and the eschatological coming in the unit Mk 8.27-9.1, see D. A. Koch, "Zum Verhältnis von Christologie und Eschatologie im Markusevangelium," *Christus in Historie und Christologie*, Festschr. Conzelmann, ed. G. Strecker (Tübingen, 1975) 395-408.

32. Origen relates Mk 9.1 to the transfiguration: "Some (i.e. exegetes) say that the words, 'there are some standing here who will not taste death before they see that the kingdom of God has come with power,' refer to the ascent after six days of Jesus with the three disciples up on a high mountain. For the three disciples having seen Jesus being transfigured before them . . . they have seen the kingdom of God coming with power," *Commentary on Matthew*, Tom. 12, 31, GCS Origen Vol. 10, 136-37. Origen, however, offers in addition other exegetical options for Mk 9.1. Exegetical suggestions relative to the one offered by Origen above, see in Chrysostom, PG 58.549; Victor 351-52; Theophylact 577; Lane 313; Schmithals 1, 397; and Montague 104-05. See also the pertinent discussion in J. Karavidopoulos, "The Beginnings of Ecclesiology in the Gospel of Mark," *ΕΕΘΣΠΘ* 17 (1972) 58-69. E. Nardoni, "A Redactional Interpretation," 384, suggests that Mk 9.1 is related both to the eschatological parousia of Mk 8.38 and to the transfiguration of Mk 9.2-8.

33. See Theophylact 577, Damalas 3.105, Nineham 231, and M. Horstmann, *Studien* (1969) 67-69. In his analysis of Mk 9.1, A. Ambrozic, *The Hidden Kingdom* (1972) 203-40, prefers the connection of this verse with the passage 8.27-38 and not with the passage 9.2-8, and thinks that the emphasis lies on the passion idea.

34. For a select bibliography on Mk 9.2-8, see M. Horstmann, *Studien zur markinischen Christologie* (1969) 72-103; J. M. Nützel, *Die Verklärungserzählung im Markusevangelium* (Würzburg, 1973); U. B. Müller, "Die christologische Absicht des Markusevangeliums und die Verklärungsgeschichte," *ZNW* 64 (1973) 159-93; F. R. McCurley, Jr., "And after six days," *JBL* 93 (1974) 67-81; B. Trémel, "Des récits apocalyptiques: Baptême et Transfiguration," *LV* 23 (1974) 70-83; R. H. Stein, "Is the Transfiguration a Misplaced Resurrection-Account?," *JBL* 95 (1976) 79-96; A. Fuchs, "Die Verklärungserzählung des Mk-Ev in der Sicht moderner Exegese," *TPQ* 125 (1977) 29-37; C. R. Kazmierski, *Jesus the Son of God* (1979) 105-26; H. J. Steichele, *Der leidende Sohn Gottes* (1980) 161-92; E. L. Schnellbächer, "Καὶ μετὰ ἡμέρας ἕξ (Mk 9.2)," *ZNW* 71 (1980) 252-57; B. D. Chilton, "The Transfiguration: Dominical Assurance and Apostolic Vision," *NTS* 27 (1980) 115-24.

35. See more in F. R. McCurley, Jr., "And after six days," 73-81 and in E. Schnellbächer, "Καὶ μετὰ ἡμέρας ἕξ," 257, who relates the phrase "and after six days" to the passion and the resurrection.

36. The two events are the resurrection of the daughter of Jairus (Mk 5.35-43) and the prayer at Gethsemane (Mk 14.33-42). In the last case the verb used is παραλαμβάνει, namely, the very same verb used in Mk 9.2. Cf. M. Horstmann, *Studien* (1969) 83-85.

37. E.g. six days, mountain, cloud. See B. D. Chilton, "The Transfiguration," 120-23. For the uniqueness of the theophany described in Mk 9.2-8 see Lohmeyer 177-81.

38. The observation is valid regardless of the general theories related to the event of the transfiguration. If the transfiguration is a variation of one of the appearances of the Risen Lord, or if it is a theophanic event which happened when and where Mark places it, the result in terms of Christology of authority does not change drastically. Cf. R. Stein, "Is the Transfiguration Misplaced?," 90-96; B. D. Chilton, "The Transfiguration," 119-24.

39. Matthew describes the radiation of the transformed face with the phrase, "his face shone like the sun" (Mt 17.2); cf. Lk 9.29. The omission of the face in the narrative of Mark is perhaps the result of a copyist's oversight. Cf. Taylor 389. Schmithals 2, 402 ascribes the omission to theological factors.

40. The indescribable whiteness is presented with the unusual phrase, "white (i.e. the garments of Jesus), as no fuller on earth could bleach them" (Mk 9.3). This phrase, according to Taylor 389 and Nineham 237, implies the heavenly origen of the glistening whiteness. Cf. Pesch 2, 73 and Gnilka 2, 33.

41. See Origen, *Commentary on Matthew*, Tom. 12, 38, GCS Origen

Vol. 10, 155, Chrysostom, *Homilies on Matthew,* Homily 56, PG 58.549, Victor 353-54, Theophylact 581, and Nineham 234-35. An analytical presentation of the pertinent opinions see in J. Nützel, *Die Verklärungserzählung im Markusevangelium* (1973) 113-22. For the unique significance of Elijah and Moses in the transfiguration narrative see M. E. Thrall, "Elijah and Moses in Mark's Account of the Transfiguration," *NTS* 16 (1970) 305-17.

42. E.g. Mk 4.41, 5.15, 5.33, 6.50. See M. Horstmann, *Studien* (1969) 81-83, for a discussion of the relevant passages. Horstmann suggests that in Mark the fear of the disciples is a dominant motif with christological significance, because it appears as a response to some glorious revelation of Jesus.

43. As Taylor 391 remarks, the fear implied in the phrase, "they were exceedingly afraid," (ἔκφοβοι ἐγένοντο), "is supernatural awe rather than fright." Pesch 2, 76 characterizes here the fear as theophanic fear or awe (Epiphanie-Furcht). Gnilka 2, 35 on the contrary speaks of human faint-heartedness.

44. Chrysostom observes here: "Why did the voice came out of the cloud? Because this is the way God always appears: 'Clouds and thick darkness are round about him' (Ps 97.2); 'The Lord is riding on a swift cloud' (Is 19.1); 'who makes the clouds thy chariot' (Ps 104.3); 'and a cloud took him out of their sight' (Acts 1.9); and 'like a Son of man coming on the clouds' (a possible conflation of two Septuagint variants of Dan 7.13). The voice comes from the cloud so that they believe that this is the voice of God . . . When he wants to issue a threatening warning, the cloud appears dark as in the case of Moses (Ex 19.16, 20.21) . . . Here, however (i.e. in the transfiguration) the cloud is luminous, because God did not want to create fear but to teach . . . There (i.e. on Sinai) smoke and vapor of the furnace; here light ineffable . . . " (*Homilies on Matthew,* Homily 56, PG 58.553). Cf. Victor 356 and Trembelas 158.

45. As W. Kelber, *Mark's Story of Jesus* (1979) 54 notes, in the declaration of Mk 9.7 crucial identifications of Jesus are involved which have been given already in the section Mk 1.1-9.1. Jesus is "figure of power over evil and death, founder of the new community, man of suffering and death, victor over death who will come at some future time."

46. For the particular significance of the phrase "listen to him" (Mk 9.7), see the insightful observations of M. Horstmann, *Studien* (1969) 88-90, who considers the divine declaration of v. 7 as the highest point of the transfiguration pericope and as the epitome of its christological meaning.

47. Nineham 234 notes that "what was vouchsafed to the three disciples was a glimpse of Jesus in that final state of Lordship and glory to which he would eventually be exalted."

48. Origen notes characteristically: Jesus "appeared to them (i.e. the three disciples) in 'the form of God' in which he was from the beginning; thus to the ones who were in the low levels (τοῖς κάτω) he appeared having the 'form of a servant,' whereas to the ones who followed him up on the high mountain he appeared having the 'form of God' " (*Commentary on Matthew,* Tom. 12, 37, GCS Origen Vol. 10, 152.

49. Victor 356: "Listen to him that he must suffer, that he must share with men death" (κοινωνῆσαι ἀνθρώποις θανάτου). Cf. Achtemeier 130 and Montague 107. U. B. Müller, "Die christologische Absicht," 175-76, 180-81, 190-93, even suggests that the reason of the existence of the transfiguration pericope at this point is the connection of the injuction "listen to him" with the predictions of the passion. Cf. H. Weinacht, *Die Menschwerdung* (1972) 60; R. Lightfoot, *The Gospel Message* (1950) 43-44; and C. F. Evans, *The Beginning of the Gospel* (1968) 73.

50. See Damalas 3.125-27 and M. Horstmann, *Studien* (1969) 101-03. It should be noted, however, that the transfiguration discloses much more than the confession of Peter and as W. Kelber, *The Kingdom in Mark* (1974) 84-85, convincingly argues, it constitutes "the true scene of recognition."

51. For a select bibliography on Mk 9.9-13, see M. Horstmann, *Studien zur markinischen Chrstologie* (1969) 106-36; P. Vassiliadis, "The Function of John the Baptist in Q and in Mark," Θεολογία 46 (1975) 405-13; H. J. Steichelle, *Der leidende Sohn Gottes* (1980) 81-108; E. Best, *Following Jesus* (1981) 62-65; M. M. Faierstein, "Why do the Scribes say that Elijah must come first?," *JBL* 100 (1981) 75-86.

52. Cf. Theophylact 581. The connection has a special significance from the viewpoint of the Christology of passion, because, the way it occurs in Mk 9.9-10, it incorporates the two motifs of the "Messianic secret" and of the "disciples' unperceptiveness.' " Cf. M. Horstmann, *Studien* (1969) 109-13, 133-34.

53. The element of martyrdom-passion is significant for the understanding of the role of John the Baptist in Mark's Gospel. See P. Vassiliadis, "The Function of John," 409-10. Cf. Victor 357-58 and Theophylact 584.

54. See Damalas 3.124, M. Horstmann, *Studien* (1969) 134-36. At any event, the two basic concepts of the passion and of the vindication of the Son of man remain co-existing, as M. Hooker, *The Son of Man* (1967) 133, plausibly argues.

55. For a select bibliography on Mk 9.14-29, see. W. Schenk, "Tradition und Redaktion in der Epileptiker-Perikope Mk. 9,14-29," *ZNW* 63 (1972) 76-94; P. J. Achtemeier, "Miracles and the Historical Jesus: A Study of Mk. 9,14-29," *CBQ* 37 (1975) 471-91; F. G. Lang, "Sola Gratia in Markusevangelium," *Rechtfertigung*, Fests. E. Käsemann (Tübingen, 1976) 321-37; G. Petzke, "Die historische Frage nach den Wundertaten Jesu," *NTS* 22 (1976) 180-204; H. Aichinger, "Zur Traditionsgeschichte der Epileptiker-Perikope," *SNTU* 3 (1978) 114-43; B. Standaert, *L'Évangile selon Marc* (1978) 140-48; M. G. Steinhauser, "Healing Stories in the Gospel," *Liturgy* 25 (1980) 27-30.

56. The exegetes mention characteristically the passage Ex 32-33. See Nineham 245 and Gnilka 2, 47.

57. The center of gravity of the narrative seems to lie on the person of the Messiah and his power rather than on the disciples and their inability to perform miracles, as P. Achtemeier, "Miracles," 478, contends. Cf. G. Petzke, Die historische Frage," 186-98.

58. In all probability expressions of amazement followed the miracle, as it is shown in the parallel pericope of Luke (Lk 9.43). But here Mark indicates that the amazement occurred before the miracle, and this is christologically significant.

59. Theophylact 584-85 offers an interesting comment: "Some exegetes say that the face of Jesus became more beautifull on account of the light of the transfiguration, and this fact attracted the crowd which ran and greeted him." Cf. Zigabenos 68; Klostermann 90; Taylor 396; and Schweizer 187.

60. The other Synoptics in the parallel pericopes are brief, Mt 17.14-20 and Lk 9.37-42.

61. Cf. Schweizer 189 and Pesch 2, 91. The supernatural, divine power is emphasized in the order given by Jesus to the evil spirit, as Severian of Gabala remarks: "The Lord did not say I give you an order (παραγγέλλω, but I (emphatic) command you (ἐγώ σοὶ ἐπιτάσσω). The order (παράγγελμα) belongs to the servant, the command and authority (τὸ ἐξουσιάζειν) to the Lord," *Sermons on the Creation of the World,* Sermon 4, 7; PG 56.466.

62. See Schweizer 189; Pesch 2, 97, Montague 111; and B. Standaert, *L'Évangile selon Marc* (1978) 145-46. Lohmeyer 189 detects here elements of a theophanic narrative.

63. From that point of view, the contention by F. C. Lang, "Sola Gratia," 328 that in Mk 9.14-29 the main subject is the faith of the believers and not the healing authority and power of Jesus, seems not to render adequately and accurately the meaning of the pericope. Cf. W. Schenk, "Tradition und Redaktion," 94.

64. For a select bibliography on Mk 9.30-32, see N. Perrin, "The Use of (παρα) διδόναι in Connection with the the Passion of Jesus in the N.T.," *Der Ruf Jesu,* Fests. J. Jeremias (Göttingen, 1970) 204-12; J. Brière, "Le Fils de l'homme livré aux hommes," *AsSeign* 56 (1974) 42-52; and E. Best, *Following Jesus* (1981) 73-74.

65. Already ancient exegetes have noticed the continuous alternation between the christological concepts. Victor 362, for instance, remarks: "When he (Jesus) speaks about his passion, he proceeds immediately to perform a miracle; and he does so both before and after the words referring to the passion. We encounter this phenomenon in many instances." Cf. Theophylact 588.

66. See N. Perrin, "The use of (παρα)διδόναι," passim. Cf. Taylor 403 and Schweizer 190.

67. See Klostermann 93 and Pesch 2, 99-101. Origen in this case makes a clear-cut distinction in regard to the meaning of the verb παραδίδοσθαι. He vigorously argues that the meaning is not the same when the verb is used for the Son in relation to the Father, and when it is used for the Son in relation to the hostile powers and Judas, *Commentary on Matthew*, Tom. 13, 8, GCS Origen Vol. 10, 202.

68. See Trembelas 166; Nineham 249; and Schweizer 190.

69. For a select bibliography on Mk 9.33-50, see J. D. M. Derrett, "Salted with Fire," *Theology* 76 (1973) 364-68; J. Karavidopoulos, "Two Collections of Jesus' Sayings in the Gospel of Mark," *ΕΕΘΣΠΘ* 20 (1975) 89-120; (in Greek);

H. Koester, "Mark 9,43-47 and Quintilian 8.3.75," *HTR* 71 (1978) 151-53; H. R. Weber, *Jesus and the Children* (Atlanta, 1979) 34-51; J. I. H. McDonald, "Mk. 9,33-50: Catechetics in Mark's Gospel," *SB 1978* 2 (Sheffield, 1980) 171-77; H. Fleddermann, "The Discipleship Discourse, Mk. 9,33-50," *CBQ* 43 (1981) 57-75; E. Best, *Following Jesus* (1981) 75-98; and D. Wenham, "A Note on Mark 9,33-42," *JSNT* 14 (1982) 113-18.

70. See the relevant discussion in Nineham 250-51 and Pesch 2, 101-02. H. Fleddermann, "The Discipleship Discourse," 73-75 at the end of his careful analysis concludes that the sayings in Mk 9.33-50 display a strong and substantial connection among themselves. Similar is the conclusion of J. Karavidopoulos, "Two Collections of Jesus' Sayings," 101-03, 120.

71. Variations of the same declaration have been preserved in Mt 18.1-5; Mt 23.11; Lk 9.46-48; and Lk 22.26-27. The variety of terminology shows the frequency and the significance of the declaration in the life of the early Church.

72. This question was important for the Jewish people of the New Testament times. See Billerbeck 1, 249-50, 773.

73. H. Fleddermann, "The Discipleship Discourse," 74 even argues that the ending of the pericope Mk 9.33-50 is in Mk 10.45.

74. See H. Fleddermann, "The Discipleship Discourse," 61-64 and J. Karavidopoulos, "Two Collections of Jesus' Sayings," 106-07.

75. The phrase "ἐν τῷ ὀνόματι" or "ἐπὶ τῷ ὀνόματι" seems to connect this pericope with the immediately preceding one. Apparently what we encounter here is a catchword technique. Cf. Nineham 253 and Montague 113.

76. Cf. H. C. Kee, *Community of the New Age* (1977) 140.

77. The phrase "you bear the name of Christ" (ἐν ὀνόματι ὅτι Χριστοῦ ἐστε) in particular, seems to belong to a rather advanced Christology of authority. Cf. 1 Cor 3.23. See Taylor 408 and Pesch 2, 111. Schmithals 2, 432 relates the above phrase to the martyrdom. For the differences between Mk 9.41 and its parallel Mt 10.42 see Damalas 2.810. The differences appear to indicate the christological emphasis in Mark.

78. Cf. J. Karavidopoulos, "Two Collections of Jesus' Sayings," 112-13, 116-18.

79. The remark holds true also for the last two verses of the pericope, i.e. Mk 9.49-50, because these verses have as chief meaning the meaning of sacrifice, as J. Karavidopoulos, "Two Collections of Jesus' Sayings," 116-19, has shown.

80. Cf. Victor 367; Schweizer 197-98; and Pesch 2, 114.

81. For a select bibliography on Mk 10.1-12, see E. Bammel, "Markus 10,11f. und das jüdische Eherecht," *ZNW* 61 (1970) 95-101; K. Berger, "Hartherzigkeit und Gottes Gesetz," *ZNW* 61 (1970) 1-47; T. A. Burkill, "Two into One," *ZNW* 62 (1971) 115-20; D. R. Catchpole, "The Synoptic Divorce Material as a Traditio-Historical Problem," *BJRL* 57 (1974) 92-127; J. Delorme, "Le mariage, les enfants et les disciples de Jésus," *AsSeign* 58 (1974) 42-51; R. H. Stein, 'Is it Lawful for a Man to Divorce his Wife?,'' *JETS* 22 (1979) 115-21; A. J. Hultgren, *Jesus and His Adversaries* (1979) 119-22; J. R. Mueller, "The Temple Scroll and the Gospel Divorce Texts,"

RevQ 10 (1980) 247-56; E. Best, *Following Jesus* (1981) 99-105; and B. Brooten, "Konnten Frauen im alten Judentum die Scheidung betreiben?," *ET* 42 (1982) 65-80.

82. This pericope presents considerable exegetical problems related to the topic of the divorce. We do not deal with them here, since they do not seem to affect the christological discussion.

83. Cf. Taylor 415, 417, and Montague 116.

84. Deut 24.1: "When a man takes a wife and marries her, if then she finds no favor in his eyes because he has found some indecency in her, and he writes her a bill of divorce and puts it in her hand and sends her out of his house . . . "

85. Christ develops his teaching on the basis of the passages Gen 1.27 and 2.24.

86. Here a substantial theological interpretation of the marriage is presented founded on the concept of man's creation. See the relevant discussion in Gnilka 2, 73-74, 76-78. Cf. Schmithals 2, 439-40 and Montague 116.

87. For a select bibliography on Mk 10.13-16, see A. Ambrozic, *The Hidden Kingdom* (1972) 136-58; J. I. H. McDonald, "Receiving and Entering the Kingdom," *SE* (T.U. 112. Berlin, 1973) 328-32; R. Péter, "L'imposition des mains dans l'Ancient Testament," *VT* 27 (1977) 48-55; H. R. Weber, *Jesus and the Children* (1979) 14-33; B. Vrijdaghs, "Werden wie Kinder . . . ," *Der Evangelische Erzieher* 32 (Frankfurt, 1980) 170-81; J. Schlosser, *Le règne de Dieu* (1980) 477-92; and J. Sauer, "Der ursprüngliche Sitz im Leben von Mk. 10,13-16," *ZNW* 72 (1981) 27-50.

88. Cf. Schweizer 207 and Schmithals. 2, 445-48.

89. Origen observes here: "The power of Jesus touches the children by simply putting the hands of his authority on them, and thus no evil touches them anymore. Perhaps this was also the purpose of those who offered the children or the babies to Jesus thinking that if Jesus touches them and through the contact imparts power to them, then no evil thing or demons can touch them," *Commentary on Matthew,* Tom. 15, 6, GCS Origen Vol. 10, 364-65. Cf. Theophylact 597; Klostermann 100; Haenchen 344; and Schweizer 206.

90. See Victor 375-76; Lagrange 263; and Pesch 2, 132.

91. The passage Mk 10.14 is the only passage in the New Testament where the strong verb ἀγανακτεῖν (to be indignant) is being used for Jesus. Cf. Taylor 422-23; Nineham 267; and Gnilka 2, 80. Some exegetes suggest that the passage Mk 10.14 makes a hint at the question of the baptism of the children, e.g. Schmithals 2, 445-46 and Montague 117.

92. See Schweizer 206; Pesch 2, 133; and A. Ambrozic, *The Hidden Kingdom* (1972) 153.

93. For a select bibliography on Mk 10.17-27, see E. P. Sanders, "Mark 10,17-31 and Parallels," *SBLMeeting 1971,* 1, 257-70; R. Köbert, "Kamel und Schiffstau," *Biblica* 53 (1972) 229-33; P. J. Riga, "Poverty as Counsel and as Precept," *BT* 65 (1973) 1123-28; J. Galot, "Le fondement évangélique du voeu religieux de pauvreté," *Gregorianum* 56 (1975) 441-67; M. L.

O'Hara, "Jesus' Reflections on a Psalm," *BT* 90 (1977) 1237-40; W. Egger, *Nachfolge als Weg zum Leben* (Klosterneuburg, 1979); J. Schlosser, *Le règne de Dieu* (1980) 541-57; E. Best, *Following Jesus* (1981) 110-19; and S. R. Boguslawski, "The Discipleship of the Young Man," *BT* 19 (1981) 234-39.

94. The most important are the ones related to Mk 10.18. See the discussion in Taylor 426-27; Pesch 2, 138; and Gnilka 2, 86. Cf. Origen, *Commentary on Matthew*, Tom. 15, 10, GCS Origen Vol. 10, 374-77.

95. E.g. the kneeling of the rich man and the address used by him (Mk 10.17), the tone of Jesus' answer in Mk 10.18, the amazement of the disciples (Mk 10.24).

96. See Taylor 429.

97. Cf. Schweizer 212; Gnilka 2, 87; and Schmithals 2, 453-54.

98. See Schweizer 210-11.

99. For a select bibliography on Mk 10.28-31, see S. Légasse, "Tout quitter pour suivre le Christ," *AsSeign* 59 (1974) 43-54; G. Theissen, "Wir haben alles verlassen," *NovT* 19 (1977) 161-96; D. Malone, "Riches and discipleship," *BTB* 9 (1979) 78-88.

100. See Lagange 272-73.

101. For a select bibliography on Mk 10.32-34, see N. Perrin, "Towards an Interpretation of the Gospel of Mark," *Christology and a Modern Pilgrimage*, ed. H. D. Betz (SBL, 1973[2]) 14-30; R. McKinnis, "An Analysis of Mark 10,32-34," *NovT* 18 (1976) 81-100; E. Best, *Following Jesus* (1981) 120-22.

102. See the detailed analysis of the christological data contained in Mk 10.32 in R. McKinnis, "An Analysis of Mark 10,32-34," 82-88.

103. Mark reports only the ascent of Jesus to Jerusalem which coincides with his passion.

104. See the elaborate discussion in Pesch 2, 150-52.

105. The verb "will be delivered" (παραδοθήσεται) here again as in Mk 9.31, has no agent from the grammatical standpoint. In discussing Mk 9.31 we noticed that this grammatical phenomenon facilitates the projection of the idea of a complex divine plan to which the passion of the Messiah belongs. Cf. Haenchen 361; Gnilka 2, 97; and N. Perrin, "Towards an Interpretation," 23-24, 28-30.

106. In the first prediction (Mk 8.31) the verb "to be delivered" is missing, and in the second (Mk 9.31) the words "chief priests" and "scribes" are missing.

107. In the first two passion predictions (Mk 8.31 and 9.31) only the verb to kill (ἀποκτείνειν) is being used in order to describe the entire process and the final outcome. In the third prediction the relevant terminology is more elaborate.

108. In the passage Mk 8.31 we encounter only the general expression "to suffer many things" (πολλὰ παθεῖν), and in Mk 9.31 the even more general expression "to be delivered into the hands of men" (παραδίδοται εἰς χεῖρας ἀνθρώπων).

109. Matthew in the parallel pericope used the verb "to crucify" (σταυ-ρῶσαι) instead of the verb "to kill" (ἀποκτενοῦσιν) (Mt 20.19).

110. Victor 383 notes: "Jesus offers this prediction of the passion to the disciples, so that they know that he suffered with a full awareness of it in advance, and not in ignorance, and that he went to the passion deliberately and not unwillingly. This is why he spoke frequently about his passion, as Mark points out." Cf. Theophylact 604-05; Zigabenos 80; Lagrange 275; Taylor 437; and Gnilka 2, 97.

111. Cf. Mk 8.31 and 9.31 where we encounter the same declaration of the resurrection at the end of the passion prediction.

112. The fullness and the precision of the passion formulations in Mk 10.33-34, the specificity of the language and syntax, and the articulation of the christological concepts, has led to the hypothesis that here we have an ancient christological hymn created on the basis of the passion events. See more in R. McKinnis, "An Analysis of Mark 10,32-34," 98-100.

113. For a select bibliography on Mk 10.35-45, see A. Feuillet, "La coupe et le baptême de la Passion," *RB* 74 (1967) 356-91; C. K. Barrett, *New Testament Essays* (London, 1972) 20-27; J. Roloff, "Anfänge der soteriologischen Deutung des Todes Jesu," *NTS* 19 (1972) 38-64; S. Légasse, "Approche de l'épisode préévangelique des Fils de Zébédée," *NTS* 20 (1974) 161-77; J. Rademakers, "Revendiquer ou servir?," *AsSeign* 60 (1975) 28-39; V. Howard, "Did Jesus Speak about His Own Death?," *CBQ* 39 (1977) 515-27; W. J. Moulder, "The Old Testament Background and the Interpretation of Mk. 10,45," *NTS* (1977) 120-27; and E. Best, *Following Jesus* (1981) 123-33.

114. Cf. Trembelas 196-97; Nineham 278; Schweizer 220; and Montague 123.

115. See Is 51.17; 51.22; Ps 75.8; 69.1-3; Lam 4.21. Cf. Theophylact 605; Schweizer 220-21; and Pesch 2, 156-58. However, as A. Feuillet, "La coupe et le baptême de la Passion," 371-90 pointed out, Jesus uses here the data from the Old Testament in a way of absolute authority, freedom, and reinterpretation of the original images, symbols, and concepts.

116. E.g. Lk 12.50 and Rom 6.1-5. Cf. Origen, *Commentary on Matthew*, Tom. 16, 2, GCS Origen Vol. 10, 483.

117. The theory that the present tense here (πίνω, βαπτίζομαι) is the result of the influence of an Aramaic original which does not distinguish between present and future, is not persuasive. In the immediately following v. 39 the very same verbs are being used with a clear-cut differentiation between present and future tense.

118. Here we deal with a statement which is not so much a *vaticinium ex eventu* (Klostermann 121; Pesch 2, 159) related to James and John, as it is a general principle which the Messiah proclaims. Cf. S. Légasse, "Approche de l'épisode," 176-77.

119. Some exegetes discern in Mk 10.42-44 even an ironic hint, particularly in the phrase "who are supposed to rule" (οἱ δοκοῦντες ἄρχειν).

120. The declaration of Jesus concerning this topic is absolute. Cf. Taylor 443; Schweizer 223; and Schmithals 2, 465.

121. See the interesting comment on Mk 10.45 by Theophylact 608, based not only on the Christology of passion but also on the Christology of authority.

122. For the particular connection between the motif of the redeeming passion and the motif of diakonia or service in Mk 10.45; see J. Roloff, "Anfänge der soteriologischen Deutung," 50-55, W. J. Moulder, "The Old Testament Background," 126-27; W. Schenk, *Der Passionsbericht* (1974) 275-76; A. Higgins, *Jesus* (1964) 36-50; and M. Hooker, *The Son of Man* (1967) 140-47.

123. See 1 Cor 9.19; 2 Cor 4.5; and Gal 5.13.

124. The specific theological nuance of the expression "in your glory" (ἐν τῇ δόξῃ σου) may vary, depending on the particular exegetical approach, but the basic meaning remains the same, namely, the meaning of a supreme authority. Cf. Taylor 440 and Pesch 2, 155.

125. For a select bibliography on Mk 10.46-52, see A. Paul, "Guérison de Bartimée," *AsSeign* 61 (1972) 44-52; V. K. Robbins, "The Healing of Blind Bartimaeus in the Markan Theology," *JBL* 92 (1973) 224-43; E. S. Johnson, Jr., "Mark 10,46-52: Blind Bartimaeus," *CBQ* 40 (1978) 191-204; B. Standaert, L'Évangile selon Marc (1978) 119-25; P. J. Achtemeier, "And he followed him: Miracles and Discipleship in Mark 10,46-52," *Semeia* 11 (1978) 115-42; J. A. Mirro, "Bartimaeus: The Miraculous Cure," *BT* 20 (1982) 221-25.

126. See Klostermann 109; Lagrange 285; Lohmeyer 225; Trembelas 203; Taylor 448; Schweizer 224; Nineham 282; Gnilka 2, 110; Montague 125-27; E. Johnson Jr., "Mk 10:46-52," 195-97, and C. F. Evans, *The Beginning of the Gospel* (1968) 35-36.

127. See Mk 1.24; 3.11; 5.7; and 8.29.

128. In view of the exegetical data of the pericope, the arguments advanced by P. Achtemeier, "And he followed him," 125-31, against the christological significance of the term "Son of David" in Mk 10.47-48, are not convincing.

129. See Victor 388. Cf. Nineham 282; Haenchen 372; Pesch 2, 172; and Gnilka 2, 112.

130. See B. Standaert, *L'Évangile selon Marc* (1978) 120-24, for the concrete correlations between the present pericope and the narratives that follow.

131. See the perceptive analysis by V. Robbins, "The Healing of Blind Bartemaeus," in 227-36, 241-43, and his observations related to the term "Son of David," in Mk 10.47.

132. Cf. E. Johnson, Jr., "Mk 10:46-52," 198-204 and P. Achtemeier, "And he followed him," 132-33, 135.

133. D. O. Via, on the basis of his structuralistic analysis of the present pericope within its immediate context (Mk 10.32-52), offers the interesting hypothesis that Mark believes in the repeated eschatological opportunities which can lead to the overcoming of the spiritual blindness and to the understanding of the real identity of Christ, "Mark 10:32-52: A Structural . . . Interpretation," *SBL 1979 Seminar Papers*, ed. P. Achtemeier, (Missoula, 1979) 2, 200.

CHAPTER THREE
THE FULFILLMENT OF THE PASSION
IN THE LIGHT OF AUTHORITY (MARK 11.1-16.20)

1. For a select bibliography on Mk 11.1-11, see J. D. M. Derrett, "Law in the New Testament: the Palm Sunday Colt," *NovT* 13 (1971) 241-58; A. Paul, "L'entrée de Jésus à Jérusalem," *AsSeign* 19 (1971) 4-26; A. Ambrozic, *The Hidden Kingdom* (1972) 32-44; J. D. Crossan, "Redaction and Citation in Mk. 11,9-10,17 and 14,27," *BR* 17 (1972) 33-50; W. Schenk, *Der Passionsbericht* (1974) 166-75; R. Bartnicki, "Il carattere messianico delle pericopi di Marco e Matteo sull'ingresso di Gesù in Gerusalemme," *RivB* 25 (1977) 5-27.

2. This could be surmised from the connection of the directions given by Jesus (Mk 11.2) to Old Testament Messianic prophecies, from the entry hymns, and from the whole event of the entry. Cf. Victor 389; Theophylact 609; Klostermann 113; Taylor 451-52; Schweizer 227, 229; Pesch 2, 187-88; Lane 395; Montague 129; and Lightfoot, *The Gospel Message* (1950) 12.

3. Schweizer 228 and Gnilka 2, 117 support the first option whereas Lagrange 289 the second.

4. Cf. Mk 2.2, 2.15, 3.10, 5.9, 6.31, 9.26, 12.5, and 14.56.

5. See, for instance, Mt 21.8-9; Lk 19.37-39; and Jn 12.12.

6. See also the expressions in John 12.18-19, "the crowd went to meet him," and "look, the world has gone after him," which underline the intensity of the impression.

7. Lk 19.38; Jn 12.13; Mt 21.9. Cf. Nineham 296.

8. Victor 390 comments on this specific expression probably because he detects its particularity. He does not seem, nonetheless, to see its special christological significance. A. Ambrozic, *The Hidden Kingdom* (1972) 39, 42-44, in spite of his careful analysis, does not appear to ascribe any particular meaning to Mk 11.10 as far as the intentions of the Evangelist are concerned.

9. R. Bartnicki, "Il carattere messianico," 5-27 argues precisely that the usage of the term kingdom (βασιλεία) instead of the term king (βασιλεὺς) in Mk 11.10, is the result of Mark's intention not to project at this point the person of the Messiah in an intense way.

10. This explanation seems to be more satisfactory than the theory of the Messianic secret (Nineham 292) which at this point of the Gospel is less plausible. Cf. Achtemeier 162 and Gnilka 2, 119.

11. For a select bibliography on Mk 11.12-14, 20-25, see R. H. Hiers, "Not the Season for Figs," *JBL* 87 (1968) 394-400; J. G. Kahn, "La parabole du figuier stérile et les arbres récalcitrants de la Genèse," *NovT* 13 (1971) 38-45; K. Romaniuk, "Car ce n'était pas la saison des figues," *ZNW* 66 (1975) 275-78; J. T. Wright, "Amos and the Sycamore Fig," *VT* 26 (1976) 362-68; J. C. Meagher, *Clumsy Construction in Mark's Gospel* (1979) 64-67; G. Biguzzi, "Mc. 11,23-25 e il Pater," *RivB* 27 (1979) 57-68; C. A. Wanamaker, "Mark 11,25 and the Gospel of Matthew," *SB* 1978 2 (Sheffield, 1980) 329-37.

12. For a select bibliography on Mk 11.15-18, see R. H. Lightfoot, *The Gospel Message* (1950) 60-69; R. H. Hiers, "Purification of the Temple: Preparation for the Kingdom of God," *JBL* 90 (1971) 82-90; N. M. Flanagan, "Mark and the Temple Cleansing," *BT* 63 (1972) 980-84; J. M. Ford, "Money Bags in the Temple," *Biblica* 57 (1976) 249-53; J. Jeremias, "Ein Widerspruch zur Pericope von der Tempelreinigung?," *NTS* 23 (1976) 179-80; J. D. M. Derrett, "The Zeal of the House and the Cleansing of the Temple," *DR* 95 (1977) 79-94.

13. Several ancient interpreters have detected another form of Jesus' authority disclosed in the episode of the withered fig tree. Victor 391 writes: "it was necessary that Jesus showed evidence of his punishing power, so that the Jews learn that he could wither them but he does not. On the contrary he forgives them willingly." Isidore of Pelusium notes: " . . . in order to show to the ungrateful Jews that he (i.e. Jesus) has the power necessary for punishment . . . and for retribution, but he does not decide such a thing because he is good," *Epistle 51 to Theopompios,* PG 78.213. See also Theophylact 613 and Zigabenos 85. For the eschatological nuances of the episode see W. Kelber, *The Kingdom in Mark* (1974) 100, 105, W. Schenk, *Der Passionsbericht* (1974) 158-66.

14. The comment by Chrysostom is characteristic: "He (i.e. Jesus) did not perform the miracle to any other tree but to the one which is more juicy than all, so that the miracle would be recognized as greater. And he did this for the disciples. How do we know? Because he said to them, 'you will do greater (miracles) if you want to believe and to rely on prayer.' You see that he did everything for them, so that they should not be afraid of the threatening plots . . . ," *Homilies on Matthew,* Homily 67, PG 58.634.

15. See R. Martin, *Mark* (1972) 110.

16. Cf. Theophylact 613-16; Damalas 3.303; Lagrange 298-99; Schweizer 230-31; and Gnilka 2, 125-26. Victor 391-93 offers an interesting selection of symbolic interpretations of the fig-tree episode.

17. The observation is valid even if the judgment has no specific application to the Jewish people but to any people who present an abundance of leaves and an absence of fruits.

18. See Schweizer 233, Schmithals 2, 491-95. R. H. Lightfoot, *The Gospel Message* (1950) 60 notes: "The cleansing (of the Temple) is according to Saint Mark the great act of the Lord as the messianic king on his arrival at His Father's house."

19. Cf. Nineham 301: "Jesus' action is therefore seen as that of the messianic king on his great final visit to his Father's house and people, and, as such, it embodies God's *ultimate* judgment upon the life and religion of Israel." According to Achtemeier 164-65, this judgment connects directly the event of the withered tree to the event of the cleansing of the Temple which interpret each other.

20. R. H. Hiers, "Purification of the Temple," 83-90, suggests that the cleansing of the Temple is directly related to the establishment of the kingdom of God. This suggestion underlines the supreme authority of Jesus. R. H. Lightfoot, *The Gospel Message* (1950) 64-65, relates the cleansing of

the Temple to the new position of the Gentiles in the worship of the true God.

21. For a select bibliography on Mk 11.27-33, see J. Kremer, "Jesu Antwort auf die Frage nach seine Vollmacht," *BibLeb* 9 (1968) 128-36; R. Schnackenburg, "Die Vollmacht Jesu," *KG* 27 (1971) 105-09; G. S. Shae, "The Question on the Authority of Jesus," *NovT* 16 (1974) 1-29; and A. J. Hultgren, *Jesus and His Adversaries* (1979) 68-74.

22. It is likely that the high priests, the elders, and the scribes raise the question of authority following orders of the Sanhedrin; cf. Nineham 306-07; Haenchen 393; Pesch 2, 210; and Achtemeier 167-68. At any rate they are its de facto representatives. See Taylor 469 and Schweizer 237.

23. There is a possibility that the phrase "doing these things" (Mk 11.28) is a reference to the cleansing of the Temple (Mk 11.15-17). See G. S. Shae, "The Question on the Authority," 25-29. In addition to that it could also be a reference to the teaching of Jesus as we could deduce from the parallels in Matthew (Mt 21.23) and in Luke (Lk 20.1-2).

24. Origen notes: "The chief priests and the elders of the people . . . saw that Jesus performed mighty works with a particular authority that he had. Therefore they wanted to know from Jesus the kind and qualities of that authority," *Commentary on Matthew,* Tom. 17, 2, GCS Origen Vol. 10, 581.

25. The main part of Jesus' answer is given in the form of a counter-question, something that was customary in the discussions among the rabbis.

26. See G. S. Shae, "The Question on the Authority," 28-29; Taylor 470-71; Nineham 306-07; and Schmithals 2, 509-11.

27. As Pesch 2, 211 notes here, Jesus' authority is "the authority of the eschatological Prophet." Damalas 3.313 draws attention to the fact that Jesus does not answer the "we do not know" of the Pharisees with a phrase like "I do not know either," but with the statement "Neither do I say to you." The changing of the verb implies the big difference of authority.

28. For a select bibliography on Mk 12.1-12, see M. Hengel, "Das Gleichnis von den Weingärtnern Mk. 12,1-12 . . . ," *ZNW* 59 (1968) 1-39; H. J. Klauck, "Das Gleichnis vom Mord im Weinberg," *BibLeb* 11 (1970) 118-45; J. D. Crossan, "The Parable of the Wicked Husbandmen," *JBL* 90 (1971) 451-65; J. D. M. Derrett, "Allegory and the Wicked Vinedressers," *JTS* 25 (1974) 426-32; K. R. Snodgrass, "The Parable of the Wicked Husbandmen," *NTS* 21 (1974) 142-44; B. Dehandschutter, "La parabole des vignerons homicides et l'évangile selon Thomas," *L'évangile selon Marc,* ed. M. Sabbe (1974) 203-19; and C. R. Kazmierski, *Jesus the Son of God* (1979) 127-38.

29. This parable has a color of allegory (according to Lagrange 305, it is a parable-allegory) and has caused numerous discussions among the exegetes. Cf. Klostermann 120-21; Taylor 472-73; Nineham 309-11; Pesch 2, 214; and Gnilka 2, 142-44.

30. The servants of the parable are in all likelihood the prophets of the Old Testament. Cf. Amos 3.7: "his servants the prophets"; Zech 1.6: "I commanded my servants the prophets." See Victor 399; Theophylact 621; Klostermann 121; Taylor 474; and Pesch 2, 216.

31. See Victor 400; Theophylact 621; Nineham 310; and Schweizer 241.

32. In Mk 12.8, in addition to the information "they took him and killed him" we read that "they cast him out of the vineyard" which probably means that they left him unburied, Trembelas 223 and Taylor 475. This emphasizes the wickedness of the tenants, Schweizer 241, and Pesch 2, 220.

33. Cf. Nineham 310, and Pesch 2, 217.

34. The formulation in Mark is clearly more emphatic (12.6: ἔτι ἕνα εἶχεν υἱὸν ἀγαπητὸν) than the parallels in Matthew (21.37: τὸν υἱὸν αὐτοῦ) and in Luke (20.13: τὸν υἱόν μου τὸν ἀγαπητόν).

35. Taylor 475 recognizes the messianic significance of the term υἱὸς ἀγαπητός; he has doubts, however, for such a significance in the passage Mk 12.6. Theophylact 621; Swete 269; Pesch 2, 218, 223; Gnilka 2, 146-47, on the contrary, discern a messianic meaning in the term υἱὸς of the same passage. Schmithals 2, 513, 523, and Montague 138-39 accept a messianic meaning but with certain qualifications.

36. M. Hengel, "Das Gleichnis von den Weingärtnern," 38-39, contends that the parable aims at presenting the definitive condemnation of the religious leaders of Israel by Jesus who acts with the authority of God.

37. For a select bibliography on Mk 12.13-17, see C. H. Giblin, "The Things of God in the Question concerning Tribute to Caesar," *CBQ* 33 (1971) 510-27; A. Stock, "Render to Caesar," *BT* 62 (1972) 929-34; W. J. Bennett, Jr., "The Herodians of Mark's Gospel," *NovT* 17 (1975) 9-14; H. Jason, "Der Zinsgroschen: Analyse der Erzählstruktur," *LingB* 41-42 (1977) 49-87; E. Güttgemanns, "Narrative Analyse des Streitgesprächs über den Zinsgroschen," *LingB* 41-42 (1977) 88-105; A. B. Ogle, "What is left for Caesar?," *TToday* 35 (1978) 254-64; A. J. Hultgren, *Jesus and His Adversaries* (1979) 41-44, 75-80; and J. R. Donahue, "A Neglected Factor in the Theology of Mark," *JBL* 101 (1982) 572-75.

38. In our analysis of Mk 3.6, the strong enmity between the Pharisees and the Herodians was pointed out. Hence their alliance against Jesus acquires a special meaning.

39. Matthew in his parallel uses the verb παγιδεύσωσιν (to entrap, Mt 22.15), whereas Luke is even more clear: "so that they take hold of what he said and thus deliver him up to the authority and jurisdiction of the governor" (Lk 20.20).

40. The κῆνσος (census) was a personal tax hated by the Jewish people, because it reminded them of their subjugation to the Romans, and because it was paid with coins which had the name and picture of Caesar. See Haenchen 406-08.

41. Victor 401: "So the Pharisees and the Herodians, having been amazed at Jesus' word which was not susceptible to catch, left the scene." A. B. Ogle, "What is left for Caesar?," 254-64, even thinks that the chief meaning of the pericope is the authority of God expressed by Jesus.

42. For a select bibliography on Mk 12.18-27, see G. Baumbach, "Das Sadduzäerveständnis bei Josephus Flavius und im N.T.," *Kairos* 23 (1971) 17-37; A. Ammassari, "Gesù ha veramente insegnato la risurrezione?," *BO* 15 (1973) 65-73; A. J. Hultgren, *Jesus and His Adversaries* (1979) 123-30;

J. R. Donahue, "A Neglected Factor in the Theology of Mark," *JBL* 101 (1982) 575-78; and F. G. Downing, "The Resurrection of the Dead: Jesus and Philo," *JSNT* 15 (1982) 42-50.

43. The Sadducees were an aristocratic priestly party, from which normally the chief priests were selected, hence they possessed plenty of power (cf. Acts 5.17). For the origin of their name, and for their ideas see *TDNT*, 7, 35-54.

44. According to Gnilka 2, 161, the ultimate reference of the theme of the resurrection is the resurrection of Jesus, and this is the reason why Mark has included the present pericope in his narrative.

45. Taylor 480, 484. Cf. Pesch 2, 229. For the significance of the teaching about the resurrection as it is presented here, and for its difference from the contemporary apocalyptic ideas see Schmithals 2, 535-37.

46. For a select bibliography on Mk 12.28-34, see M. Miguens, "Amour, alpha et oméga de l'existence," *AsSeign* 62 (1970) 53-62; R. H. Fuller, "Das Doppelgebot der Liebe," *Jesus Christus in Historie und Theologie*, Festsch. Conzelmann, ed. Strecker (Tübingen, 1975) 317-29; W. Diezinger, "Zum Liebesgebot Mk. 12,28-34 par.," *NovT* 20 (1978) 81-83; and J. R. Donahue, "A Neglected Factor in the Theology of Mark,'" *JBL* 101 (1982) 578-81.

47. The parallel pericopes in Matthew (Mt 22.34-40) and in Luke (Lk 10.25-28) are much shorter and introduce the discussion in a different way.

48. "There is no other instance in the Gospels where a teacher of the law is found agreeing with Jesus," Schweizer 252.

49. Various exegetes have observed that in Mk 12.34 Jesus is projected not only as a teacher but as Lord with supreme authority. Cf. Taylor 490 and Schweizer 253.

50. For a select bibliography on Mk 12.35-37, see G. Schneider, "Die Davidssohnfrage (Mk 12,35-37)," *Biblica* 53 (1972) 65-90; F. Neugebauer, "Die Davidssohnfrage und der Menschensohn," *NTS* 21 (1974) 81-108; F. J. Moloney, "The Targum on Ps. 8 and the New Testament," *Salesianum* 37 (1975) 326-36; B. Moriconi, "Chi è Gesù? Mc. 12,35-37 momento culminante di rivelazione," *EC* 30 (1979) 23-51; and B. Chilton, "Jesus ben David," *JSNT* 14 (1982) 88-112.

51. The phrase "David himself inspired by the Holy Spirit declared" (Mk 12.36), denotes a solemn declaration of the divine truth, as it happened with the prophets of the Old Testament when they spoke in the place of God. Cf. Klostermann 129; Lagrange 326; Pesch 2, 253 and Schmithals 2, 548.

52. Cf. Nineham 329-30; Achtemeier 178; and Schmithals 2, 548-49.

53. Cf. Mt 9.27, 12.35, 15.22, 20.30; Mk 10.47; Lk 18.38; Jn 7.42. One could add that the title "son of David" was a Christological title for the early Church (Mt 1.1; Rom 1.3). For the messianic ideas inherent or expressed in Mk 12.35-37, see F. Neugebauer, "Die Davidssohnfrage," 82-90, 101-08.

54. Chrysostom comments here: "Because he (i.e. Jesus) was going towards the passion, he brings in the prophecy which declares him to be the Lord . . . He asked them before and they did not offer the right answer. They said that he was merely a man. He then contradicts their erroneous opinions by having David proclaiming his divinity. They thought that he

was merely a man, hence they said that he was son of David. He, however, corrects their error by having David the prophet witnessing to the fact that he (i.e. Jesus) possesses the lordship, and the genuine sonship, and the equal honor to the Father," *Homilies on Matthew*, Homily 71, PG 58.663. Cf. Taylor 492-93; Haenchen 415; Pesch 2, 253-55; Lane 437-38; and Gnilka 2, 171-72.

55. Cf. G. Schneider, "Die Davidssohnfrage," 89-90. B. Moriconi, "Chi è Gesù," 23-51, argues that the question of Jesus about David and Christ implies that he is in essence the Son of God.

56. This is apparent in the relevant New Testament formulations such as Jn 1.1-14; Phil 2.6-11; and Heb 1.1-11.

57. For a select bibliography on Mk 12.38-40, see P. Ternant, "La dévotion contrefaite," *AsSeign* 63 (1971) 53-63; J. D. M. Derrett, "Eating up the Houses of Widows," *NovT* 14 (1972) 1-9; H. Fleddermann, "A Warning about the Scribes," *CBQ* 44 (1982) 52-67.

58. The transgressions and sins mentioned in Mk 12.38-40 were considered by the Jews as serious and punishable by God (Taylor 495; cf. Jas 3.1), but Jesus' statement reveals a personal eschatological judgment. Cf. Pesch 2, 257, 260.

59. For a select bibliography on Mk 12.41-44, see L. Simon, "Le sou de la veuve," *ETR* 44 (1969) 115-26; G. M. Lee, "The Story of the Widow's Mite," *ExpTim* 82 (1971) 344; J. Jeremias, "Zwei Miszellen . . . ," *NTS* 23 (1977) 177-80; B. Standaert, *L'Évangile selon Marc* (1978) 149-52; and A. G. Wright, "The Widow's Mite," *CBQ* 44 (1982) 256-65.

60. See Schweizer 259. Cf. Isidore of Pelusium, *Epistle 193, to Neilos*, PG 78.1281: " . . . The Judge did not count what she put to the treasury, but he crowned her disposition which dedicated her entire fortune."

61. See B. Standaert, *L'Évangile selon Marc* (1978) 151; Nineham 335; and Achtemeier 180-81.

62. For a select bibliography on Mk 13, see R. Lightfoot, *The Gospel Message* (1950) 48-59; W. Marxsen, *Mark the Evangelist* (1969) 151-206; L. Hartman, *Prophecy Interpreted* (Lund, 1966); R. Pesch, *Naherwartungen* (Düsseldorf, 1968); C. B. Cousar, "Eschatology and Mark's Theologia Crucis," *Interpretation* 24 (1970) 136-54; F. Flückiger, "Die Redaktion der Zukunftsrede in Mk. 13," *TZ* 26 (1970) 395-409; T. Weeden, *Mark: Traditions in Conflict* (Philadelphia, 1971) 70-100; K. Grayston, "The Study of Mark 13," BJRL 56 (1974) 371-87; W. Kelber, *The Kingdom in Mark* (Philadelphia, 1974) 109-28; K. Tagawa, "Marc 13," *FoiVie* 76 (1977) 11-44; A. Feuillet, "La signification fondamentale de Mc. 13," *RT* 80 (1980) 181-215; and F. Nierynck, *Evangelica* (1982) 565-608.

63. An analysis of the pertinent material in Mk 13 with an emphasis on the Christology of passion, see in C. B. Cousar, "Eschatology and Mark's Theologia Crucis," 136-54.

64. For a select bibliography on Mk 13.1-2, see N. Walter, "Tempelzerstörung und synoptische Apocalypse," *ZNW* 57 (1966) 38-48; J. Dupont, "Il n'en sera laissé pierre sur pierre," *Bilica* 52 (1971) 301-20; B. Reicke, "Synoptic Prophecies on the Destruction of Jerusalem,' *Studies in New*

Testament and Early Christian Literature, Festschr. A. P. Wikgren, ed.
D. E. Aune (Leiden, 1972) 121-34.

65. E.g. Mic 3.12; Jer 26.18 (= LXX 36.18). See examples from non-canonical Jewish texts in Klostermann 132 and Schweizer 267.

66. For a discussion on this question and on the question of the eschatological contents of Mk 13.2, see N. Walter, "Tempelzerstörung," 38-45. Cf. Nineham 344; Schweizer 267; Gnilka 2, 182; and Schmithals 2, 558.

67. For a select bibliography on Mk 13.3-13, see J.W. Thompson, "The Gentile Mission as an Eschatological Necessity," *RQ* 14 (1971) 18-27; A. Satake, "Das Leiden der Jünger um meinetwillen," *ZNW* 67 (1976) 4-19; J. Dupont, "La persécution comme situation missionaire," *Die Kirche des Anfangs*, Festschr. H. Schürmann, ed. R. Schnackenburg (Freiburg, 1978) 97-114; G. Hallbäck, "Der anonyme Plan," *LinguB* 49 (1981) 38-53.

68. W. Marxsen, *Mark the Evangelist* (1969) 188-89, comments characteristically that the affliction (θλῖψις) in Mark 13 has a "theological and eschatological content. The community endures the θλῖψις of its Lord."

69. See L. Hartmann, *Prophecy Interpreted* (1966) 71-101 for the language in Mk 13.7-8 and its relationship to the language of the apocalyptic texts.

70. Attention should be drawn to the fact that the verb "to deliver up" (παραδιδόναι) occurs three times in the pericope Mk 13.3-13 (vv. 9, 11, and 12).

71. Cf. Pesch 2, 288 and Gnilka 2, 190.

72. This idea appears clearer in the Lukan parallel: "I will give you a mouth and wisdom, which none of your adversaries will be able to withstand or contradict" (Lk 21.15).

73. See Pesch 2, 287. Cf. Theophylact 636; Lohmeyer 272; and Lane 464. It should be noted that the sacrifice-martyrdom does not happen only for Jesus' sake but also for the sake of the promotion of the Gospel, as J. Dupont, "La persécution," 111-12 has shown.

74. For a select bibliography on Mk 13.14-23, see M. Simon, "La migration à Pella. Legende ou réalité?," *RSR* 60 (1972) 37-54; V. K. Robbins, "Dynameis and Semeia in Mark," *BR* 18 (1973) 5-20; F. Dexinger, "Ein Messianisches Szenarium als Gemeingut des Judentums in nachherodianischer Zeit," *Kairos* 17 (1975) 249-78; W. D. Dennison, "Miracles as Signs," *BTB* 6 (1976) 190-202; and D. Ford, *The Abomination of Desolation in Biblical Eschatology* (Washington, D.C., 1979).

75. The phrase "the sacrilege of desolation" (τὸ βδέλυγμα τῆς ἐρημώσεως) has been used in the Old Testament (Dan 12.11, 1 Mac 1.54) with a reference to the profanation of the Temple. For its plausible interpretations in Mk 13.14 see Victor 410-11; Taylor 511; L. Hartman, *Prophecy Interpreted* (1966) 151-54; and W. Marxsen, *Mark the Evangelist* (1969) 179-82, 185-86.

76. The passage Mk 13.22 has been rightly viewed as a parallel to the passage 2 Thes 2.8-9, in which the element of the Antichrist is more pronounced. Such a way to look at Mk 13.22 is more convincing than the one proposed by T. Weeden, *Mark: Traditions in Conflict* (1971) 98, according to which here we have to do with Christians who believe and preach a "theios aner" Christology. Cf. L. Hartman, *Prophecy Interpreted* (1966) 195-205, and W. Marxsen, *Mark the Evangelist* (1969) 185-86.

77. W. Kelber, "Mark and Oral Tradition," *Semeia* 16 (1979) 40-46, has tried to demonstrate the decisive role that the appearance and activities of the "false prophets" (Mk 13.22) has played in the origin and formation of the Gospel of Mark. Kelber's theory contains elements and observations worth discussing, and in certain way corroborate our own christological observations on Mk 13.14-23, but as a whole it is a debatable theory.

78. Cf. Gnilka 2, 198-99.

79. For a select bibliography on Mk 13.24-27, see L. Hartmann, "La Parousie du Fils de l'homme (Mc. 13,24-32)," *AsSeign* 64 (1969) 47-57; T. J. Weeden, *Mark: Traditions in Conflict* (1971) 126-37; O. F. J. Seitz, "The Future Coming of the Son of Man," *SE* 6 (Berlin, 1973) 478-94; L. Sabourin, "The Biblical Cloud," *BTB* 4 (1974) 290-311; and G. Hallbäck, "Der anonyme Plan," *LinguB* 49 (1981) 38-53.

80. See Is 13.10, 34.4; Zech 2.10; Ezek 32.7; Dan 7.13; 1 Enoch 80.4-7; 4 Ezra 5.4 et al. Cf. Billerbeck 1, 955-60.

81. Cf. Damalas 3.495, Trembelas 252-53. Victor 413 observes "And immediately Christ will come and the creation will be transformed. The sun will be darkened not by way of its elimination but because of its defeat by the light of Christ's presence. The stars will be falling. What is the use of them when night will be no more?"

82. L. Hartmann, *Prophecy Interpreted* (1966) 157 notes: "It is in keeping with the fact that there the Son of Man appears in place of God that the celestial phaenomena which accompany this appearance are associated in the Old Testament with theophanies on the Day of Yahweh." Cf. G. Schille, *Offen für alle Menschen* (1974) 25-26.

83. Victor 413: "The angels belong to God, and their being sent out is a prerogative of God." Cf. Theophylact 640: "Do you see that the Son sends out the angels like the Father does?"

84. Pesch 2, 304 makes the right observation that the existence of one, common subject for the verbs ἀποστελεῖ (he will send out) and ἐπισυνάξει (he will gather) underlines the supremacy and excellence of the Son of Man.

85. Judged from that point of view, the contention by Taylor 517, that in Mk 13.24-27 there are no traces of eschatological judgment, seems at least excessive. Cf. Pesch 2, 302; Gnilka 2, 201-02; and G. Schille, *Offen für alle Menschen* (1974) 24-27.

86. Taylor 518 remarks that "in Mark (Mk 13.26) the description is that of a superhuman person invested with divine authority and clothed with heavenly light. His divine origin is suggested . . . " Cf. Gnilka 2, 201 (" . . . heavenly, divine Being").

87. Cf. Mk 8.38, 10.37, 14.62.

88. As Gnilka 2, 202 states, this Son of Man in Mk 13.24-27 "is identified with Jesus of Nazareth," and does not constitute another supernatural being. Cf. Montague 158 and M. Hooker, *The Son of Man* (1967) 157-58.

89. This does not mean that Mark 13 is related only to chs. 14 and 15 which follow. Mark 13 has an essential christological connection with the 12 chapters that preceded. Cf. W. Kelber, *The Kingdom in Mark* (1974) 110, 126-28.

90. For a select bibliography on Mk 13.28-37, see J. Dupont, "La parabole du figuier qui bourgeonne," *RB* 75 (1968) 526-48; J. Winandy, "Le logion de l'ignorance," *RB* 75 (1968) 63-79; A. Weiser, "Von der Predigt Jesu zur Erwartung der Parusie," *BibLeb* 12 (1971) 25-31; R. Bauckam, "Synoptic Parousia Parables and the Apocalypse," *NTS* 23 (1976) 162-76; M. Künzi, *Das Naherwartungslogion* (1977); D. Peabody, "A Pre-Markan Prophetic Sayings Tradition and the Synoptic Problem," *JBL* 97 (1978) 391-409; C. R. Kazmierski, *Jesus the Son of God* (1979) 139-50.

91. W. Marxsen, *Mark the Evangelist* (1969) 187-88, makes a persuasive association between the imperatives in Mk 13.33-37 and the imperatives in Mk 1.15. In both cases we encounter declarations which reveal a divine authority.

92. The expression "to all" (πᾶσιν) could be a reference to all the readers of the Gospel (Taylor 524), or to all the believers in general, Swete 319; Pesch 2, 316; and Montague 159.

93. As Lane 480 suggests here, "this claim of high dignity of Jesus' words implies a christological affirmation: what is said of God in the Old Testament may be equally affirmed of Jesus and his word. The prophecy developed on Olivet (Mk 13.30-31) will surely come to pass."

94. E.g., Jn 5.47, 6.63, 14.10, 17.8. Cf. Mt 5.18.

95. See the pertinent discussions in Taylor 522-23; Pesch 2, 309-10; and J. Winandy, "Le logion de l'ignorance," 63-79. For an anthological presentation of the relevant patristic interpretations, see Trembelas 255-56.

96. According to the excellent formulation by Athanasios of Alexandria, "He (i.e. Christ) as Logos knows, but as man (ἄνθρωπος) ignores. It is appropriate (ἴδιον) for man to ignore, and all the more such things," *Against the Arians*, Discourse 3, 43, PG 26.413f. Similarly Cyril of Alexandria, *Letter to Euoptios Against Theodoret*, Anath. 4, PG 76.412: "Therefore the ignorance is not that of the God Logos but of the 'form of the servant,' who at that time knew as much as the indwelling Divinity (ἐνοικοῦσα Θεότης) has revealed to him." Chrysostom in this instance proposes an interpretation of pastoral nature, *Homilies on Matthew*, Homily 77, PG 58.703. Cf. Trembelas 255-56.

97. The organic continuity between Mk 14-16 and Mk 1-13 is so obvious that the hypothesis by E. Trocmé, *The Formation of the Gospel according to Mark* (1975) 215-59, that the Gospel of Mark is the result of a synthesis of two different texts (i.e. Mk 1-13 and Mk 14-16) cannot be persuasively defended.

98. This and the parallel case in Mt 26.4 are the only instances where the term δόλος (stealth) is used in the Gospels with reference to the passion. The only other passage in Mark (7.22) in which the word δόλος occurs belongs to an ethical context.

99. Cf. Pesch 2, 319 and Montague 160.

100. For a discussion concerning the date of the passion, and for a recent bibliography on this topic, see Pesch 2, 323-28.

101. For a select bibliography on Mk 14.3-9, see J. Delobel, "L'onction par la pécheresse," *ETL* 42 (1966) 417-75; L. Schenke, *Studien zur Passionsgeschichte des Markus* (Würzburg, 1971) 67-118; H. Schlier, *Die Markuspassion* (Einsiedeln, 1974) 11-21; J. K. Elliot, "The Anointing of Jesus," *ExpTim* 84 (1974) 105-07; W. Schenk, *Der Passionsbericht nach Markus* (Gütersloh, 1974) 175-80; E. E. Platt, "The Ministry of Mary of Bethany," *TToday* 34 (1977) 29-39; D. Dormeyer, *Der Sinn des Leidens Jesu* (Stuttgart, 1979) 34-48; and C. Schedl, "Die Salbung Jesu in Bethanien," *BLit* 54 (1981) 151-62.

102. Cf. Pesch 2, 328, 331. Schmithals 2, 589-90, argues that Mark has placed the anointing episode at this point of the narrative in order to gain one day in the passion week. The argument does not seem to be convincing.

103. In Mark's text there is no mentioning of the disciples; in the parallel, however, Matthean passage the disciples are explicitly mentioned (Mt 26.8).

104. Pesch 2, 333-35 argues that in Mk 14.7 the contrast is between "you always have" and "you will not always have," and not between Jesus and the poor, and consequently that here Jesus is portrayed as the poor (cf Ps 41), a fact that implies ideas of passion Christology. Cf. Gnilka 2, 224-25.

105. Cf. Schweizer 289-91.

106. For a select bibliography on Mk 14.10-11, see L. Schenke, *Studien zur Passionsgeschichte* (1971) 119-40; W. Schenk, *Der Passionsbericht* (1974) 143-50; L. P. Trudinger, "Davidic Links with the Betrayal of Jesus," *ExpTim* 86 (1975) 278-79; and D. Dormeyer, *Der Sinn des Leidens Jesu* (1979) 34-48.

107. It should be noted that the verb παραδιδόναι (to deliver up) occurs also in the passion predictions (Mk 9.31 and 10.33), and, therefore, could be considered as a basic technical term related to the killing of the Messiah.

108. The dryness of the information does not mean an absence of pain. The phrase "one of the twelve" is indicative of the inherent deep sorrow. Chrysostom draws attention to another significanct aspect when he writes: "The Evangelists, as you see, do not hide anything even from things considered the most shameful. They could have said simply 'one of his disciples' . . . but now they add 'of the twelve' as if they wanted to say of the highest group, of the outstandingly selected, of the ones who were with Peter and John. The Evangelists were interested in one thing, namely, the truth alone, not on covering up the events. This is the reason why they bypass many of the miracles, but they do not conceal anything considered shameful, be it a word, a thing, or anything else, which they proclaim with frankness," *Homilies on Matthew*, Homily 80, PG 58.727.

109. See Mt 26.15: "What will you give me, if I deliver him to you?," and Lk 22.3: "Then Satan entered into Judas called Iscariot . . . he went away and conferred with the chief priests."

110. For a select bibliography on Mk 14.12-16, see L. Schenke, *Studien zur Passionsgeschichte* (1971) 152-98; H. Schlier, *Die Markuspassion* (1974) 22-36; W. Schenk, *Der Passionsbericht* (1974) 182-85; and V. K. Robbins, "Last Meal: Preparation, Betrayal and Absence," *The Passion in Mark*, ed. W. H. Kelber (Philadelphia, 1976) 21-40.

111. Jesus' foreknowledge in Mk 14.13-16 has been compared with that in Mk 11.1-6 on account of a number of word similarities. The two cases, however, are totally different in terms of events, although they have the same meaning in terms of the amazing foreknowledge of Jesus. Cf. V. K. Robbins, "Last Meal," 27.

112. Schweizer 297 speaks here about "the miraculous foreknowledge of Jesus" and explains that "the miracle consists in the precise prediction of what follows." Cf. Nineham 376 ("supernatural foresight").

113. Also in Luke (22.7-14), and less in Matthew (26.17-18) who has shortened the narrative.

114. Chrysostom notes: "Why Jesus sends the disciples to an unknown person? In order to show through that event that he had the power not to suffer. He was able to speak to the mind of an unknown person so that he would receive the disciples . . . What then could he (i.e. Jesus) have done to those who crucified him, if he wanted not to suffer?," *Homilies on Matthew,* Homily 81, PG 58.730. Cf. Victor 420; Theophylact 648; and Gnilka 2, 233.

115. For a select bibliography on Mk 14.17-21, see L. Schenke, *Studien zur Passionsgeschichte* (1971) 199-285; K. Hein, "Judas Iscariot: Key to the Last-Supper Narratives?," *NTS* 17 (1971) 227-32; F. C. Synge, "Mk. 14,18-25: Supper and Rite," *JTSA* 4 (1973) 38-43; W. Schenk, *Der Passionsbericht* (1974) 185-89; V. K. Robbins, "Last Meal," *The Passion in Mark,* ed. Kelber (1976) 21-40; and F. Kermode, *The Genesis of Secrecy* (1980) 84-93.

116. The image of the communion and bond emerges from the three phrases in which the preposition μετά (with) occurs with genitives: μετὰ τῶν δώδεκα (with the twelve), μετ' ἐμοῦ (with me) (vv. 17, 18, 20).

117. This is a characteristic verb in the Gospel of John (8.21-22, 13.3, 13.33-36, 16.5, 16.10). Cf. Lohmeyer 301-02.

118. This is already known from Mk 9.12, "How it is written of the Son of man that he should suffer many things . . . "

119. Taylor 539 characterizes the pericope Mk 14.17-21 as "a little more than a prophecy in a narrative setting."

120. The verb ὑπάγει (he goes) suggests the idea of a deliberate and conscious march towards the passion. Cf. Victor 421: "this word interprets the voluntary."

121. For a select bibliography on Mk 14.22-25, see N. A. Beck, "The Last Supper as an Efficacious Symbolic Act," *JBL* 89 (1970) 192-98; L. Schenke, *Studien zur Passionsgeschichte* (1971) 286-347; J. Jeremias, "This is my Body . . . ," *ExpTim* 83 (1972) 196-203; D. Palmer, "Defining a Vow of Abstinence," *Colloquium* 5 (1973) 38-41; D. Flusser, "The Last Supper and the Essenes," *Immanuel* 2 (1973) 23-27; W. Schenk, *Der Passionsbericht* (1974) 189-93; V. K. Robbins, "Last Meal," *The Passion in Mark,* ed. Kelber (1976) 21-40; H. Merklin, "Erwägungen zur Überlieferungsgeschichte der neutestamentlichen Abendmahlstraditionen," *BZ* 21 (1977) 88-101; R. Pesch, *Das Abendmahl und Jesus Todesverständnis* (Freiburg, 1978); D. Peabody, "A Pre-Markan Prophetic Sayings Tradition and the Synoptic Problem," *JBL* 97 (1978) 391-409; J. Schlosser, *Le règne de Dieu*

dans les dits de Jésus (Paris, 1980) 374-98; R. J. Daly, "The Eucharist and Redemption," *BTB* 11 (1981) 21-27; and X. Léon-Dufour, "Prenez! Ceci est mon corps," *NRT* 104 (1982) 223-40.

122. The passage Mk 14.22-25 presents the exegetes with problems of text and interpretation which lie outside the scope of the present study. Long discussion of the pertinent opinions and recent bibliography, see in Pesch 2, 364-77.

123. Schweizer 300 notes here: "The style is terse, listing only the words and actions that have liturgical importance, in a manner which is almost ceremonious."

124. For the variant readings of Mk 14.24, see Nestle-Aland, ed. 26 (1979).

125. Victor 423: "When he says 'my blood . . . which is poured out for many,' he speaks about all, because many are all." Cf. Trembelas 269; E. C. Maloney, *Semitic Interference in Markan Syntax* (Chico, 1981) 57-58, 139-42; C. Schedl, "Fragen zur revidierten Einheitsübersetzung," *BLit* 54 (1981) 226-28; F. Werner, "Theologie und Philologie," *BLit* 54 (1981) 228-30.

126. See variants in Nestle-Aland, ed. 26 (1979).

127. Cf. Taylor 544 and Nineham 381-82.

128. See Gregory of Nyssa, *The Great Catechetical Oration* 37, PG 45.96-97. Cf. Pesch 2, 361; Gnilka 2, 249; and J. Karavidopoulos, "Beginnings of Ecclesiology in the Gospel of Mark," 81-82.

129. V. K. Robbins, "Last Meal," 27, 34-36, argues that the Eucharist emphasizes the absence rather than the presence of Christ. Such an assumption does not seem to account convincingly for the data of the pericope Mk 14.22-25. The same critique applies to the relative thesis advanced by J. D. Crossan, "A Form of Absence: The Markan Creation of Gospel," *Semeia* 12 (1978) 44-46.

130. See A. Ambrozic, *The Hidden Kingdom* (1972) 189-91, 197-201; Swete 337; Klostermann 148; and Gnilka 2, 246. Victor 424 sees here the resurrection: "He (Jesus) called here the resurrection kingdom of God and Father. From the resurrection the kingdom was given to him, a kingdom shared by the rest of humankind." Cf. Theophylact 652.

131. For a select bibliography on Mk 14.26-31, see M. Wilcox, "The Denial-Sequence in Mk. 14,26-31, 66-72," *NTS* (1971) 426-36; L. Schenke, *Studien zur Passionsgeschichte* (1971) 348-460; R. H. Stein, "A short Note on Mk. 14,28 and 16,7," *NTS* 20 (1974) 445-52; R. P. Schroeder, "The Worthless Shepherd. A study of Mk. 14,27," *CurTM* 2 (1975) 342-44; D. Brady, "The Alarm to Peter in Mark's Gospel," *JSNT* 4 (1979) 42-57; and E. Best, *Following Jesus* (Sheffield, 1981) 199-204, 210-13.

132. The text of the prophecy Zech 13.7 seems to follow the Hebrew original. In the Septuagint, the variant from Codex B offers a somehow different reading, whereas the variant from Codex A approximates the Hebrew reading.

133. The variant readings of Mk 14.27 do not affect the basic meaning of this verse.

134. According to M. Wilcox, "The Denial-Sequence," 427-36, the meaning of Mk 14.26-31 in conjunction with Mk 14.66-72 is not the denial by the disciples but the prediction of that denial by Jesus. Cf. Nineham 387 and Haenchen 489.

135. The theory that here the emphasis falls on Galilee as the place of the eschatological parousia of the Messiah (Lohmeyer) is not convincing. The chief point in Mk 14.28 is the resurrection of Christ and the subsequent meeting with the disciples, as R. H. Stein, "A short Note," 447-52, has shown.

136. In Mk 14.28 we observe something similar to what we have seen in Mk 8.31, 9.31, 10.33-34, namely, that the prediction of the passion is accompanied by the prediction of the resurrection. The difference is that in Mk 14.28 the prediction of the resurrection is presented in the first person ("after I am raised up"), hence it becomes more emphatic.

137. For a select bibliography on Mk 14.32-42, see R. S. Barbour, "Gethsemane in the Tradition of the Passion," *NTS* 16 (1970) 231-51; L. Schenke, *Studien zur Passionsgeschichte* (1971) 461-551; W. H. Kelber, "Mark 14,32-42: Gethsemane. Passion Christology and Discipleship Failure," *ZNW* 63 (1972) 166-87; W. Mohn, "Gethsemane," *ZNW* 64 (1973) 194-208; H. Schlier, *Die Markuspassion* (1974) 37-51; W. H. Kelber, "The Hour of the Son of Man and the Temptation of the Disciples," *The Passion in Mark*, ed. Kelber (1976) 41-60; A. Feuilet, *L'agonie de Gethsémane* (Paris, 1977); C. R. Kazmierski, *Jesus the Son of God* (1979) 151-64; and J. Thomas, "La scène du jardin, selon Marc 14,32-42," *Christus* 28 (1981) 350-60.

138. See W. Kelber, "The Hour of the Son of Man," 50-56.

139. Cf. R. Martin, *Mark* (1972) 119-20.

140. The meaning of the phrase περίλυπος . . . ἕως θανάτου is "sorrow which almost kills," or "sorrow so great that death could be preferable," Nineham 391. R. S. Barbour, "Gethsemane in the Tradition of the Passion," 236-38, sees the intensity of the sorrow as a manifestation of the confrontation between the Son of God and the power of the evil.

141. The repetition does not seem to mean a confusion of the sources, or a clumsiness in the narrative technique, but rather a deliberate emphasis on the part of Mark. Victor 427 notes that "to say twice and three times the same thing is for the Scriptures strongly indicative of the truth." Cf. also Chrysostom, *On the Incomprehensible Nature of God*, Homily 7,6, PC 48.766.

142. See Schweizer 310-12, 315; Schmithals 2, 637: "The sorrow is not a preparation for the passion of Jesus, but part of the passion itself. The passion has begun . . . "; W. Kelber, "The Hour of the Son of Man," 52: "At Gethsemane, therefore, Mark's christological explication of the suffering Son of Man has reached a high point . . . Gethsemane summarizes the suffering Son of Man Christology."

143. See Theophylact 653. Cf. Swete 341; Lagrange 387; and Gnilka 2, 259, 264.

144. Cf. Lohmeyer 316-18; Klostermann 149; Schweizer 313-14; and Pesch 2, 392. Schmithals 2, 636 even argues that the antithetical presentation of

Jesus and his disciples constitutes the central point of the narrative, a thesis already proposed by W. Kelber, "The Hour of the Son of Man," 47-50.

145. Luke offers a philanthropic justification of the disciple's sleep: "He (Jesus) found them (the disciples) sleeping for sorrow," (Lk 22.45). Chrysostom remarks: Jesus "speaks to all, reproving them for their weakness. For the people who declared that they were ready to die with Jesus were unable to be with him in his sorrow because they were under the power of sleep," *Homilies on Matthew,* Homily 83, PG 58.745. Cf. Victor 426-27.

146. One of the concepts operative here is the direct and intimate communion between Jesus and the Father, as it is disclosed in the address, "Abba, Father," (Mk 14.36). Cf. Lohmeyer 315-16.

147. See Theophylact 653.

148. As Chrysostom points out, Jesus "taught the disciples through all that happened that the passion was not a matter of necessity nor of weakness, but of ineffable dispensation (οἰκονομία ἀπόρρητος). For he knew that the passion was coming, yet not only did he not leave but he went toward it," *Homilies on Matthew,* Homily 83, PG 58.747. See also Victor 427.

149. For a select bibliography on Mk 14.43-52, see G. Schneider, "Die Verhaftung Jesu," *ZNW* 63 (1972) 188-209; R. Scroggs and K. I. Groff, "Baptism in Mark: Dying and Rising with Christ," *JBL* 92 (1973) 531-48; L. Scenke, *Der gekreuzigte Christus* (Stuttgart, 1974) 111-24; B. Standaert, *L'Évangile selon Marc* (1978) 153-68; F. Neirynck, "La fuite du jeune homme en Mc. 14,51-52," *ETL* 55 (1979) 43-66; H. Fleddermann, "The Flight of a Naked Young Man," *CBQ* 41 (1979) 412-18; and F. Kermode, *The Genesis of Secrecy* (1980) 55-63, 84-93.

150. The phrase "one of the twelve" appears also in the parallel accounts of Matthew (26.47) and Luke (22.47), a fact suggestive of the deep impression left on the memory of the early Church. Cf. Victor 428 and Klostermann 152.

151. Cf. Lk 22.48: "Judas, would you betray the Son of man with a kiss?" As G. Schneider, "Die Verhaftung Jesu," 206-07, shows, Judas' kiss belongs to the very archaic elements of the tradition which lies behind the narrative in Mk 14.43-52.

152. The episode with the young man belongs to the general theme of the flight of the disciples according to G. Schneider, "Die Verhaftung Jesu," 205-06, and to H. Fleddermann, "The Flight of a Naked Young Man," 415-18. Other scholars like R. Scroggs and K. I. Groff, "Baptism in Mark," 533, 544-46, suggest that the episode should be interpreted on the basis of the baptismal theology and praxis of the Early Church. A. Vanhoye, "La fuite du jeune homme nu," *Biblica* 52 (1971) 401-06, argues that the said episode is symbolically related to the burial and the resurrection of Jesus. A combination of all the above mentioned theories has been attempted by B. Standaert, *L'Évangile selon Marc* (1978) 163-67.

153. See Theophylact 657 and Pesch 2, 403.

154. Cf. Victor 429; Theophylact 657; Nineham 394; Pesch 2, 401; Gnilka 2, 273; and Schmithals 2, 646.

155. For a select bibliography on Mk 14.53-65, see G. Schneider, "Gab es eine vorsynoptische Szene Jesus vor dem Synedrium?," *NovT* 12 (1970) 22-39; S. Légasse, "Jésus devant le Sanhédrin," *RTL* 5 (1974) 170-97; L. Schenke, *Der gekreuzigte Christus* (1974) 23-46; G. Theissen, "Die Tempelweissaussagung Jesu," *TZ* 32 (1976) 144-58; J. R. Donahue, "Temple, Trial and Royal Christology," *The Passion in Mark*, ed. Kelber (1976) 61-79; N. Perrin, "The High Priest's Question and Jesus' Answer," *The Passion in Mark*, ed. Kelber (1976) 80-95; P. Lamarche, *Révélation de Dieu* (1976) 105-18; R. Kempthorne, "The Markan Text of Jesus' Answer to the High Priest," *NovT* 19 (1977) 197-208; D. Juel, *Messiah and Temple* (Missoula, 1977); R. T. Fortna, "Jesus and Peter at the High Priest's House," *NTS* 24 (1978) 371-83; O. Genest, *Le Christ de la Passion. Perspective Structurale* (Montreal, 1978) 29-56; D. Dormeyer, *Der Sinn des Leidens Jesu* (1979) 49-61; R. Kazmierski, *Jesus the Son of God* (1979) 165-90; C. Walters, Jr., *I, Mark, a Personal Encounter* (1980) 132-34; R. T. France, "Jésus devant Caïphe," *Hokhma* 15 (1980) 20-35; and D. Lührmann, "Markus 14,55-64: Christologie und Zerstörung des Tempels . . . ," *NTS* 27 (1981) 457-74.

156. A long and detailed discussion on the trial of Jesus and a rich recent bibliography see in Pesch 2, 404-24. Cf. Schmithals 2, 657-69; J. R. Donahue, *Are You the Christ?* (Missoula, 1973); and D. Juel, *Messiah and Temple* (Missoula, 1977) 1-39.

157. D. Lührmann, "Markus 14.55-64," 460, connects the motif of the false witnesses to the motif of the suffering righteous of the Old Testament. Cf. J. R. Donahue, "Temple, Trial and Royal Christology," 66-71.

158. The provocation lies in the distortion of a relevant teaching of Jesus so that he is presented as raising messianic claims. Cf. Swete 356-57 and D. Lührmann, "Markus 14:55-64," 465-69. The theme of the Temple, however, is very significant as D. Juel, *Messiah and Temple* (1977) 117-209, has demonstrated.

159. The question of the high priest, "Are you the Christ?," has a discernible nuance of contempt. Cf. Taylor 567.

160. The "tearing of the garments" is a typical juridical gesture of condemnation according to the Talmud (cf. Billerbeck 1, 1007-08). This, however, does not mean any absence of emotional outburst and intense irritation. Cf. Schweizer 331. Gnilka 2, 282 argues for the opposite. For a detailed discussion on the subject, see D. Juel, *Messiah and Temple* (1977) 95-106.

161. There has been a long debate among the exegetes concerning the question whether or not the declaration by Jesus could be considered a blasphemy according to the prevailing Jewish religious practices. Mark, nonetheless, is very clear on this point, and his witness emphasizes the nature of Christ's passion. Cf. Billerbeck 1, 1008-09; *TDNT* Vol. 1, 623; Taylor 569-70; Schweizer 331; Gnilka 2, 283; and Montague 174-75.

162. Chrysostom characteristically observes: "What could be found equal to that outrage? They were striking and spitting on the face (of Christ) which the sea had respected, from which the sun had turned away its rays out of reverence. They were making the wounds even worst by striking, slapping, and by adding insult to the injuries through spitting. They were using

mocking words . . . Even the servants were treating him with the same drunken violence . . . Those are the things of which I am very proud, not only of the many dead whom He raised but also of the sufferings which He suffered. Those are the things for which Paul is constantly speaking: the cross, the death, the sufferings, the mockery, the insults, the scoffing,'' *Homilies on Matthew,* Homily 85, PG 58.757-58.

163. There are other elements of the authority Christology, but less apparent. One could mention, for instance, the passage Mk 14.65 which constitutes a fulfilment of Jesus' prediction in Mk 10.34, and, therefore, becomes an evidence of his supernatural knowledge.

164. Victor 431: "Jesus declares himself God." W. Wrede, *The Messianic Secret* (1971) 75: "Son of God in a supernatural and metaphysical sense . . . " Cf. Damalas 3.645; Lohmeyer 328-29; Trembelas 285; Schweizer 331; Lane 536-37; Lagrange 402; Taylor 568-69; Gnilka 2, 281-82; and Schmithals 2, 662. See extensive discussion in J. R. Donahue, "Temple, Trial and Royal Christology," 72-79, and N. Perrin, "The High Priest's Question," 81-91.

165. As Victor 430 notes, this has happened so that there would remain no excuse on the part of the Jewish religious leaders that they did not hear Jesus declaring himself the Messiah of God. Cf. P. Lamarche, *Révélation de Dieu* (1976) 109, 115-17.

166. D. Lührmann, "Markus 14:55-64," 462, suggests that the Christology of Mark is the result of a combination of those three titles. Cf. H. C. Kee, *Community of the New Age* (1977) 129. See also the interesting observations by J. R. Donahue, "Temple, Trial and Royal Christology," 71-79, and by D. Juel, *Messiah and Temple* (1977) 77-107.

167. See M. Hooker, *The Son of Man* (1967) 172-73.

168. N. Perrin, "The High Priest's Question," 95, argues that Mk 14.61-62 with its christological ideas "functions both retrospectively and prospectively. Retrospectively it is the climax of the christological concerns of the Evangelist and it marks the formal disclosure of the Messianic Secret. Prospectively, it prepares the way for the christological climax of the centurion's confession, it interprets the crucifixion/resurrection of Jesus as the enthronement/ascension of Jesus as Christ and Son of Man, and it anticipates the parousia.

169. Nineham 399 cites here Dibelius who "rightly describes this as a climax in Mark's passion narrative, and speaks of Jesus' glorious divine status shining out in the midst of all the abasement."

170. For a select bibliography on Mk 14.66-72, see M. Wilcox, "The Denial-Sequence in Mark 14,26-31,66-72," *NTS* 17 (1970) 426-36; G. W. H. Lampe, "St. Peter's Denial," *BJRL* 55 (1973) 346-68; L. Schenke, *Der gekreuzigte Christus* (1974) 15-22; J. Ernst, "Noch einmal: Die Verleugnung Jesu durch Petrus," *Catholica* 30 (1976) 207-26; K. E. Dewey, "Peter's curse and cursed Peter," *The Passion in Mark,* ed. Kelber (1976) 96-114; D. Gewalt, "Die Verleugnung des Petrus," *LinguB* 43 (1978) 113-44; and F. Kermode, *The Genesis of Secrecy* (1980) 115-23.

171. Theophylact 661 notes in addition that Peter was scared by a maid!

172. This is more intense in the description by Mark, as K. E. Dewey, "Peter's curse and cursed Peter," 108-13, has shown.

173. It is not accidental that the event is presented in details by all the Evangelists (Mt 26.69-75, Lk 22.56-62; Jn 18.15-18, and 25-27) as an indispensable part of the passion narrative. See the relevant analysis in Schmithals 2, 652-57 and K. E. Dewey, "Peter's curse and cursed Peter," 96-105, 113-114.

174. See Victor 431-32.

175. For a select bibliography on Mk 15.1-15, see H. Z. Maccoby, "Jesus and Barabbas," *NTS* 16 (1969) 55-60; L. Marin, "Jésus devant Pilate," *Languages* 22 (1971) 51-74; P. Winter, *On the Trial of Jesus* (Studia Judaica 1, Berlin, 1974) 131-43; W. Schenk, *Der Passionsbericht* (1974) 243-50; L. Schenke, *Der gekreuzigte Christus* (1974) 47-52; G. M. Lee, "Mark 8,24. Mark 15,8," *NovT* 20 (1978) 74; O. Genest, *Le Christ de la Passion* (1978) 57-96; and D. Dormeyer, *Der Sinn des Leidens Jesu* (1979) 62-75.

176. As Pesch 2, 455, 461, points out, Jesus here again appears as the suffering righteous. Cf. Schweizer 335.

177. This second official meeting underlines the fact that the decision for the execution of Jesus was not the result of a spontaneous excitement but of a premeditated, cool plot.

178. This is the first time in the Markan narrative when we are informed that "they bound Jesus." The information reveals the magnitude of the involvement of the high priests.

179. The constant use of the verb "to deliver up" (παραδιδόναι) is very impressive in the passion narrative: 7 times in Mk 14, and 3 times in Mk 15.1-15. As the narrative progresses, the verb "to deliver up" becomes christologically more and more intensive.

180. The narration in Mk 15.1-15 implies the responsibility of the Jewish religious authorities. Victor 435 puts it plainly: "The Jews proved themselves to be more impious than a pagan (i.e. Pilate). For Pilate released Jesus from every accusation . . . whereas they intensified their shouts "crucify him.""

181. For the historical aspects of the Barabbas episode, see Taylor 580 and Pesch 2, 461-62. For its theological significance, see Schmithals 2, 674-76.

182. This comparison will remain alive in the memory of the early Church, as it is evidenced from its use by Peter in his speech in Acts 3.13-15. Cf. Victor 435.

183. At any rate Mark seems to indicate that the high priests were decisively responsible for the frenetic animosity of the crowd. See Gnilka 2, 305.

184. See Victor 434-35, Klosterman 161, and Nineham 412. Schmithals 2, 676, on the contrary, thinks that the decision taken by Pilate is in accordance with the existing law.

185. Swete 373 argues that Pilate, by the scourging, aimed at the satisfaction of the crowd so that the crucifixion could be avoided. The argument, however, is not convincing (the passage Lk 23.16 does not verify it). Cf. Victor 435: "Why Pilate having scourged Jesus delivered him to be crucified? He did it because Jesus was already a convict, or because he wanted to put a frame to the decision, or because he wanted to do a favor to the crowd."

186. Taylor 580 and Pesch 2, 458 detect here echoes from Old Testament texts, for instance, from Is 52.15, 53,7; Ps 37 (LXX)13, 14 and 108 (LXX) 2-4. Gnilka 2, 300 believes that the amazement of Pilate suggests the unusual, the divine of Jesus' person. Cf. Trembelas 293.

187. The silence of Jesus with its multifaceted theological meaning has remained deeply imprinted in the memory of the early Church. See Nineham 412 and Schmithals 2, 672-73.

188. Cf. Victor 434; Theophylact 664; Taylor 579; Schweizer 336; and Montague 177.

189. N. Perrin, "The High Priest's Question," 93-94, argues that from Mk 15.1 on, the Evangelist does not lose any opportunity to connect the title "king" with Jesus, because "for Mark the crucifixion narrative is the narrative of the enthronement of Christ as King." Cf. W. Kelber, *Mark's Story of Jesus* (1979) 81-83.

190. For a select bibliography on Mk 15.16-20, see H. Schlier, *Die Markuspassion* (1974) 52-71; P. Winter, *On the Trial of Jesus* (Studia Judaica 1, Berlin 1974) 100-06; W. Schenk, *Der Passionsbericht* (1974) 250-53; L. Schenke, *Der gekreuzigte Christus* (1974) 51-54; and O. Genest, *Le Christ de la Passion* (1978) 123-45.

191. The scoffing scene is so terrible that, as Victor 436 remarks, "it is understandable that the disciples are not present lest they take offense. For what happened is beyond any logic." Chrysostom observes here: "As if following a signal, the devil was leading all to a (frenzied) dance. Let us assume that the Jews inflamed by envy and evil eye treated him (i.e. Jesus) with drunken violence. But what was the reason for the Roman soldiers' attitude? Is it not obvious that it was the devil who was leading all to a frenzy-stricken behavior?," *Homilies on Matthew,* Homily 87, PG 58.769.

192. See Lagrange 421-23 and Taylor 646-48.

193. The feast of Saturnalia could have influenced the soldiers in the scene of mockery as Taylor notes. For further details see Taylor 646-48.

194. In the scene described in Mk 15.16-20 there are possible echoes from Old Testament texts like Is 50.6. Cf. Mt 27.27-31.

195. For a select bibliography on Mk 15.21-32, see J. A. Dvoracek, "Vom Leiden Gottes," *CV* 14 (1971) 231-52; W. Schenk, *Der Passionsbericht* (1974) 13-64; L. Schenke, *Der gekreuzigte Christus* (1974)83-110; J. H. Reumann, "Psalm 22 at the Cross," *Interpretation* 28 (1974) 39-58; G. M. Lee, "Mk. 15,21. The Father of Alexander and Rufus," *NovT* 17 (1975) 303; T. J. Weeden, "The Cross as Power in Weakness," *The Passion in Mark,* ed. Kelber (1976) 115-34; M. De Burgos Nunez, "La communion de Dios con el crucificado," *EstBib* 37 (1978) 243-66; O. Genest, *Le Christ de la Passion* (1978) 97-122; D. Dormeyer, *Der Sinn des Leidens Jesu* (1979) 76-89; and H. J. Steichele, *Der leidende Sohn Gottes* (1980) 193-266.

196. "This is a picture drawn with dark lines against a dark background," notes Haenchen 531. Pesch 2, 481-83 thinks that the deep sorrow of Jesus is described in such a way as to project his image as the image of the "suffering righteous" of the Old Testament. T. J. Weeden, "The Cross as Power in Weakness," 116-21, 129-34, contends that the multifaceted drama of the

crucifixion promotes exclusively the Christology of the suffering Son of man.

197. The occurrence of this specific information here may be due to other reasons (cf. Lohmeyer 342; Gnilka 2, 315; Schmithals 2, 685-87); its main function, nonetheless, seems to be the presentation of Jesus as being bodily exhausted.

198. Plutarch offers the characteristic statement that "each of the condemned criminals carries his own cross," *On the delays of the divine punishment* 554 AB, Loeb ed. Moralia 7, 214. Cf. Lagrange 424-25 and Haenchen 525.

199. This was a custom with roots in the past as it is hinted at in Prov 31.6, "Give strong drink to him who is perishing, and wine to those in bitter distress . . . " Cf. Billerbeck 1, 1037-38.

200. The crucifixion constituted one of the most terrible and most abominable forms of execution invented by human beings. Cicero notes succinctly that crucifixion is "crudelissimum taeterrimumque supplicium," *In Verrem*, 64.

201. Luke in his parallel passage uses the term criminals (κακοῦργοι) for the two robbers (Lk 23.32). Pesch 2, 485 and Montague 181 suggest that the two robbers were political convicts ("zealots"), whereas Lagrange 429 speaks of common robbers. Gnilka 2, 318 considers both assumptions as plausible.

202. The terminology used in Mark's narrative, Mk 15.29 in particular, is reminiscent of Old Testament texts like Ps 22.8-9, Lam 2.15.

203. T. J. Weeden, "The Cross as Power in Weakness," 116-17, 120, 128, 132, while admitting the presence of elements of authority Christology in Mk 15.21-32, claims paradoxically that Mark mentions them in order to reject them.

204. Cf. Haenchen 531 and Pesch 2, 490.

205. E.g. Nineham 421, citing Dibelius.

206. Cf. Schweizer 346-47, 351.

207. For a select bibliography on Mk 15.33-41, see F. W. Danker, "The Demonic Secret in Mark," *ZNW* 61 (1970) 48-69; H. A. Guy, "Son of God in Mk. 15,39," *ExpTim* 81 (1970) 151; P. B. Harner, "Qualitative Anarthrous Predicate Nouns: Mk: 15,39 and John 1,1," *JBL* 92 (1973) 75-87; H. Schützeichel, "Der Todesschrei Jesu," *TTZ* 83 (1974) 1-16; G. M. Lee, "Two Notes on St. Mark," *NovT* 28 (1976) 36; P. Lamarche, *Révélatoin de Dieu chez Marc* (1976) 119-44; K. Stock, "Das Bekenntnis des Centurio, Mk. 15,39," *ZKT* 100 (1978) 289-301; C. R. Kazmierski, *Jesus the Son of God* (1979) 191-210; H. J. Steichele, *Der ledende Sohn Gottes* (1980) 267-79; H. Chronis, "The Torn Veil: Cultus and Christology in Mark 15,37-39," *JBL* 101 (1982) 97-114; D. Cohn-Sherbok, "Jesus' Cry on the Cross," *ExpTim* 93 (1982) 215-17; and W. Munro, "Women Disciples in Mark?" *CBQ* 44 (1982) 225-41.

208. See the relevant discussion in J. H. Reumann, "Psalm 22 at the Cross," *Interpretation* 28 (1974) 39-58. Reumann's article is offering interesting data but seems weak in its conclusions. Also interesting aspects are encountered in D. O. Via, *Kerygma and Comedy in the New Testament* (Philadelphia, 1975) 146-47.

209. See Damalas 3.699; Lohmeyer 345; Schweizer 353; Taylor 594; Achtemeier 222; R. Martin, *Mark* (1972) 120; and W. Kelber, *Mark's Story of Jesus* (1979) 81. Victor 439, on the contrary, finds that the basic thing here is "Jesus' unanimity (ὁμόνοια) with the One who has begotten him." Cf. Theophylact 669-72 and Gnilka 2, 321-22.

210. There are exegetes who think that the phrase "Eloi, Eloi, lama sabachtani" points to the entire Psalm 22, and, therefore, is expressive of the trust of the suffering righteous to the love and protection of God. Cf. discussion in Nineham 427-29; Schmithals 2, 696-97; and W. Schenk, *Der Passionsbericht* (1974) 56. The context of Mk 15.34, however, does not seem to suggest that the above opinion is the most convincing exegetical option for Mk 15.34. Klostermann 166 supports a combination of the forsaking and of the trusting elements in Mk 15.34. Cf. Trembelas 304-05; Lagrange 434; Pesch 2, 495; and Montague 183.

211. Taylor 595-96 and Nineham 429 think that the word "saying (λέγων) in v. 36 is a copyist's error or a result of confusing different traditions (cf. Mt 27.48-49; Lk 23.36; Jn 19.29). The phrase "wait, let us see . . . ," however, is sarcastic no matter who said it. Cf. Klostermann 166-67; Lagrange 434-35; and Pesch 2, 497.

212. The description of the death as well as of the crucifixion is offered in a laconic way, with only one verb. Mark here is absolutely reluctant in adding any comments.

213. See the pertinent comments by Chrysostom: "Think at what time the eclipse of the sun happened. It occurred in the middle of the day, so that all the people could know . . . This event was sufficient to help them (i.e. the Jews) to repent, not only because of the magnitude of the miracle but also because of the time of its occurrence. For the fact that Jesus being on the cross was able to perform such things (like the eclipse of the sun) was more amazing than his coming down from the cross . . . The darkness was not a (natural) eclipse but wrath and indignation as it becomes evident from the time of the event," *Homilies on Matthew,* Homily 88, PG 58.775. Cf. Victor 439 ("a sign from heaven"); Lohmeyer 345; and Trembelas 303.

214. The darkness here seems to be an apocalyptic and eschatological sign as it is in Mk 13.24. Mk 15.33 has been seen as a parallel to Amos 8.9: "And on that day, says the Lord God, I will make the sun go down at noon, and darken the earth in broad daylight." Cf. Nineham 426; Schweizer 352-53; Lane 571; Gnilka 2, 321; and Schmithals 2, 694-95.

215. See analytical discussion and presentation of the christological elements implied in the event of the tearing of the curtain in H. Chronis, "The Torn Veil," 107-14, and in P. Lamarche, *Révélation de Dieu* (1976) 121-29.

216. As Eusebios of Caesarea notes: " . . . when, because of his (i.e. Christ's) passion the veil of the Temple was torn asunder, the worship of God there according to the Law was in essence abolished," *Evangelical Demonstration* 8.2, PG 22.629. Cf. Victor 441; Theophylact 672; Taylor 596; Schweizer 355; and Gnilka 2, 323-24. Pesch 2, 499 disagrees with such a symbolic interpretation.

217. Victor 440 notes: " . . . he died with authority, for he uttered a loud cry, namely, a glorious cry which did not have traces of death." Similarly Theophylact 672 comments: "Jesus uttered a loud cry and breathed his last as if inviting death, and dying as Lord in his own authority." Cf. Origen, *Commentary on John,* Tom. 19, 16, G.C.S. Origen Vol. 4, 316.

218. The great or loud voice (φωνὴ μεγάλη) of Mk 15.37 is the voice of a supreme authority as rightly interpreted in Origen, Victor, Theophylact and others, and not an apocalyptic voice as W. Schenk, *Der Passionsbericht* (1974) 45-46, claims.

219. Cf. Swete 388; Klostermann 167; Taylor 597; and Schweizer 355-56. For the co-existence of elements of authority Christology and of Passion Christology in the confession by the centurion, see P. B. Harner, "Qualitative Anarthrous Predicate Nouns," 79-81.

220. As Taylor 597 points out, Mark read in the centurion's confession "a confession of the deity of Jesus in the full Christian sense." Cf. H. Chronis, "The Torn Veil," 101; H. Weinacht, *Die Menschwerdung* (1972) 68; G. Schille, *Offen für alle Menschen* (1974) 50-53; Dan O. Via, *Kerygma and Comedy* (1975) 155; Nineham 430-31; Lane 575-76; Gnilka 2, 324-25; and Schmithals 2, 692-93.

221. Lohmeyer 347 observes that in Mark the centurion's confession is superior to Peter's confession (Mk 8.29), and that it asserts what was a blasphemy for the high priest (Mk 14.61-63). Cf. W. Wrede, *The Messianic Secret* (1971) 75-76.

222. For a select bibliography on Mk 15.42-47, see R. H. Smith, "The Tomb of Jesus," *BA* 30 (1967) 74-90; J. Schreiber, *Die Markuspassion* (1969); H. Schlier, *Die Markuspassion* (1974) 72-85; W. Schenk, *Der Passionsbericht* (1974) 77-83; J. Blinzler, "Die Grablegung Jesu in historischer Sicht," *Ressurrexit,* ed. E. Dhanis (Rome, 1974) 108-31; B. Standaert, *L'Évangile selon Marc* (1978) 168-71; and J. Schreiber, "Die Bestattung Jesu," *ZNW* 72 (1981) 141-77.

223. See Nineham 432; Gnilka 2, 336-37; Schmithals 2, 704; and B. Standaert, *L'Évangile selon Marc* (1978) 170.

224. The variant πτῶμα instead of σῶμα appears in numerous codices and has been the preference of Nestle-Aland (26 ed., Stuttgart, 1979). Pesch 2, 514 underlines the use of the word πτῶμα as an indicator of the certainty of death.

225. For a select bibliography on Mk 16.1-8, see E. Güttgemanns, "Linguistische Analyse von Mk. 16,1-8," *LinguB* 11-12 (1972) 13-53; J. D. Crossan, "Empty Tomb and Absent Lord," *The Passion in Mark* ed. Kelber (1976) 135-52; A. Lindemann, "Die Osterbotschaft des Markus," *NTS* 26 (1980) 298-317; F. Neirynck, "Marc 16,1-8 Tradition et rédaction," *ETL* 56 (1980) 56-88; N. R. Petersen, "When Is the End Not the End?," *Interpretation* 34 (1980) 151-66; T. E. Boomershine, "Mark 16,8 and the Apostolic Commission," *JBL* 100 (1981) 225-39; M. Gourgues, "A propos du symbolisme christologique et baptismal de Mc. 16,5," *NTS* 27 (1981) 672-78; and L. Schottroff, "Maria Magdalena und die Frauen am Grabe Jesu," *EvT* 42 (1982) 3-25.

226. See Schweizer 371; Taylor 605; Nineham 444; and Pesch 2, 527, 531-32.

227. The "young man" (νεανίσκος) here is an angel according to most exegetes. Cf. Klostermann 171; Trembelas 315; Taylor 606-07; Schweizer 372; Pesch 2, 532; Schmithals 2, 710-11; Lane 587; and F. Neirynck, "Marc 16,1-8 Tradition et rédaction," 56ff. The theory by J. D. Crossan, "Empty Tomb and Absent Lord," 148, that the νεανίσκος is the "Markan community of those reborn in the resurrected Christ," does not seem persuasive.

228. This co-existence of the two christological concepts will be characteristic of the basic creedal formulations of early Christianity. See, for instance, Ignatios of Antioch, *To the Trallians* 9.1-2 and Justin Martyr, *1 Apology* 21.1. Cf. A. Lindemann, "Die Osterbotschaft des Markus," 304-05.

229. Cf. Pesch 2, 535 and Lane 589.

230. Cf. Theophylact 677; Lane 590; and Pesch 2, 535-36. T. E. Boomershine, "Mark 16.8 and the Apostolic Commission," 230, recognizes the "sacred awe" of the women, yet he does not see it as a fundamental narrative element related to the resurrection of Christ.

231. Gregory of Nyssa, for instance, writes: "In the copies the more accurate, the Gospel of Mark ends with the phrase "for they were afraid" (ἐφοβοῦντο γάρ), *On Holy Easter,* Sermon 2, PG 46.644-45.

232. See detailed presentation and discussion of the relevant date in W. R. Farmer, *The Last Twelve Verses of Mark* (London, 1974) and J. Hug, *La finale de l'évangile de Marc* (Paris, 1978).

233. For a select bibliography on Mk 16.9-20, see J. K. Elliot, "The Text and Language of the Endings of Mark's Gospel," *TZ* 27 (1971) 255-62; G. W. Trompf, "The First Resurrection Appearance and the Ending of Mark's Gospel," *NTS* 18 (1972) 308-30; W. R. Farmer, *The Last Twelve Verses* (1974); R. H. Fuller, "Longer Mark: Forgery, Interpolation, or Old Tradition?," *Colloquy* 18 (Berkeley, 1975); P. Lamarche, *Révélation de Dieu chez Marc* (1976) 149-54; J. Hug, *La finale de Marc* (1978); and H. Lubsczyk, "Kyrios Jesus," *Die Kirche des Anfangs,* Festschr. H. Scchürmann, hersg. R. Schnackenburg (Freiburg, 1978) 133-74.

234. P. Lamarche, *Révélation de Dieu* (1976) 150, detects here traces supporting the archaic origin of the pericope. Cf. Swete 403-04; Taylor 611-12; and Schweizer 375-76.

235. Pesch 2, 549 suggests that the emphasis on the unbelief and the hardness of heart of the disciples in Mk 16.11-14 serves the purpose of underlining the certainty of the resurrection. Such a suggestion seems plausible, but even more plausible is the opinion that Mk 16.11-14 constitutes a natural continuation of the line of the passages in Mark in which the disciples' unbelief or hardness of heart is the chief motif (Mk 4.40; 6.52; 7.18; 8.15-21). Cf. J. Hug, *La finale de l'évangile de Marc* (1978) 183-84.

236. Schweizer 378 comments here that the real purpose of mentioning Jesus' resurrection is the proclamation of the gospel to the entire world. Cf. Achtemeier 233 and Schmithals 2, 741-42. For the essential continuity between the phrase "preach the gospel" in Mk 16.15 and "preaching the

gospel" in Mk 1.14, see J. Hug, *La finale de l'évangile de Marc* (1978) 180-83 and W. Farmer, *The Last Twelve Verses in Mark* (1974) 94-96.

237. See Pesch 2, 553 for the eschatological perspectives of Mk 16.16.

238. Cf. Schmithals 2, 748-49.

239. Irenaios sees in Mk 16.19 the verification and confirmation of Ps 110.1, *Haereses* 3.10,6, Sources Chrétiennes 211 (1974) 136-39.

240. Cf. P. Lamarche, *Révélation de Dieu* (1976) 152.

241. Pesch 2, 555 remarks that this short report in Mk 16.20 "correctly has been characterized as 'Acts of the Apostles in miniature.' "

Select Bibliography

The bibliography that follows offers a selection of works directly related to the topic and the content of the present book. The selection is representative of various theological and exegetical tendencies, and lists works published mostly during the last two decades. Additional bibliographical material can be found in the endnotes of this book. The present Bibliography of the English translation has been enriched with several new items which appeared after the publication of the original Greek edition.

A. COMMENTARIES

Achtemeier, P. J., *Invitation to Mark. A Commentary on the Gospel of Mark* (Garden City, 1978).

Beda Venerabilis, *In Marci Evangelium Expositio*, PL 92.131-302.

Carrington, P., *According to Mark: A Running Commentary on the Oldest Gospel* (Cambridge, 1960).

Cranfield, C. E. B., *The Gospel according to Saint Mark* (Cambridge, 1959).

Damalas, N. M., Ἑρμηνεία εἰς τὴν Καινὴν Διαθήκην, Vols. 2 and 3 (Athens, 1892).

Gnilka, J., *Das Evangelium nach Markus*, 2 vols. (Zurich, 1978-1979).

Haenchen, E., *Der Weg Jesu. Eine Erklärung des Markus-Evangeliums und der kanonischen Parallelen* (Berlin, 1968[2]).

Klostermann, E., *Das Markusevangelium* (Tübingen, 1949[4]).

Lagrange, M. J., *L' Évangile selon Saint Marc* (Paris, 1966 repr.).

Lane, W. L., *Commentary on the Gospel of Mark* (Grand Rapids, 1974).

Lohmeyer, E., *Das Evangelium des Markus* (Göttingen, 1967[17]).

Mann, C. S., *Mark* (Garden City, 1986).

Montague, G. T., *Mark: Good News for Hard Times* (Ann Arbor, 1981).

Nineham, D. E., *Saint Mark* (Baltimore, 1963).

Pesch, R., *Das Markusevangelium. Theologischer Kommentar zum Neuen Testament*. I Teil (Freiburg, 1976), II Teil (Freiburg, 1977).

Schmithals, W., *Das Evangelium nach Markus*, 2 vols. (Gütersloh, 1979).

Schweizer, E., *The Good News according to Mark*, English trans. D. H. Madvig (Richmond, 1970).

Strack, H. L. und Billerbeck, P., *Kommentar zum Neuen Testament aus Talmud und Midrasch I-VI* (Munich, 1969[5]).

Swete, H. B., *The Gospel according to St. Mark* (London, 1898 —repr. 1977).

Taylor, V., *The Gospel according to St. Mark* (London, 1963).

Theophylact of Bulgaria, Ἑρμηνεία εἰς τὸ κατὰ Μᾶρκον Εὐαγγέλιον, PG 123.491-682.

Thomas Aquinas, *Catena aurea in quatuor Evangelia*, Vol. 1 (Rome, 1953) 433-566.

Trembelas, P. N., Ὑπόμνημα εἰς τὸ κατὰ Μᾶρκον Εὐαγγέλιον (Athens, 1951).

Victor, presbyter of Antioch, "Σύντομος Ἑρμηνεία εἰς τὸ κατὰ Μᾶρκον εὐαγγέλιον," in J. Cramer, *Catenae in Evangelia,* Vol. 1 (Oxford, 1844).

Zigabenos, Euthymios, Ἑρμηνεία τοῦ κατὰ Μᾶρκον Εὐαγγελίου, PG 129. 765-852.

B. SPECIAL STUDIES AND ARTICLES

Achtemeier, P. J., "He Taught Them Many Things: Reflections on Markan Christology," *CBQ* 42 (1980) 465-81.

Ambrozic, A. M., *The Hidden Kingdom. A Redaction-Critical Study of the References to the Kingdom of God in Mark's Gospel* (Washington, D.C., 1972).

Belo, F., *A Materialist Reading of the Gospel of Mark* (English trans.) (Maryknoll, 1981).

Best, E., *The Temptation and the Passion: The Markan Soteriology* (Cambridge, 1965).

Best, E., *Following Jesus: Discipleship in the Gospels of Mark* (Sheffield, 1981).

Best, E., *The Gospel as Story* (Edinburgh, 1983).

Betz, H. D. (ed.), *Christology and a Modern Pilgrimage* (SBL, 1973[2]).

Bilezikian, G. G., *The Liberated Gospel. A Comparison of the Gospel of Mark and Greek Tragedy* (Grand Rapids, 1977).

Blackwell, J., *The Passion as Story. The Plot of Mark* (Philadelphia, 1986).

Blevins, J. L., *The Messianic Secret in Markan Research 1901-1976* (Washington, D.C., 1981).

Booth, R., *Jesus and the Laws of Purity* (Sheffield, 1986).

Boring, M. E., "The Christology of Mark: Hermeneutical Issues for Systematic Theology," *Semeia* 30 (1984) 125-53.

Bowman, J., *The Gospel of Mark: The New Christian Jewish Passover Haggadah* (Leiden, 1965).

Brandenburger, E., *Markus 13 und die Apokalyptik* (Göttingen, 1984).

Breytenbach, C., *Nachfolge und Zukunftserwartung* (Zurich, 1984).

Brown, R. E., "Who Do Men Say That I Am? — Modern Scholarship on Gospel Christology," *Horizons* 1 (1974) 35-50.

Burkill, T. A., *New Light on the Earliest Gospel* (Ithaca, 1972).

Busemann, R., *Die Jüngergemeinde nach Markus 10* (Bonn, 1983).

Calloud, J., "Toward a Structural Analysis of the Gospel of Mark," *Semeia* 16 (1979) 133-65.

Cangh, J. M. van, "La Galilée dans l'évangile de Marc: un lieu théologique?," *RB* 79 (1972) 59-75.

Cancik, H., *Markus-Philologie* (Tübingen, 1984).

Carroll, W. D., "The Jesus of Mark's Gospel," *BT* 103 (1979) 2105-12.

Carlston, C. E., *The Parables of the Triple Tradition* (Philadelphia, 1975).

Casey, M., *Son of Man. The Interpretation and Influence of Daniel 7* (London, 1979).

Chordat, J. L., *Jésus devant sa mort dans l'évangile de Marc* (Paris, 1970).

Church, I.F., *A Study of the Marcan Gospel* (New York, 1976).

Cook, M. J., *Mark's Treatment of the Jewish Leaders* (Leiden, 1978).

Cousar, C. B., "Eschatology and Mark's Theologia Crucis," *Interpretation* 24 (1970) 321-35.

Crossan, J. D., "Empty Tomb and Absent Lord," *The Passion in Mark*, ed. W. H. Kelber (Philadelphia, 1976) 135-52.

D'Arc, J., *Évangile selon Marc* (Paris, 1986).

Danker, F. W., "The Demonic Secret in Mark: A Reexamination of the Cry of Dereliction," *ZNW* 61 (1970) 48-69.

Delling, G., *Der Kreuzestod Jesu in der Urchlistlichen Verkündigung* (Göttingen, 1972).

Delorme, J., "Lecture de l'Évangile selon saint Marc," *Cahiers Evangile* 54 (1973) 3-123.

Derrett, J. D. M., *The Making of Mark* (Shipston, 1985)

Dewey, Joanna, *Markan Public Debate* (Chico, 1980).

Donahue, J. R., *"Are you the Christ?" The Trial Narrative in the Gospel of Mark* (Missoula, 1973).

Donahue, J. R., *The Theology and Setting of Discipleship in the Gospel of Mark* (Milwaukee, 1983).

Dormeyer, D., *Der Sinn des Leidens Jesu* (Stuttgart, 1979).

Doughty, D. J., "The Authority of the Son of Man (Mk 2:1-3:6)," *ZNW* 74 (1983) 161-81.

Dschulnigg, P., *Sprache, Redaktion und Intention des Markus-Evangeliums* (Stuttgart, 1986).

Duling, D. C., "Interpreting the Markan Hodology," *Nexus* 17 (1974) 2-11.

Dumitriu, P., *Comment ne pas l'aimer! Une lecture de lÉvangile selon saint Marc* (Paris, 1981).

Dungan, D. L., "The Purpose and Provenance of the Gospel of Mark According to the 'Two Gospels' Hypothesis," in *Colloquy on New Testament Studies*, ed. B. Corley (Macon, 1983) 133-79.

Dunn, J. D. G., "Le secret Messianique chez Marc," *Hokhma* 18 (1981) 34-56.

Dupont, J., *Études sur les évangiles synoptiques*, 2 vols. (Leuven, 1985).

Egger, W., *Frohbotschaft und Lehre* (Frankfurt, 1976).

Egger, W., *Nachfolge als Weg zum Leben* (Klosterneuburg, 1979).

Englezakis, B., "Markan Parable: More than Word Modality a Revelation of Contents," *ΔBM* 2 (1973-74) 349-57.

Evans, C. A., "The Hermeneutics of Mark and John: On the Theology of the Canonical Gospels," *Bib* 64 (1983) 153-72.

Evans, C. F., *The Beginning of the Gospel* (London, 1968).

Farmer, W. R., *The Last Twelve Verses of Mark* (New York, 1974).

Feneberg, W., *Der Markussprolog: Studien zur Formbestimmung des Evangeliums* (Munich, 1974).

Feuillet, A., *L'agonie de Gethsémani* (Paris, 1977).

Ford, D., *The Abomination of Desolation in Biblical Eschatology* (Washington, D.C., 1979).

Fowler, R. M., *Loaves and Fishes: The Function of the Feeding Stories in the Gospel of Mark* (Chico, 1981).

Fusco, V., *Parola e regno. La sezione delle Parabole nella Prospettiva Marciana* (Brescia, 1980).

Gaboury, A., "Christological Implications Resulting from a Study of the Structure of the Synoptic Gospels," *SocBibLit Meeting 1972* (Los Angeles) Vol. 1, 97-146.

Genest, Olivette, *Le Christ de la Passion. Perspective Structurale* (Montreal, 1978).

Hahn, F., (ed.), *Der Erzählung des Evangeliums* (Stuttgart, 1985).

Harrington, D. J., *The Gospel according to Mark* (New York, 1983).

Harrington, D. J., "A Map of Books on Mark (1975-1984)," *BTB* 15 (1985) 12-16.

Harrisville, R. A., *The Miracle of Mark. A Study in the Gospel* (Minneapolis, 1967).

Hartman, L., *Prophecy Interpreted* (Lund, 1966).

Higgins, A. J. B., *Jesus and the Son of Man* (Philadelphia, 1964).

Hooker, M. D., *The Son of Man in Mark* (London, 1967).

Hooker, M. D., *The Message of Mark* (London, 1983).

Horstmann, M., *Studien zur markinischen Christologie* (Münster, 1969).

Hug, J., *La finale de l' évangile de Marc* (Paris, 1978).

Hultgren, A. J., *Jesus and His Adversaries* (Minneapolis, 1979).

Humphrey, H. M., *A Bibliography for the Gospel of Mark, 1954-1980* (New York, 1981).

Johns, E. and Major, D., *Witness in a Pagan World. A Study of Mark's Gospel* (London, 1980).

Juel, D., *Messiah and Temple. The Trial of Jesus in the Gospel of Mark* (Missoula, 1977).

Karavidopoulos, J., "'Απαρχαὶ 'Εκκλησιολογίας εἰς τὸ κατὰ Μᾶρκον Εὐαγγέλιον," *ΕΕΘΣΠΘ* 17 (1972) 45-93.

Karavidopoulos, J., "Δύο συλλογαὶ λογίων τοῦ 'Ιησοῦ εἰς τὸ κατὰ Μᾶρκον Εὐαγγέλιον," *ΕΕΘΣΠΘ* 20 (1975) 89-120.

Kazmierski, C. R., *Jesus the Son of God. A Study of the Markan Tradition and its Redaction by the Evangelist* (Würzburg, 1979).

Kealy, S. P., *Mark's Gospel: A History of its Interpretation. From the Beginning Until 1979* (New York, 1982).

Keck, L. E., "Mark 3,7-12 and Mark's Christology," *JBL* 84 (1965) 341-58.

Kee, H. C., *Community of the New Age. Studies in Mark's Gospel* (Philadelphia, 1977).

Kelber, W. H., *The Kingdom in Mark. A New Place and a New Time* (Philadelphia, 1977).

Kelber, W. H. (ed.), *The Passion in Mark. Studies on Mark 14—16* (Philadephia, 1976).

Kelber, W. H., *Mark's Story of Jesus* (Philadelphia, 1979).

Kermode, F., *The Genesis of Secrecy. On the Interpretation of Narrative* (Cambridge, 1980^3).

Kertelge, K., *Die Wunder Jesu im Markusevangelium* (Munich, 1970).

Kesich, V., *The Gospel Image of Christ* (Crestwood, 1972).

Kingsbury, J. D., *The Christology of Mark's Gospel* (Philadelphia, 1983).

Koester, H., *Synoptische Überlieferung bei den Apostolischen Vätern* (Berlin, 1957).

Koester, H., "History and Development of Mark's Gospel," in *Colloquy on New Testament Studies,* ed. B. Corley (Macon, 1983) 35-85.

Kolenkow, A. B., "Healing Controversy as a Tie Between Miracle and Passion Material for a Proto-Gospel," *JBL* 95 (1976) 623-38.

Kühschelm, R., *Jüngerverfolgung und Geschick Jesu* (Klosterneuburg, 1983).

Lamarche, P., *Christ Vivant* (Paris, 1977).

Lamarche, P., *Révélation de Dieu chez Marc* (Paris, 1976).

Lemcio, E. E., "The Intention of the Evangelist Mark," *NTS* 32 (1986) 187-206.

Lightfoot, R. H., *The Gospel Message of St. Mark* (Oxford, 1950).

Linnemann, E., *Studien zur Passionsgeschichte* (Göttingen, 1970).

Longstaff, T. R. W., *Evidence of Conflation in Mark?* (Missoula, 1977).

Lührmann, D., "Biographie des Gerechten als Evangelium," *Wort und Dienst,* N.F. (1977) 25-50.

Luz, U., "Das Geheimnismotiv und die markinische Christologie," ZNW 56 (1965) 9-30.

Malbon, E. S., "Galilee and Jerusalem: History and Literature in Marcan Interpretation," *CBQ* 44 (1982) 242-55.

Malbon, E. S., "Disciples/Crowds/Whoever: Markan Characters and Readers," *NovT* 28 (1986) 104-30.

Marxsen, W., *Der Evangelist Markus* (Göttingen, 1959^2). English trans. *Mark the Evangelist* (Nashville, 1969).

Matera, F. J.,*The Kingship of Jesus: Composition and Theology in Mark 15* (Chico, 1982).

Matera, F. J., *Passion Narratives and Gospel Theologies* (New York, 1986).

Maloney, E. C., *Semitic Interference in Marcan Syntax* (Chico, 1981).

Martin, R. P., *Mark: Evangelist and Theologian* (Exeter, 1972).

Marcus, J., "Mark 4:10-12 and Marcan Epistemology," *JBL* 103 (1984) 557-74.

Marcus, J., *The Mystery of the Kingdom of God* (Atlanta, 1986).

McCowen, A., *Personal Mark* (New York, 1985).

Meagher, J. C., *Clumsy Construction in Mark's Gospel* (New York, 1979).

Meye, R. P., *Jesus and the Twelve. Discipleship and Revelation in Mark's Gospel* (Grand Rapids, 1968).

Minette de Tillesse, G., *Le secret messianique dans l'évangile de Marc* (Paris, 1968).

Neirynck, F., *Evangelica. Gospel Studies. Collected Essays*, ed. F. van Segbroeck (Leuven, 1982).

Nickelsberg, G., "The Genre and Function of the Markan Passion Narrative," *HTR* 73 (1980) 153-84.

O'Grady, J. F., *Mark: The Sorrowful Gospel. An Introduction to the Second Gospel* (New York, 1981).

Peabody, D. B., *Mark as Composer* (Macon, 1987).

Perrin, N., "Towards an Interpretation of the Gospel of Mark," in *Christology and a Modern Pilgrimage,* ed. H. D. Betz (SBL, 1973²).

Perrin, N., "The Interpretation of the Gospel of Mark," *Interpretation* 30 (1976) 115-24.

Pesch, R., *Naherwartungen: Tradition und Redaktion in Mk 13* (Düsseldorf, 1968).

Pesch, R., *Das Abendmahl und Jesu Todesverständnis* (Freiburg, 1978).

Petersen, N. R., "When is the End not the End? Reflections on the Ending of Mark's Narrative," *Interpretation* 34 (1980) 151-66.

Pryke, E. J., *Redactional Style in the Markan Gospel* (Cambridge, 1978).

Quesnel, M., *Comment lire un évangile. Saint Marc* (Paris, 1984).

Quesnell, Q., *The Mind of Mark. Interpretation and Method through the Exegesis of Mark 6,52* (Rome, 1969).

Räisänen, H., *Das Messiasgeheimnis im Markusevangelium. Ein Redaktionskritischer Versuch* Helsinki, 1976).

Reardon, P. H., "Kenotic Ecclesiology in Mark," *BT* 70 (1974) 1476-1482.

Roads, D. and Michie, D., *Mark as Story* (Philadelphia, 1982).

Robbins, V. K., "Summons and Outline in Mark: The Three-Step Progression," *NovT* 23 (1981) 97-114.

Robbins, V., *Jesus the Teacher,* (Philadelphia, 1984).

Robinson, J. M., *The Problem of History in Mark* (London, 1971⁴).

Sabbe, M. (ed.), *LÉvangile selon Marc. Tradition et rédaction* (Gembloux, 1974).

Schenk, W., *Der Passionsbericht nach Markus* (Gütersloh, 1974).

Schenke, L., *Der gekreuzigte Christus* (Stuttgart, 1974).

Schenke, L., *Die wunderbare Brotvermehrung* Würzburg, 1983).

Schille, G., *Offen für alle Menschen. Redaktionsgeschichtliche Beobachtungen zur Theologie des Markus-Evangeliums* (Stuttgart, 1974).

Schlier, H., *Die Markuspassion* (Einsiedeln, 1974).

Schlosser, J., *Le règne de Dieu dans les dits de Jésus* (Paris, 1980).

Schmidt, K. L., *Der Rahmen der Geschichte Jesu: Literarkritische Untersuchung zur ältesten Jesusüberlieferung* (Darmstadt, 1964[repr.]).

Schweizer, E., "Towards a Christology of Mark," *God's Christ and His People,* Festschr. N. A. Dahl (Oslo, 1977) 29-42.

Senior, D., *The Passion of Jesus in the Gospel of Mark* (Wilmington, 1984).

Senior, D., "The Struggle to be Universal: Mission as Vantage Point for New Testament Investigation," *CBQ* 46 (1984) 63-81.

Smith, M., *The Secret Gospel. The Discovery and Interpretation of the Secret Gospel According to Mark* (New York, 1973).

Smith, M., *Clement of Alexandria and a Secret Gospel of Mark* (Cambridge, 1973).

Standaert, B., *LÉvangile selon Marc. Composition et genre littéraire* (Zevenkerken-Brugge, 1978).

Steichele, H. J., *Der leidende Sohn Gottes* (Regensburg, 1980).

Stock, A., *Call to Discipleship.* (Wilmington, 1982).

Strecker, G., "Zur Messiasgeheimnistheorie im Markusevangelium," *Studia Evangelica III* (T.U. 88, Berlin, 1964) 87-104.

Swartley, W. M., *Mark: The Way for all Nations* (Scottdale, 1981).

Tanehill, R. C., "The Gospel of Mark as Narrative Christology," *Semeia* 16 (1979) 57-95.

Telford, W. (ed.), *The Interpretation of Mark* (Philadelphia, 1985).

Theissen, G., *Urchristliche Wundergeschichten* (Gütersloh, 1974).

Tödt, H. E., *The Son of Man in the Synoptic Tradition.* English trans. D. M. Barton (London, 1965).

Trockmé, E., *The Formation of the Gospel according to Mark.* English trans. P. Gaughan (Philadelphia, 1975).

Vassiliadis, P., "Behind Mark: Towards a Written Source," *NTS* 20 (1974) 155-60.

Vassiliadis, P., "The Function of John the Baptist in Q and Mark," *Θεολογία* 46 (1975) 405-13.

Via, D. O. Jr., *Kerygma and Comedy in the New Testament. A Structuralist Approach to Hermeneutic* (Philadelphia, 1975).

Via, D. O. Jr., *The Ethics of Mark's Gospel* (Philadelphia, 1985).

Vielhauer, P., "Erwägungen zur Christologie des Markusevangeliums," in *Aufsätze zum Neuen Testament* (Munich, 1965) 199-214.

von Wahlde, U. C., "Mark 9:33-50: Discipleship: The Authority that Serves," *BZ* 29 (1985) 49-67.

Weber, H. R., *Jesus and the Children* (Atlanta, 1979).

Weeden, T. J., "The Heresy that Necessitated Mark's Gospel," *ZNW* 59 (1968) 145-58.

Weeden, T. J., *Mark: Traditions in Conflict* (Philadelphia, 1971).

Weinacht, H., *Die Menschwerdung des Sohnes Gottes im Markus-evangelium* (Tübingen, 1972).

Wilder, A. N., "The Parable of the Sower: Naiveté and Method in Interpretation," *Semeia* 2 (1974) 134-51.

Williams, J. G., *Gospel against Parable: Mark's Language of Mystery* (Sheffield, 1985).

Williamson, L. Jr., *Mark* (Atlanta, 1983).

Wrede, W., *Das Messiasgeheimnis in den Evangelien* (Göttingen, 1901) English trans. *The Messianic Secret* (Cambridge, 1971).

General Outline and Particular Pericopes of the Gospel of Mark

1. The Manifestation of Authority and the Prelude to the Passion (Mark 1.1-8.26)

2. Balance within the alternating Concepts of Authority and Passion (Mark 8.27-10.52)

3. The fulfillment of the Passion in the light of Authority (Mark 11.1-16.20)

Index of the Markan Passages

Index of the O.T. and N.T. Passages

Index of Authors

Ancient

Modern